Readers Respond to
Dolphin Love ... *From Sea to Land*

I'm still enjoying your book and it's the neatest thing, I feel the beautiful dolphins all around me while I read!! ~ Ann A., Arizona

When I read your book, I was also reading two other spiritual adventure stories about alternate worlds and realities. When I put those books down, I returned to my normal life. When I put your book down, I was altered. And so was my world. For the better! I get the feeling you are guiding me away from mere rational comprehension, toward experiencing the deeper mystery. You tantalize the reader with life filled with spiritual adventure. You shift our focus into life that is totally and joyfully immersed in spiritual purpose. Reading this, I feel inspired, and challenged. ~ Michael Eason, Arizona

I put your book down once, then I could not put it down again until the end. Linda, I received a healing while reading your book. I felt waves of energy tingling through my body from head to toe. This occurred several more times as I continued to read. Your book was a serendipitous experience! ~ Brenda K., Arizona

WOW. I am really awe-struck; not just by the depth and vastness of your own journey, but by how you have written about it. Completely you, completely entertaining, and yet full of silence, authenticity, and love. ~ Cynthia C., Hawaii

I just want to say once again, how much I enjoyed your book. I absolutely loved your conversations with Keiko, and it was so interesting to see how similar they were to mine and other communicators'. You are an excellent communicator! This is information and experience that needs to be out there. And I am so glad that you are doing this. ~ Mary Getten, Animal Communicator; author of *Communicating with Orcas: The Whales' Perspective*

I finished reading your book last night. What a story! I really enjoyed it and didn't want it to end. Your book opened up a whole new world to me. There's so much I didn't realize about the dolphins and the ocean. It really has helped me with exploring my own dolphin connection. ~ Emily

Been reading your book ... it is so wonderful. I feel like I am on the awakening journey with you! ~ Pamela B., Florida

Your book, your sharing, felt like a personal gift from the dolphins to me. As I began reading your book, the tears began to flow opening me up to all the sadness I have been holding since leaving my beloved water and dolphins, the one place I feel is home and where I belong. Your story, so simple, so beautiful, reminded me of the real message of the dolphins: that we are not meant to be loners. We must learn to live in pods also ... human pods that love and touch and support and dance and play together. My heart longs for this and now, perhaps, I can allow for this in my life. It is time! ~ Sariah M.

Dolphin Love ...
From Sea to Land

My Interdimensional Journey to my Heart,
with the Dolphins by my Side

♡

A True Story of Dolphin Consciousness,
Dolphin Energy Healing,
and Joy

Linda Shay

DANCING SEAS MEDIA

*Beloved Sherrie —
What a Joy
to meet you &
hug you in person!
Thank you for your
Presence & Light!
Dolphin Love &
Joy!
♡ Linda*

ISBN: 978-0-9847431-0-0
Library of Congress Control Number: 2011941264
Copyright information available upon request.

Editor: David Rosenthal
Copyeditor: Sharon K. Garner
Interior design: J. L. Saloff
Cover design: Manjari Graphics
Typography: Garamond Premier Pro, Gabriola, Gill Sans, Spirals, Cocktail Script.

All photographs and illustrations are the copyright of the author except for: Dolphin photographs by Anna Emich, pgs. 31, 151, 152, 217, and back cover. Whale photographs by Marta Diaz, courtesy of Whale Watching Panama, pgs. 258, 259. Back cover author photograph by KFM Design. Dolphin outline images ©iStockphoto.com/ColbaltMoon.

v. 1.0
First Edition, 2012
Printed on acid-free paper.

This is a true story. Some names have been changed to protect privacy.

Dancing Seas Media
Minden, NV 89423

For Alana

Contents

Dolphin Love

♡

A Message From Linda

This book is not meant to be a scientific examination of the dolphin species. There are many resources available out there that do a far better job at that than I ever could.

Rather, this is my personal spiritual adventure story—and my love story—with the dolphins. This is a true story. It takes place on land, in the sea, and in the realm of spirit ... in other dimensions of reality.

I invite you to float through these pages with an open mind, a receptive heart, and an adventurous spirit. Many of my readers have told me they received transmissions of dolphin energy while reading this book. This may happen for you too! Invite the dolphins to play with you. Open your heart and let them in ... and then pay attention to your life. Since you were attracted to this book, I suspect your personal dolphin adventure story has already begun!

May this story inspire you on your own unique path upon planet Earth. Open your eyes, your heart, and your mind, and look around you. Who or what are your special teachers? Follow the beauty. Follow the magic. Follow your joy. In so doing, you will discover your own precious heart, your own true nature. And, in this, we will all find freedom. I know that to be the wish for all of humanity from our dolphin brothers and sisters.

Dolphin Love

It is a joy and a privilege for me to be in service to my fellow humans, and to this precious planet, by bringing the gifts of the dolphins ... from sea to land.

In Dolphin Love and Joy!
Linda Shay

Prologue

I was standing at the ocean's edge. The sultry, pungent ocean air activated my senses, awakening every cell of my being. The sun's rays warmed me, while the bright midday light transformed the gentle rippling water into a dazzling display of sparkling diamonds for as far as the eye could see. Curling and uncurling my toes in the soft, warm sand, I watched my feet slowly disappear with each lapping wave. A giggle bubbled up inside.

The day was exquisite. My mind was quiet and clear as I gazed into the distance. The ocean was magnificent; she beckoned me to enter. As if pulled by an invisible magnetic force, I stepped into the warm tropical water. As the silky liquid enveloped me, the tension in my body dissolved. The resulting lightness of being was intoxicating. I felt giddy. I walked and walked, as effortlessly as if through air. My destination seemed to be the horizon. I was in total peace and harmony.

I simultaneously sensed and saw movement in my periphery. A fin sliced silently through the water, heading my way. *A shark?* Curiously, I felt no fear. Rather, a feeling of familiarity and anticipation rose up inside.

Gliding to a stop beside me was ... a dolphin! In the blink of an eye, I was riding alongside him with my arm cupped around his dorsal fin, like I'd seen so many times on TV. I laughed and laughed as we swam around and around, moving through the pristine water with grace and ease. Oh, did we play! I hadn't felt this free in ages, if ever. I felt so alive!

I was also in awe. The dolphin was big, immensely strong, and agile. His skin was incredible … firm, smooth, sleek, and silky. He seemed to be pure muscle. Our bodies were in full contact as we undulated through the water. *He is magnificent!*

When I felt absolute trust and safety, we dove. We hovered just beneath the surface while I acclimated to his world. Somehow, breathing was not an issue for me. When I was ready, slowly and gently, we dove deeper. I saw this exquisite underwater world through his eyes. I felt deeply honored to be invited into his home. The trust I felt was apparently mutual.

Deeper still, the water became dark and cold. The silence was deafening. The lack of light and sensory input became claustrophobic. I felt a prickle of fear. Sensing my fear, the dolphin changed course. We swam back up toward the light of day, while my new friend bathed me in feelings of love and peace. We communicated mind-to-mind. He assured me that I was safe. Harm would not come to me while I was in his care. That was his solemn promise.

My heart swelled with love for this being. In this brief span of time, this dolphin became a precious friend. He seemed to know everything about me. I trusted him completely.

We played again at the surface and soon my adventurous spirit returned. Soaring through the water with him was one outrageous ride! I never knew such joy.

When I was warm and relaxed, we dove once more into the depths of his world. This time I saw more, and feared less. Then, as the colors deepened to black and the water chilled me to my bones, my fear arose again. The mystery and vastness of this underwater world was overwhelming. Blackness and nothingness was all there was. It was too much.

Again, the dolphin turned. As we swam toward the surface, my anxiety subsided. Wave upon wave of peace and calm flowed through me. I knew this nurturing energy was coming from the dolphin. He soothed my body and soul.

We sped to the surface, leapt into the spectacular sunshine and exhaled with great force, gasping in lungfuls of wonderfully crisp, clean air. We were back in *my* world now.

"Everyone gently begin coming back into the room ..."

Softly, from far away, a woman's voice began to penetrate my consciousness. Two vastly different realities swirled around and around, shifting and separating. My dolphin friend and his world slowly dissolved away as my awareness returned to a warm, cozy room in the foothills of the Sierras, in northern California.

*Where am I? Where **was** I?* I opened my eyes to see a handful of people sitting around the softly lit room. *Where is my dolphin?* I wanted him to come back. I felt disoriented and confused ... and sad.

I looked at the meditation facilitator. Wonder and questioning poured forth from my eyes. She returned my gaze knowingly, exuding compassion. Eye contact with this woman brought me back, quietly and gently, into present time and space.

We sat in silence for a few moments, and then we took turns sharing our experiences. The group was fascinated by my dolphin journey. I was too. It was so real! In a strange way, the dolphin's world felt more real than the world I returned to.

The next day, life returned to normal. My life experience up until that time gave me no frame of reference for my experience in that meditation. I didn't give it, or the dolphins, another thought. Until a few years later, when they swam back into my life ...

ONE

Before the Dolphins

I was living the American Dream. I was married to my best friend. We had recently purchased and moved into a brand new 3,050-square-foot house, with a swimming pool and Jacuzzi, in Sacramento, California. Norman drove a gold-toned BMW convertible; I drove a turquoise baby Mercedes-Benz. We were overextended financially, but who wasn't? That was how the system was set up. When we married, I moved into his house. When we wanted to move into another house, we had to buy a bigger house or get creamed with capital gains taxes.

Norman was a lobbyist in the state capital. He had an image to maintain. My banking career was on a surprisingly fast upward trajectory—every nine months I got promoted. We were seduced by a lifestyle that was beyond our means. We had all the material trappings, and precious little disposable income.

My seemingly stable and satisfying life began to unravel in 1987, when the bank that I worked for, Security Pacific Bank, brought in its first senior executive from outside the organization. Up until then, this huge corporation had my unconditional loyalty. I thought that was rather remarkable for an organization of that size. I used to say I would have jumped off the Golden Gate Bridge if they'd asked me to. I knew the top executives personally, from my earliest days in Los

Angeles, when I was a cute and perky 21-year-old executive secretary on the top floor. The grandfatherly CEO affectionately called me "giggles and wiggles." We were a family.

By 1987, I was assistant vice president and manager of a medium-sized banking office in Sacramento. I loved my job. Then this outside executive came in, and the entire corporate culture of the bank changed overnight. It no longer mattered how well I managed my staff, or treated my customers, or administered the business of banking. Now, all that mattered was bringing in the numbers—loans, deposits, new customers. And the quotas kept increasing. The culture changed so radically, so fast, that I became physically ill. My gut told me that my symptoms were caused by stress. Many, many nights, I cried myself to sleep. I was miserable.

During this time, I had a cut-and-color appointment with my favorite hairdresser. Doreen was sweet, personable, and fun—and really talented with hair. I'd been going to her for five years, and I looked forward to my appointments. We always laughed a lot, and I left feeling joyful and uplifted.

On this particular day, midway through the cut, Doreen asked me if I'd ever had a massage.

"No," I replied.

"You *must* give this woman a call and book an appointment for a massage. Her name is Patricia. She's amazing. Before you leave, I'll give you her number."

As I was preparing to leave, Doreen wrote Patricia's number on the back of one of her business cards and handed it to me, asking for my assurance that I'd make the call.

"Sure!" I lied.

I thanked her, stuck the card into my purse, and left with my usual smile and a wave. *I don't need a massage ... I'm fine!* I thought to myself. I walked to my car, got in, and drove back to my perfectly *fine* life.

Six weeks later, I'm back in Doreen's chair, and the first question she asks me is, "Did you see Patricia?"

"No."

"You must! This woman is *amazing*. What she does is so much more than massage. She gets into your head!" she said mysteriously, peering deeply into me with her big brown eyes.

And that's a good thing? But I nodded and smiled, to be polite. Doreen went on and on about this woman, Patricia, but I felt no inclination to make an appointment for a massage.

Days later, I found myself with the business card with Patricia's phone number in one hand, and the telephone receiver in my other. Almost as if I was in a trance, I dialed the number, talked to the woman who answered, and made an appointment for the following week.

What am I doing? I asked myself, as I hung up the phone.

As the day of the appointment approached, I became increasingly uncomfortable about the whole thing. I was raised conservatively in a small, sheltered community just outside of Pittsburgh, Pennsylvania. I was in uncharted territory here. Since I had no idea what to expect, thoughts began churning around in my head. *Getting a massage means you have to get naked, right? I don't get naked in front of strangers. What is she going to do to me? Do I have to get totally naked? Why did I say yes to this? What have I gotten myself into?*

The day arrived. I had gotten myself pretty worked up and stressed out, but I decided to follow through with this. Doreen did arouse my curiosity, and I trusted her. Mainly, I couldn't face sitting in her chair again and admitting that I was too chicken to get a massage!

I drove to Patricia's house, which was situated in a quiet, well-kept residential neighborhood. I rang the doorbell and a kind-looking, friendly, middle-aged woman with short, reddish hair, a warm smile, and sparkly eyes opened the door.

Patricia welcomed me into her home, showed me into her treatment room, and instructed me to get undressed and then lie on the massage table, on my back, under the sheets. Seeing the deer-in-the-headlights look on my face, she amended herself and said that if I felt more comfortable leaving my underwear on, that would be okay. She assured me that my privates would be covered the whole time, and that receiving a massage was totally safe. While undressing, I decided to live dangerously. I'd come this far. The underwear, along with everything else, came off.

Dolphin Love

During the massage, I was hyperaware of everything. I can't say that I relaxed at all during that first massage, because it was all so new to me. Patricia had told me that sometimes her clients fall asleep on the table. Not me! I was wide awake, every moment, noticing each stroke and touch, all the while wondering and worrying about where and how she would touch me next.

 "There's no accident that you came here ... I'm not just a massage therapist ... My real job is to wake people up ..."

When the massage was over, I was relieved. I got off the table, dressed, and went out to meet her at her dining room table, to pay and leave.

With checkbook in hand and pen poised to write, I sat down in the chair that was waiting for me. And then Patricia started to talk. And she talked, and she talked, and she talked. She was saying very strange things like, "There's no accident that you came here ... I'm not just a massage therapist ... My real job is to wake people up ..."

Wake people up? I'm awake. What's she talking about?

"When the student is ready, the teacher will appear."

Student? What student? I'm a professional businesswoman. What's she talking about?

I sat in this strange woman's dining room, listening to her talk. She was speaking English, but she might as well have been speaking a foreign language. I had no idea what she was saying. I just sat there and nodded, and smiled, and nodded and smiled some more. I honestly had nothing to say. It was the strangest thing.

Finally, after about forty minutes of her talking and me sitting, she looked at me and said, "Your eyes are glazed over. That's enough for now."

I asked her how much I owed her, wrote the check, thanked her for the massage, and turned to leave, feeling utterly perplexed by the whole experience.

Following me, Patricia reached past me and opened her front door to let me out. When my foot crossed the threshold of her doorway and landed on the pavement outside, the thought entered my mind, *My life will never be the same ...*

I had no idea what that meant. Dazed, I walked to my car. I started the car, began the drive home, and noticed that the colors looked brighter. The cars and people looked different somehow. Driving on the freeway toward home, a Whitney Houston song came on the radio—"The Greatest Love." I burst into tears. I cried and cried. I was driving home, but I didn't want to go home. I loved my husband, but I didn't want to go home to him. This song was about self-love, and I became aware, for the first time, that I did not truly love myself. I grieved my lack of self-love, intensely.

That was the beginning. The time I spent with Patricia did, indeed, wake me up! I didn't know at the time just how "asleep" I had been. The word "spirituality" wasn't in my vocabulary. I marvel now at how I could not have known that this whole other world—the world of energy and spirit—existed. How was that even possible?

The moment I left Patricia's house, my inner doorway to spirituality cracked open. And once that doorway was open just a little bit, spirit came through and blasted it wide open. Things just started happening—so quickly, so intensely. It was as if I was on the fast track of my own unique spiritual path, and there was nothing I could do to stop it.

A few days after my massage, a small ad in a local newspaper caught my eye. It was for a Kundalini yoga class. I'd heard of yoga, but I'd never heard of Kundalini yoga. I was curious, so I decided to check it out. I walked into the house where the classes were being held and saw an American man wearing a white turban wrapped around his head. *Weird.* At the end of the first class, he had us all standing in a big circle singing songs that he called chants. I was squirming in discomfort by the foreignness of it all, but something caused me to keep coming back.

My third class, I arrived late. My day had been distressing and majorly stressful. Entering into the large living room, I scanned the space. The only spot left open in the whole room was right next to the ... teacher ... yogi ... the strange man with the turban on his head. *Great* ... I thought to myself. But everyone had already seen me. I couldn't very well turn around and leave.

Right after I took my seat, he had us stand up in a circle and hold hands. Then he had us chant, which set off my squirming. I couldn't help wondering what my friends and family would think if they saw me standing here, doing this, in this roomful of people. But I persevered. No one else seemed to be having a problem with it.

When we stopped chanting, this man instructed us to remain standing, close our eyes, and continue holding hands in silence. After a minute or two, I began to feel a tingling sensation in my right hand, the hand that was holding his. My left hand, that was holding the hand of the woman on the other side of me, felt normal. The tingling sensation grew stronger and stronger, and then began to move up my hand and into my wrist, then up my forearm, and finally all the way up to my elbow. When the tingling sensation reached my elbow, he instructed us to disconnect our hands and sit down.

What was that? What just happened? I was freaked out, and completely distracted for the rest of the class. The moment the class was over, I was out of there. I thought about going back to ask what had happened, but I was too chicken. I stopped going to those classes.

The very next day, I had an even more intense experience at the local community college where I was taking some classes. I felt very attracted to my psychology professor, and I had a feeling he was also attracted to me. Neither of us acknowledged this, though. We were both married. We kept our interactions and communications professional.

After this particular psych class, I was standing just outside the college building talking to Elizabeth, a classmate. I was in my thirties; she was in her fifties. Being the only two middle-aged women in the midst of all of these young people was a connecting point for us. As our professor walked by, Elizabeth stopped him and we all began talking. Soon she was asking him some pretty personal questions, so I excused myself and walked away.

The moment I turned away from this man, waves of intense tingling sensations began pouring through my body, from the top of my head to the tips of my toes. This intense stream of energy flowed continuously through me as I made the long walk across campus to my car. It was all I could do to walk normally with these orgasmic waves of energy rushing through me, all the while passing masses of young people bustling about in between classes. When I got into my car, I had to sit for quite a while until the sensations stopped and I felt able to drive. *What's happening to me?*

These kinds of experiences just started to happen, suddenly and unexpectedly. I didn't understand any of it, but somehow I knew to trust what was happening. I no longer felt in control of my life ... and that was okay. These new experiences were exhilarating and exciting. Every day was brand new. I never knew what was going to happen next!

♡

Norman and I decided to take a Love Boat cruise, a short three-day cruise down the coast of Mexico, with day excursions to Cabo San Lucas, Mazatlán, and Puerto Vallarta. We were both growing increasingly disenchanted with our jobs. We needed a break from the rat race.

On the first night, at dinner, we were seated next to a man who told us an extraordinary story. He was a Mormon, had been married, had five children living in Utah, a lucrative career—and, one day, he walked away from it all. He left his "normal" life behind, went to Belize, bought a small island and a boat, and started a charter business sailing tourists around the Caribbean coast. "Life is simple. I couldn't be happier." He was glowing.

Norman and I left our encounter with this man, fascinated. Who does that? Who just leaves their life and buys a tropical island and starts anew? This man wasn't famous and wealthy, he seemed pretty ordinary. Throughout the duration of the cruise, we found ourselves drawn into deeper conversations with him. We were so curious about what his life was like. He talked occasionally about the pangs of guilt he felt sometimes, particularly in regard to his children, but he seemed truly, genuinely happy!

Neither of us had ever met anyone like this man. While we may not have condoned his choices, we were intrigued by his lifestyle, and we were certainly attracted to the sense of freedom and joy that radiated from him.

Every night, we returned to our tiny cabin and began imagining ... *What would life be like if ... What could life be like if ... we made a radically different choice?* A seed had been planted. All of the sudden, we started meeting really interesting people, who were living really interesting lives. The seed was being nurtured.

When we returned home, I continued my explorations into the world of metaphysics and spirituality, my eyes now wide open to an even wider array of possibilities. My first foray into a new age bookstore was much like the first time I ventured into a serious weightlifting gym, full of sweaty, hunky jocks. I felt totally out of my element—intimidated, uncomfortable, a stranger in a strange land. Everything was totally foreign. But I persisted!

Soon I discovered the world of psychic readings. If a mini reading was offered, I got one. Several readers gave me the same message: "You are a healer." This was new information; I didn't even know what being a healer meant! The third time a reader told me this, he followed it up with some practical advice. "Take a course in massage therapy. That would be a good place to start." I laughed to myself, thinking of my very first massage experience. *If he only knew!*

I was looking for a way to create a new life for myself, and this young man's suggestion stayed with me. Norman and I agreed that massage was something that I could do anywhere, and it sure was a change from banking! He was supportive of the idea, so I did some research. I found a massage school nearby that offered a 100-hour course in massage therapy. I made an appointment to meet the staff, tour the facility, and learn more. I liked what I saw, so I signed up.

The day I walked into the first class, there was a group of about fifteen students and a teacher already seated in a circle on the floor. I sat down and introduced myself.

A young man responded, "Wow, you really look like you belong here!"

My new classmates all eagerly agreed. I smiled and thanked them. I was surprised to already feel so welcomed.

The training was a wonderful experience. Learning therapeutic massage was the perfect first step in the creation of my new life.

Before the Dolphins

♡

In 1993, Norman and I made that radical decision that we had flirted with ever since the Love Boat cruise. We were both miserable in our jobs. What did we have to lose? We quit our jobs, sold our house, and purchased a large RV. With our beloved cats, Oscar and Chester, and our Jeep Wrangler in tow, we set out on a cross-country trip in search of the perfect place to begin anew.

Ultimately, we landed in mystical, magical Sedona, Arizona. I had first heard about Sedona from my hairdresser, Doreen. Once again, Doreen was a pivotal person in my life. When she learned that Norman and I were taking this trip, she said, "You *must* go to Sedona!" I'd never heard of the place.

The first time I saw Sedona, it took my breath away. Stunning red rock monuments thrust out of the earth, creating a landscape that exudes sacredness. But the magic of Sedona is more than just the spectacular scenery. The land is dotted with special power spots, called energy vortexes. These are anomalies in the earth where energy is amplified. Many people report having mystical experiences while visiting them. To me, all of Sedona is one big vortex. You can't help but be influenced by the unique quality of energy of this place—whether you are aware of it, or believe in it, or not.

> Stunning red rock monuments thrust out of the earth, creating a landscape that exudes sacredness.

Sedona is a creative vortex. It attracts a wide variety of artists and spiritual seekers. Spiritual and metaphysical shops and activities abound. By the time I arrived, I was completely open. Like a kid in a candy store, I relished exploring the various treats this place had to offer. With a voracious curiosity and lust for life, I was fertile soil for Sedona to work her magic.

Norman's dream was to buy a small business that we could manage together until we could retire. We looked for that; but I was also out there every day, meeting people, hiking on the land, exploring this new world, and creating an exciting new life for myself.

Dolphin Love

♡

Living among the red rocks amplifies your internal experience, and often the first six months in Sedona can be intense. We heard this frequently from Sedona locals when they learned we were newcomers.

"The first six months are the test. If you survive that, you'll be okay."

Sedona is a small town of around 10,000 residents, and it's surrounded by protected forest and wilderness land. You're never far from a trail. Walking for hours alone on the land became my cherished daily ritual. The desert landscape was new to me. I wandered aimlessly, selected a spot and just sat, sometimes for hours. I looked deeply into the seemingly barren desert landscape and marveled at all the life I saw. Captivated by the untamed beauty of the desert, I fell in love with her wildness. I felt utterly safe in her midst.

It did not take long to unwind from my previous life in the corporate world and let my guard down. On the land, I was free to be me. The land did not judge me; it simply witnessed me. My mind began to quiet. For the first time in my life, I learned how to just *be*. What a tremendous gift!

Very early on during these sojourns, I experienced a deep catharsis. I cried every day for two weeks. The moment I stepped onto the land, I burst into tears. I cried and cried. The tears seemed to come from the very depth of my being, from my soul. I didn't know what this flood of emotion was about. All I could do was surrender to the tears. It seemed like I was releasing lifetimes of pain. I figured I was better off allowing this energy to leave my body than keeping it buried deep inside. I was grateful for the release.

After the tears ebbed every day, nature began to reveal her mystical side to me. I began to feel and see subtle energies ... of the land, the plants, and the sky. I was even seeing energy fields, in the form of a white light, around inanimate objects in our home. Every day, nature unveiled a new aspect of her invisible self to me. I was fascinated. I became passionate about the unseen world, the world of energy and spirit. Nature became my teacher and the land my classroom. I was a most willing and enthusiastic student.

My parents visited one weekend from Pittsburgh. While standing together in my living room, with a large picture window that looked out upon the red rocks, my dad asked me, "Do you go to church?"

I lifted my arm and swept my hand toward the window. Looking out toward the red rocks, I replied, "That's my church."

I loved Sedona. I loved the place, I loved the people. But mostly, I loved the land.

I wish I could say that our move to Sedona resulted in a fairy tale second phase of Norman's and my life together. But that's not what happened. We were not immune from the intense energies of this place having their way with us. My inner world was rockin' and rollin'. My belief systems were collapsing; all I knew to be true was being challenged. Events occurred that were wake-up calls for me that our marriage was not what I wanted ... needed ... it to be.

At the end of a yoga class, a woman came up to me, softly touched my shoulder, and whispered, "Tell me about your relationship."

A dam burst, and tears flowed. I cried and cried for an embarrassingly long time, before I was able to talk. This woman was a psychic. She saw a truth in me that I wasn't willing to see—or feel—myself. Her mere touch, and the speaking of those five words, brought this painful truth to the surface.

"Norman is my best friend, and I love him dearly, but what we have together is not a marriage," I uttered, in between sobs.

I returned home from that fateful class, with the words ... *Something has to change, something has to change* ... resounding in my heart and mind.

The months that followed were a wild pendulum swing. At one extreme there was hell and craziness in my rapidly unraveling relationship with Norman. At the same time, there were exquisite spiritual openings and wondrous connections within the warm and welcoming community of Sedona, and my ever-deepening connection to the land.

With Norman, it wasn't long before things escalated to the point that it became impossible to continue living together without doing more damage. We made the difficult decision to separate, so that we could have the time and space to heal, each in our own timing and each in our own way.

I told him at one point, "Once we're healed and whole, we can come back together and see where we are ... see if we still want to be together."

Separating from Norman was probably the hardest decision I'd made in my life. I loved him deeply. He was a good man. He was good to me. And I knew he loved me with all his heart. How is it that sometimes love is not enough?

And then, a few months after we separated, Norman suddenly died. Almost six months to the day after we arrived together in Sedona, full of hope, excitement, and optimism for the new life we would create together, he was gone. The life I had known was over.

Six months after the tragedy, I moved to the Hawaiian island of Maui, to grieve and to heal. Being in the soft, nourishing energy of the island was a tremendous gift. Months passed. The shock of Norman's passing slowly subsided, and my heart began to heal. A newfound sense of freedom began to emerge inside of me. In a holy moment, the realization dawned that there were no ties or connections left to hold me back from being or doing anything I wanted. My life was a blank canvas. I was free to create my life anew. After all that I'd been through, I felt this to be a sacred gift.

TWO

The Call of the Dolphins

I unexpectedly landed back in Sedona. I'd been away for a year—living in Hawaii for five months, traveling through Southeast Asia for the next five months, and then touring the U.S. in search of my next home. Sedona wasn't even on my radar screen as a place to live. I had no interest in going back. It was time for a new experience.

As my travels wound down, I fell in love with a tiny, rustic log cabin in the sweet little mountain town of Nederland, fifteen miles west of Boulder, Colorado, snuggled in the foothills of the Rocky Mountains. I saw myself living there, spending the cold winter months in front of a cozy fire, writing.

I was discouraged to discover that the cabin wouldn't be available for two weeks. The idea of staying in a nearby motel for two weeks wasn't appealing. A friend of mine, who owned a beautiful second home in Sedona—a luxurious log cabin—popped into my mind. When I had visited him last, he extended the invitation for me to stay at his cabin anytime, whether he was there or not. I gave my friend a quick call. The cabin was available, and he was more than happy for me to stay there for as long as I needed to.

With a few boxes of my worldly possessions stashed in the back of my Jeep, I was on the road again ... to Sedona. I made the fourteen-hour drive in one day.

It was 9:30 at night as I passed through Flagstaff, the mountain community thirty miles north of Sedona. Driving along I-17, I leaned forward, folded my arms on top of the steering wheel, and looked up into the ink black night sky. The blackness was perforated with a dazzling array of brilliantly shining stars. *It's the sky that gets to me here—both the daytime sky and the nighttime sky.*

As my love for the sky expanded inside of me and filled me up, the biggest, brightest shooting star I'd ever seen descended from the heavens, directly in front of me, on a vertical trajectory straight down toward the earth. The shooting star was pointing in the direction of my destination—Sedona. This felt like a message. *Uh-oh. No ... don't tell me I'm going to live in Sedona again.*

I felt it in my bones. Sedona was to be my home once more. An internal struggle of yes-no ensued inside of me. My first six months there were way too intense. Driving down through Oak Creek Canyon, the last leg of the trip, my internal struggle raged on. I loved Sedona, and I was grateful for all the magic that occurred for me there, but I really didn't want to live there again! I thought about turning around and driving back to Colorado. *I've already come this far. It's ludicrous to turn around and go back to Colorado now ...*

I continued on until I arrived at my friend's cabin. I fumbled around in the dark for the key, let myself in, and got situated. One question floated alongside the stirred-up emotions of my past: *Whatever shall I do here?*

My travels had been fun and exciting, but it was time to settle down and do something meaningful with my life. I knew what I didn't want to do—go back to my earlier life of banking, business suits, and the 9-to-5 workday. I'd left that world behind, spread my wings, traveled to distant lands, and tasted the intoxication of freedom.

My bank account was dwindling. That 401(k) nest egg money wasn't going to last forever. I hadn't a clue what I could do that would suit the new me I was still in the process of discovering, that would nourish and fulfill me ... and also pay the bills.

As my head dropped onto the pillow for my first night's sleep of this apparent return to Sedona, I had a firm talk with spirit. *"If you want me to live here, tell me what*

to do with my life. I want to do something fulfilling and purposeful, and I want to know
what that something is by the time I wake up tomorrow!"

I was awakened at dawn by a vivid, involved dream that showed me working
with young people. That dream was enough to stimulate my imagination and open
me to the idea of living in Sedona again. I jumped out of bed, full of energy and
excitement, and padded outside to catch the sunrise bathing the magnificent red
rocks in soft, apricot light. I was so happy, I couldn't contain myself. I walked down
the rock pathway to the street to see more of the red rocks, and found myself spinning down the middle of the street like a kid, giggling and laughing. Thankfully,
not a soul was around. In that moment, I felt like I had Sedona all to myself. *Oh,
Sedona. You've captured my heart ... again.*

That very day, the magic began. But events took a completely unexpected turn.
What actually happened had nothing to do with my waking dream of working
with young people. No dream could have prepared me for how my life was about
to unfold.

What started happening was very strange. Wherever I went, almost everyone
I met, whether I knew them or not, immediately started talking to me ... about
dolphins! I didn't bring up the subject, they did. This happened to me over and
over again. It was the strangest thing. I didn't have anything to contribute to these
conversations, because I didn't know much, or care much, about dolphins at all. I
liked dolphins, but I didn't perceive them as having anything to do with my life.
Why are you talking to me about dolphins? We live in the desert, for heaven's sake, was
the thought that kept rolling around in my head.

Looking back on it, though, there were two earlier experiences that foreshad-
owed the connection I was about to discover.

The first one happened in 1992, as I was just beginning to awaken to my
spirituality. I accepted a friend's invitation to attend a weekly meditation group in
the foothills, just north of Sacramento, California. There were only a few of us,
and the facilitator led us into meditation using guided visualization techniques.

Dolphin Love

Meditation was new to me, and I was wide open, in that sublime place of "beginner's mind." I knew nothing and had no expectations, the prerequisite for magic to occur.

It was during one of these meditations that I had my first spirit dolphin encounter—the one I describe in the Prologue to this book. It was as clear and real as could be. I'd never had an experience like that in my life. It didn't occur to me at the time to derive a meaning or message from the meditation. It was just a really cool experience that kept me going back for more. The dolphin did not visit me again in those meditations, and my awareness of him quickly faded.

The second experience happened off the coast of Lanai, Hawaii, in 1994. Accompanied by a friend on a tourist boat, we departed Lanai for the return trip to Maui. I had heard that there was a pod* of spinner dolphins that hang out in that bay, so we were on the lookout for them. Sure enough, as we left the dock, dolphins appeared and surrounded the boat. Everyone got superexcited and rushed to the railings to get a good look at them, causing the boat to list slightly to one side.

Before I could move, a stream of energy passed through me, from the top of my head down through my toes, gluing me to my spot. It was as if something else took over. My eyes closed and I heard myself asking the dolphins, in my mind:

"Why are you here? What do you have to teach us?"

The reply came instantly, and I heard it clearly:

"Unity ... Community."

The dolphins left, and the boat continued on its way. This was after my earlier experiences in Sedona, where I had communicated with various aspects of the natural world—plants, trees, rocks, some animals. I considered this event to be just one more of the many unusual experiences I'd been having on my spiritual journey, and I didn't take it very seriously. I didn't even think to share that communication with my friend.

That was it. Those were my two dolphin experiences. They were interesting, but I didn't perceive them to be particularly significant to me, personally.

---

* Dolphins live and travel in groups called pods. A pod is like an extended family.

♡

Once I was back in Sedona, though, the dolphins were quite ingenious in getting my attention.

I was wearing a small rutilated quartz crystal dolphin necklace that I had purchased on Maui. I didn't buy it because of the dolphin. I bought it because of the crystal. The people selling the necklaces performed a muscle-testing technique to determine which, from a big pile of necklaces they were selling, was best for me. They told me that rutilated quartz crystal carries the qualities of grounding and protection. That sounded good to me! So I bought it, and wore it every day. I never took that necklace off.

When I returned to Sedona, things started happening to the necklace. One day it disappeared. I was wearing it, and then it was just gone. Days later, walking through a public parking lot, I noticed something sparkling on the ground. I walked over to see what it was, and I was shocked to discover my dolphin necklace lying there! I had no idea how it got there, but I was so happy to have it back.

Even though it was broken, I had an irrational, strong feeling that I needed to keep the necklace close to me for some reason.

The necklace disappeared and reappeared again, and then one day I noticed it was broken. I found a tiny piece of the crystal lying on my kitchen floor—a part of the dolphin's tail. I had no idea how it could have broken. I continued wearing the broken necklace until it mysteriously broke even more. Still, I kept wearing the necklace, even though the crystal no longer bore any resemblance to a dolphin. Finally, one day, I decided it was enough. Wearing this broken necklace seemed ridiculous. So I took it off—reluctantly—and put it in my purse, where it remained for a long time. Even though it was broken, I had an irrational, strong feeling that I needed to keep the necklace close to me for some reason.

Months later, I attended a weekend retreat on energy healing with a friend. On Saturday, the spiritual healer and psychic called on me to stand in front of the roomful of seventy-five people. He proclaimed, "There's a broken necklace in your purse that's important to you."

"Yes! What does it mean?" I asked, hoping that this man could solve this mystery for me.

"I don't know. I only know it's important to you," he replied.

That wasn't very helpful.

Meanwhile, I kept meeting people who spontaneously started talking to me about dolphins. It was weird.

Then, one day, I was introduced to a man named Matisha at the local natural foods store. He is a singer-songwriter who lives in Hawaii and swims with dolphins frequently. Matisha was in Sedona to give a concert.

When we met, Matisha said to me, "You're totally a dolphin."

"How do you know?" I asked, reflexively wrapping my hand around the broken dolphin necklace I was wearing.

"I can totally see it. Their energy is all around you!"

I didn't know what he meant by that. But, by now, the dolphins had my attention. Something was clearly going on between the dolphins and me. I wanted to know what.

Upon returning home to my Sedona townhouse, I paced the length of my living room, pondering this whole dolphin phenomenon. Frustrated and exasperated, I exclaimed out loud to the universe, "What is it about the dolphins? I'm in the desert. I don't get it! What do I have to do with dolphins, and what do dolphins have to do with me?"

Within weeks of shouting my plea, a messenger was sent. The dolphins' message was delivered, loud and clear. And my life was turned inside out and upside down ... again! **

** Years later, the dolphins gave me their point of view: *"What we really did was turn your life right side up!"*

THREE

The Message

In January 1996, my friend Nickie cajoled me into taking an amateur acting class with her. I didn't perceive myself as remotely artistic or creative. Taking an acting class was not something I would have chosen to do on my own. But I was open for a new adventure that would bring more fun and play into my life, so I agreed to go.

We went to the first class, made grand fools of ourselves, and had a great time. I even met a nice guy named David during the break. We talked for a few minutes and discovered we had a few things in common—we were both eating a PowerBar, and we were both wearing the same brand of essential oils.

"We're a match made in heaven!" we joked.

He asked me for my phone number, and I gave it to him.

Throughout the second half of the class, I noticed David watching me. Every once in a while, our eyes met, and we smiled at one another from across the room. I was flattered. Receiving that kind of attention was fun. I was single now. Why not enjoy it?

When the class was over, all of the students were mingling, hugging, and saying goodbye. Hugging is very big in Sedona. It was like a big party. Joy was in the air.

David walked toward me with a big smile on his face, his arms outstretched wide. I stepped forward to hug him, and the moment he wrapped his arms around me, I felt a sensation of familiarity ... of *home*. Before I could fully register that feeling, he lifted me up and swung me around enthusiastically.

"Wow!" I responded when he put me down, held me at arm's length, and beamed me his big smile. I didn't know what to say.

A mixture of thoughts and feelings were tumbling around inside of me. I was definitely disconcerted by that fleeting feeling of being "home" in his arms. David's uncensored expression of attraction and excitement was a bit overwhelming—and also nice! *Who is this man?*

I pulled myself together to thank him for that enthusiastic hug, giggling to cover my embarrassment. I then excused myself to find Nickie ... to take me away from there.

When we got to the car, Nickie and I were both so energized, we decided to go out for a cup of tea to unwind. We arrived at Cups, a small café in West Sedona. It was late at night by Sedona standards. We had the place to ourselves. We found the perfect table in a quiet corner and sat down.

The lighting was soft and dim, and the atmosphere was warm and cozy. The tables were draped with cotton floral tablecloths and topped with a single candle and a small clear glass vase sprouting a few stems of wildflowers. Perched against the vase in the center of our table was a small white card: "$5, 5-minute psychic reading by Antarah Rose."

In this haven for spiritual and new age seekers, this casual invitation into the psychic realm was not unusual. We looked at each other and grinned. "This could be fun! For five dollars, what have we got to lose?" We ordered one dessert, two herbal teas, and two psychic readings. Only in Sedona!

Nickie went first, and the reading was all about relationship. It seemed pretty generic, and quite honestly, I was not impressed with the reader. Then it was my turn.

Antarah looked into my eyes, closed her eyes, opened her eyes, and called out, "DOLPHINS!"

I was shocked! It felt like the room shook.

She continued, "You need to go to them, swim with them, be with them, be healed by them ..."

She said so much so quickly, I don't believe she took one breath! Out poured a steady stream of information about my connection with the dolphins, and what I was supposed to do about it.

This was so out of left field for me that I was hardly hearing her. *Me?? Swim with dolphins? **Other** people do dolphins ... **I** don't do dolphins!* This is what my mind was saying.

I looked at Nickie at one point during the reading and saw tears streaming down her face. She told me later that she saw me turn into a dolphin right before her eyes! She felt sad because she knew I would be leaving Sedona again. It all felt very true to her.

I didn't know what to make of this. I had just returned to Sedona and had finally committed to staying there. I had already lived in Hawaii once and felt complete with that. *Now I'm supposed to go back?*

As we left the restaurant, I said to Nickie, "Usually I jump when spirit tells me to do something—and I've been doing a lot of jumping lately—but this is too far out for me. I'm not going to do anything to make this happen. For me to go through with it, this trip has to create itself."

Two weeks later, I was on a plane, headed for Hawaii.

Immediately following the reading, all the information came to me ... where to go to swim with the dolphins, where to stay, what to expect from an underwater encounter in the wild ... it all came. How did this happen? It started with a phone call.

The day after the reading, my friends Paula and David Green called from Maui. They were getting married in February and I had agreed to fly there early to make Paula's wedding dress. While we talked, I told them about this perplexing psychic reading I'd just received. David revealed to me, for the first time, that when I had given him a massage when I lived on Maui, he opened his eyes at one point and saw me as a dolphin.

Dolphin Love

"You're telling me this *now?*" I replied in exasperation.

They went on to tell me about a bay on the Big Island of Hawaii where human-friendly dolphins hang out. People kayak out and swim with them in the wild there. Paula and David swam with the dolphins there several months earlier. *Oh, geez. Okay ... so this is where to go to swim with dolphins.*

Then Paula told me about a beautiful retreat center with inexpensive lodging that was on the hill overlooking the bay. She'd research the information and call me back with it. She did, that afternoon. *This is where to stay.*

Later that day, I was shopping in a local metaphysical store. From across the room, the magazine stand grabbed my attention. I felt magnetically pulled toward the magazines, to the *Sedona Journal of Emergence* in particular. Without even thinking, I picked it up and bought it. This magazine is a compilation of channeled material. When I first moved to Sedona, I bought the magazine regularly, and inhaled its contents. I hadn't bought an issue for quite some time.

In big, bold print the words "Swimming With Wild Dolphins" stared up at me. I was stunned.

I returned home, made a cup of tea, and sat down to skim through the magazine. This time, nothing interested me; I just flipped the pages. About two-thirds of the way through, I turned a page, saw the article title, and froze. In big, bold print, the words "Swimming With Wild Dolphins" stared up at me. I was stunned.

There was even a note from the publisher, right underneath the article title, acknowledging that the inclusion of this article in the magazine was a policy departure. Ordinarily, this magazine only prints channeled information. This wasn't channeled information, but they felt it was an important story and that the material was timely. *I'll say ... timely for me!*

I devoured the article. The writer had just returned from his first encounter swimming with wild dolphins off the coast of Oahu, Hawaii. He described the transformational experiences of the various group members, as well as his own in-water adventures with the dolphins. It was all there.

Okay! Okay! I'll go! I'll do it! Clearly the universe wanted me to do this. The energy around it seemed huge, and there was a palpable sense of urgency in the air. I felt an enormous ball of energy behind me, propelling me forward into this experience.

I already had plans to fly to Hawaii in a month for Paula and David's wedding. Why not go to the Big Island a week or two early to check out the dolphins? That seemed the reasonable and practical thing to do. But Antarah told me I was to live there, which made sense. If I'm to swim with the dolphins and be healed by them, shouldn't I live there so I can be with them as much as possible?

I had two months left on my lease. In the various moves I'd made since beginning my life anew, I'd let go of most of my material possessions. I had become a master of letting go! The one exception was my beloved Jeep. I was fondly attached to this vehicle. He had traveled with me across the ocean once already, to Hawaii and back, and was sporting a few small rust spots as souvenirs. I didn't want to ship him there again. It just didn't feel right. I had half-heartedly attempted to sell him a few times in the past, but there were no nibbles. This was the last big test. If my Jeep sold, there would be no doubt that I was supposed to make this move.

With resolve and more than a bit of curiosity, I placed an ad in the local paper to appear that Wednesday. At the stroke of midnight Wednesday, I was shaking hands with the proud new owners of my Jeep. They came, saw, drove, and said YES by the light of a mere flashlight. *That's it ... I'm moving to Hawaii. Again!*

I surrendered the remainder of my lease and stored my small stash of belongings in a friend's basement. There was nothing left to handle. I was leaving Sedona for the second time, this time to embark upon a mysterious adventure with wild dolphins.

Am I nuts?

Four

The Gift

The stark landscape that greeted me upon arrival on the Kona side of the Big Island was startling and disconcerting. I didn't know much about this island. I had only visited it once before, and then I stayed on the Hilo side, the "wet side," which is lush and tropical, the way Hawaii is supposed to be.

All I saw here, besides the glistening ocean off in the distance, was black lava rock covering the earth like a scorched crust. It was not remotely appealing. I wasn't sure I liked it here at all.

Thankfully, as I drove toward my destination, the landscape changed. Ah ... green ... lots of green. This was more like it. It felt like old Hawaii here. Even the tourist area was more laid-back than what I'd seen on Maui. I felt my body relax. The awe and excitement of this new adventure washed through me.

Following the directions to the retreat center where I was staying, I drove down a narrow, winding road, passing lush tropical flora that spilled onto both sides of the road. The air was thick with moisture and heavily laden with tropical scents.

Suddenly, the world seemed very small to me. It was all right here ... the whole world, fully contained in this spot. This place had its own sense of time. Clocks, calendars, day planners—these linear timekeepers did not belong here. I could feel the rhythm and pulse of the natural world. My body and mind shifted naturally into resonance with this rhythm. Ever so subtly, I entered into an altered state of consciousness.

At a bend in the road, I spotted the faded and tattered rainbow flag that marked the entrance to the retreat center. Turning onto the steep, grassy driveway, I descended into the property and parked my rental car beside the only other car there. As I took my first steps on the rich, moist soil, the earth yielded under my feet. I was enveloped in a profusion of new scents, sounds, and sights. I could smell the earth here, a distinctive damp, musty aroma. I inhaled deeply and felt a stirring inside. There was something familiar about this earthy scent. It was comforting and grounding.

I wandered through lush gardens and various outbuildings in search of the property manager. When I found her, she greeted me warmly, showed me to my room, and gave me a brief tour of the grounds. My room was small and clean, with only a screened window (no glass) to the Garden of Eden outside. The showers were outdoors, which I loved. I was thrilled. This was the perfect place to stay while embarking on my new adventure!

I looked forward to exploring the retreat center grounds more thoroughly, but that would have to wait. I was feeling pulled by the dolphins. It was time to go to the bay and meet them!

Brimming with excitement and enthusiasm, I told the property manager that I was there to swim with the dolphins! The way she looked at me, I could tell she was unimpressed. Apparently, I was not the first to come here to do that, nor would I be the last. She asked if I had snorkel gear. *Oops! I didn't think about that.* She let me borrow hers that afternoon, and told me where to go to rent some for the rest of my stay.

I got back into my car and drove down the hill to the bay. My body was buzzing in anticipation. It was very strange. I knew I was being guided to meet the dolphins, yet I had absolutely no idea why, or what to expect. I had no previous life experience to prepare me for what I was about to do.

As a result, my mind was not *thinking* much. This was all so new to me that my mind couldn't wrap around what was happening. Rather, I was feeling my body sensations and being in the moment, taking one step at a time.

I felt an underlying sense of trust. I had no idea what was about to transpire; yet I felt completely safe. It was as if someone else had taken over, and I was following that someone else's lead. A benevolent force seemed to be guiding me.

I arrived at the bay in midafternoon, parked my car in the parking area at the end of the road, and stepped out, noticing black lava rock again. Scanning the rocky shoreline, there was not a speck of sand in sight. *Where's the beach?* I saw people in kayaks out in the bay, but I couldn't see how they got there. This bay didn't seem very user-friendly.

A young man approached me, one of the Kona Kayak boys who rents kayaks to tourists. He told me that I had just missed the dolphins by half an hour.

Darn! My heart sank. I walked away and surveyed the scene for a while, getting a feel for this place. I was uncertain what to do. It hadn't occurred to me to hire a guide.

This was a large, protected bay, and the water was calm. The weather was exquisite ... warm, sunny, and clear. The water sure looked inviting! I decided to rent a kayak and go out into the bay to get acclimated.

I'd never been in a sea kayak before. It was a hollow shell of dense plastic— light, easy to maneuver, but still tippy. The young man assisted me into the water and assured me that he would be there when I returned to help me out, as the access point was tricky to navigate alone.

Gliding quietly on the bay was heavenly. I paddled gently, with no particular destination in mind. I was just getting used to being in ... on ... the ocean. The soft lapping of the water against the kayak helped me unwind. I breathed the peace and serenity of this place into my body.

Soon I sensed excitement farther out in the bay. There was a lot of splashing and commotion happening around a cluster of kayaks about a half-mile away. I just knew the dolphins were there. I kicked into high gear and paddled vigorously to reach them before they disappeared again. In my mind, I called out to them, *"I'm coming! I'm coming! Don't go away!"* My heart was racing. It seemed like

Dolphin Love

I was getting nowhere fast. It was taking me forever to make any progress toward them.

I slowed down to catch my breath, and remembered the article I'd read about that man's experiences swimming with the Hawaiian spinner dolphins. He said these dolphins are very sensitive to our energies. They respond better to humans when we are in a peaceful, meditative state.

I was far from peaceful, and I certainly wasn't meditative, so I stopped paddling and let the kayak drift. Closing my eyes, I went inside and focused on breathing slowly and deeply. I calmed down and stayed right where I was for what seemed like a long time. I slipped into a meditative state.

I felt alone in the bay. I was in my own little world again, in total bliss. My intentions and expectations about this trip, and the dolphins, dissolved away. I was just *being*.

When I opened my eyes, I was deeply peaceful and relaxed. In my peripheral vision, I spotted movement under the water. A long, dark shape swam by ... then another ... then another. *The dolphins! They're here!* They were swimming right under my kayak. I watched them for a while, mesmerized. Then I remembered. *Oh! I'm supposed to swim with them. I have to go in! That's why I came here, after all. It's time!*

I was nervous and excited. I had no idea what to expect, but I wasn't afraid at all. Shaking a bit, I donned the slightly-too-big borrowed snorkel gear and tumbled into the water. I meant to enter the water gracefully. That didn't happen. So much for first impressions!

Once I steadied myself, I regained some semblance of dignity. I was a fish as a kid ... all four of us kids were. We lived in the community swimming pool from dawn until dusk, every day of every summer. I was as comfortable in the water as I was on land. But that was a long time ago.

The turquoise water was warm, clear, and highly buoyant. After adjusting my mask, snorkel, and flippers, I took my first look underwater. What I saw took my breath away—brilliant rays of colored light for as far as I could see. It was as though there were masses of clear quartz crystals lining the ocean floor, creating this spectacular liquid light show. I'd swum in many oceans, and I'd never seen anything like this before. This water felt truly magical. Floating effortlessly at the surface in the midst of rays of purple and pink, blue and green, and yellow and white, I completely forgot about the dolphins.

Bliss enveloped me as I connected to the energy of the ocean. I invited all the colors and all the rays of light to wash over and through me, to penetrate and heal me. The warmth of the sun on my back melted me into an even deeper state of relaxation. I no longer felt where my body left off and the water began. I didn't have a care in the world. I felt like I could float there forever.

Then the dolphins returned, startling me out of my reverie. They were all around me! It seemed like there were hundreds of them in the bay. *They're so beautiful! This is amazing! Breathe, Linda.* They swam beneath me in pairs and triads. There was no sound, yet their movements were in perfect harmony and synchronicity. *How do they do that?*

Captivated by the beauty, elegance, and grace of these magnificent beings, I floated at the surface for a long time, watching their exquisite underwater ballet. Nothing else existed in the entire world except this ocean, these dolphins, and me.

After a while, I remembered the dolphin kick I'd read about. It's the kicking part of the butterfly swim stroke, where both legs kick in unison while the arms stay at the sides of the body, or hands clasp together behind the back. Kicking in this manner creates an undulating movement in the body that simulates the way dolphins move.

I practiced swimming this way at the surface. It felt clumsy at first, and I was glad no other humans were around to see me. Then I got the rhythm or, rather, the rhythm got me. *Ah ... this feels ... melodic.* I tried swimming freestyle, to compare sensations, and that felt like I was attacking the water. In contrast, the dolphin kick felt fluid and harmonious in this liquid environment. I practiced this style of swimming for a long time. I'd swim and rest, swim and rest, all the while watching dolphins languidly swim by beneath me.

I was in awe of these beautiful beings. Here we were, two different species coexisting peacefully and harmoniously in the same time and space. I knew they were aware of my presence, and I was most certainly aware of them. It seemed very natural to be here together in this way. It was very sweet.

As I was swimming the dolphin kick at the surface, a group of three dolphins rose beside me and broke the surface to breathe. We swam side by side, making close eye contact for the first time. I was spellbound by their presence at my side. I couldn't take my eyes off those dolphin eyes, peering deeply into me. Their pace was a bit faster than mine, and I soon fell behind, but those few moments we were together were amazing! It was as if I was one of them. *I want to do that again!*

I watched expectantly for another opportunity to swim by their side. Soon a group below me began to surface. I kicked hard, in an effort to be where they would be when they surfaced to breathe. When I realized I wouldn't reach them, I stopped and floated, waiting for the next group to arrive.

When I stopped, my head moved, as if on its own. Looking below and behind me, I saw one lone dolphin floating there. We made eye contact, and suddenly he swam right for me, at full speed. I thought he was going to hit me! In a split second, my eyes closed, my body shifted from its horizontal floating position to vertical, with my head fully submerged. When my eyes opened, I saw this dolphin hover-

ing vertically just inches in front of me, looking at me! I was face-to-face, body-to-body with a wild dolphin!

I laughed out loud through my snorkel and face mask. This dolphin was in my face, and all I could do was laugh! This was so unexpected!

I could reach out and touch him! My intuition told me to keep my arms at my sides. That was hard!

Laughing and snorkeling don't go together. Water flooded my mask. I had to surface to clear it. I didn't want to … I wanted to stay here longer and commune with my new friend. As I surfaced, the dolphin made some clicking sounds and swam away.

I was alone in the water with these wild dolphins for about two hours. It seemed timeless. I kept remembering that dolphin face looking right at me.

The dolphins are inviting me into their world. It feels natural to be here with them. There is nothing extraordinary about it. This is just one more exploration into the natural world; only this time I am exploring the world of dolphins, in their home, the ocean.

I had no idea of the magic and mystery that was about to unfold in my life. I am still discovering the magnitude of the gift my dolphin friend gave me that day.

FIVE

Transcending Time and Space

Upon my return to the retreat center after my magical dolphin encounter, I crossed paths with Henry, the only other person staying there at the time. He'd swum with the dolphins the day before, and we talked briefly about our experiences. I accepted his invitation to join him and his friends in a dolphin swim the following day. We said goodnight and I floated back to my room, feeling soft, mellow, and deeply peaceful. I slept like a baby.

The next morning, while I was eating breakfast in the communal kitchen, Henry came in and gave me some startling news. "Do you know that when we talked last night, the dolphins transmitted energy through you into me?"

"What?" I asked, incredulous.

He repeated his statement. "Last night when we talked, the dolphins transmitted energy ... *to* me, *through* you."

I felt my brain cock a fraction of an inch counterclockwise, and a stream of energy ran through my body from my head to my feet. Inside myself I heard the words, **"Listen to him, he speaks the truth."**

I'd never heard words so clearly inside myself before.

I deluged Henry with questions in an effort to understand what he was saying.

Dolphin Love

Henry is a Buddhist, and he meditates a lot. He knows a lot about energy. But he had no answers for me.

Finally, he said, "Look, all I know is that I received a transmission of energy last night, and it came *from* the dolphins and it came *through* you. That's all I know."

I didn't know what to make of this, so reluctantly I let it go, and we headed out for my second swim with the dolphins. Once again, the weather was sunny and warm, and the water was pristine. This time we swam from shore, taking a narrow overgrown path to a tiny spot of sand that Henry's friends showed us. I was excited to discover this path. I much preferred swimming the half-mile from shore to dealing with a kayak.

The swim was a long one, so we paced ourselves. When we finally reached the dolphins, I was thrilled to see so many of them! The four of us went our separate ways to have our own encounters.

I alternated between floating and swimming at the surface, enjoying watching the dolphins be dolphins. This was a totally different experience from the day before, when I was all alone with them. When it was just the dolphins and me, we were one harmonious pod. Our interactions were peaceful, silent, and elegant. Today, with other humans around, there was a lot going on.

There were kayaks floating in the midst of where we were all swimming. I needed to take frequent breaks from looking down into the water below, where the dolphins were, to look up and scan the surface for kayaks and other swimmers. That took some getting used to.

The swimmers were at varying skill levels. Some obviously had extensive experience swimming with dolphins. They were extraordinary to watch. Many were able to hold their breath for a really long time, and dive deeply to interact with the dolphins below the fray of us inexperienced swimmers. They were so graceful and fluid in the water, they looked like dolphins themselves!

It was swimmers like me—the inexperienced ones—that I had to watch out for, and to navigate around. There were a few bumps, after which we'd nod our apologies to one another through our face masks, and return to why we were there—swimming with the dolphins.

On this day, rather than swimming as a cohesive pod, the dolphins formed smaller groups, and some dolphins swam alone. Some dolphins seemed to be greatly enjoying interacting with us humans. Others, including several sets of mamas and babies, remained at the ocean floor, only surfacing to breathe. The water was quite clear, so even though many dolphins stayed far below, I could still observe them. The dolphins that did interact with us humans spread themselves around, giving each of us high-quality encounters.

Henry and I bumped into each other at one point. We were both giggling, thoroughly enjoying ourselves. I received an inner prompting to ask Henry to meditate with me in the water while holding hands. Now that felt too weird to me. *I've just met this man!* I wasn't at all comfortable with that idea, so I let it go. The inner prompting came again. I ignored it again. When it came the third time, it was very strong. The energy of the request filled up my whole body. *Okay, okay. I'll do it!*

It felt awkward, but I asked Henry if he would be open to meditating with me in the water. He liked that idea. We joined hands and floated at the surface together, our heads underwater, breathing through our snorkels. This felt very strange. Here I was, floating in the ocean, with dolphins and other swimmers all around, holding hands with a guy I barely knew. *I'm supposed to be able to meditate?* I focused on my breathing and did my best to calm down. Finally, I did surrender, and I did meditate. It was a very sweet experience, actually, once I allowed it. I was glad my guidance was persistent, and proud of myself for following through, despite my initial discomfort.

When the meditation felt complete, we disconnected our hands and turned our attention back to the dolphins. A large group of dolphins was on the ocean floor directly beneath us, making quite a racket! It sounded like many mice squeaking. They were very loud. I didn't know what was going on down there, but they were fascinating to watch.

Then one dolphin approached us. He seemed like a young one. Hovering motionless beside us, just beneath the surface, he looked directly at us. I couldn't help but giggle. *They're so cute!* The spinner dolphins are petite. They're about our size, which may be one reason it feels so safe to be in the water with them. I noticed a leaf floating in the water between us and the dolphin. The leaf seemed significant somehow. I looked back and forth between the leaf and the dolphin, the leaf and the dolphin. The dolphin seemed to be communicating something, but I didn't get it. I knew I was missing something. After a little while, the dolphin swam away.

The four of us emerged from the bay after two hours, exhilarated from our dolphin encounters.

Two days later, a woman was visiting the retreat center where I was staying. She had just come from a lecture by Joan Ocean, the amazing woman on the island who pioneered this whole human-dolphin swim phenomenon. Just as I walked into the communal kitchen, she began talking about "the leaf game" that Joan described during her talk. This is a game the dolphins made up to play with humans. They hook a leaf (or a piece of seaweed, or a plastic bag) on their pectoral fin, rostrum,* or tail and make sure the swimmer sees it. The dolphin swims with it, close by, and then releases it. The human is to then swim to the leaf, acquire it and swim with it for a ways, and release it for the dolphin to catch. It's like tag.

That dolphin was trying to play the leaf game with us! I realized, with a thrill. I was really disappointed that I missed that opportunity; but I was glad that I'd know what to do the next time I got the chance to play the leaf game with a dolphin!

After experiencing optimal weather two days in a row, I thought it was like that in the bay every day. I soon discovered otherwise. It rained the next day, and the next day, and the next.

One night, Henry knocked on my door pretty late, asking me to help him with a painful muscle spasm in his back. He saw my light on and hoped I didn't mind him coming by so late. He wasn't able to sleep due to the pain. He knew I was a massage therapist. Once I saw the look of pain on his face, of course I offered to help.

After doing some massage, I placed one hand at the base of his spine and one hand at the base of his head, allowing energy to flow between my hands, along his spine. The energy that came through was the highest, finest frequency I'd ever

---

* The rostrum is the "beak" or "nose" of the dolphin.

experienced. Gently and naturally lulled into an exquisite meditative state, we lost all sense of time. The night was silent and still.

In one moment, the silence was shattered by an eruption of thunderous bird-song right outside my screened window. It lasted just moments, and then promptly stopped, leaving us in total silence again.

"What was that?" I whispered.

Henry said that just before the birdsong erupted, a stream of energy was activated in him. It surged up from the base of his spine and flowed to the top of his head. He recognized this as the kundalini energy talked about in yoga. Apparently the birds felt this ripple of energy and responded!

That woke us out of our trance state, and we realized it was late. Henry went back to his room and I drifted into a deep sleep. The understanding did not dawn on me until later. *That experience of the "highest, finest frequency" flowing through me was my first experience of healing with dolphin energy!*

My days on the Big Island were winding down, and still the rains came. I did not enter the bay again for the duration of my stay on that island. There was, however, a growing awareness inside of me that the dolphins were still with me, even as I went about my daily activities on the island. It was as if I was contained in an energy bubble of that very high, fine frequency, all the time. The cells of my body seemed to be in a perpetual state of buzz.

The best times were when I was in my room alone —reading, writing, meditating, or just being. That was when I felt the dolphin energy moving through me intensely and strongly. Even though I wasn't in the water, swimming with the dolphins physically, I sensed them all around me. Despite all the rain, my final days on the Big Island were a sublimely peaceful and uplifting time.

> Even though I wasn't in the water, swimming with the dolphins physically, I sensed them all around me.

While I was curious about not having another opportunity to swim with the dolphins, I sensed that this was not the island where

Dolphin Love

I would live. I felt drawn to the island of Kauai. I thought the dolphins that lived there would be the ones with whom I would establish a deep relationship. They were the ones that would heal me.

When the time came to leave the Big Island, I was ready. I was off to Maui to make a wedding dress!

SIX

Visions of Dolphins and Whales—Oh, My!

Once on Maui, I dove right into the wedding dress project. The ceremony was in ten days; there was not a moment to spare. The dolphin-swim experience was behind me, and every moment of every day leading up to the wedding was full of sewing, talking, laughing, crying, and sharing with my two dear friends, Paula and David. These days, too, were full of magic and mystery.

The big day arrived, and I was up early putting finishing touches on the dress. The wedding dress project was quite an adventure for Paula and me. In the end, we were both thrilled with the result. Paula looked amazing.

The outdoor ceremony was exquisite. Several friends and family members were invited to give readings during the ceremony. When it was my turn to speak, I opened my mouth, spoke my first words, and all the birds in the surrounding trees erupted into wild birdsong! Unable to hear myself speak, I stopped, looked up into the trees, laughed, and waited for the birds to quiet. The second time I spoke, I was able to complete the reading without interruption. I didn't realize, at the time, that the birds were responding to the dolphin energy that was transmitted through my voice!

During the reception, I spoke with a woman named Leslie. She shared that she was being drawn to the islands by the whales and didn't know why. I told her about my mysterious connection with the dolphins, and that I didn't know what that was about. As I talked, the top of my head became all tingly, and the hairs on her arms stood straight up.

She touched my arm and said, "You have something to share with me."

I went into performance anxiety. "I don't channel. I don't do anything like that," I responded.

She looked at me expectantly. She wasn't taking no for an answer. "You have something to share."

Okay!

"I meditate," I told Leslie. "The only thing I can think for us to do is to hold hands, meditate together, and see what happens."

She was open to the idea. While the reception festivities proceeded on the deck of this beautiful bed-and-breakfast with an ocean view, Leslie and I retreated into the lobby in search of a quiet place to meditate. We sat on a sofa, held hands, and closed our eyes. The moment I closed my eyes, I felt energy enter the top of my head and flow down my arms, out my hands, and into hers. She began talking and telling me what she was experiencing.

She became a dolphin. She believed she was in Atlantis, as there were underwater temples and crystals. She felt the rush of water against her dolphin skin as she swam. She described her experience in great detail, sensing that she was reliving a past life. I was amazed by what I was hearing. All I felt was energy moving through me. I received no pictures or messages at all.

Then her vision shifted, and she was in another lifetime, again as a dolphin. There were other dolphins with her this time. She thought I was one of the other dolphins in her pod. Again, she described her experience in great detail. She truly was having an experience of herself in a dolphin body, living as a dolphin!

She went into a third lifetime. This time she was an indigenous man who spent much of his life on the water in a small boat, in telepathic communication with the dolphins.

Finally, she received a communication about her connection with the whales in this lifetime, and what that was about. The whales were going to help her heal.

Visions of Dolphins and Whales—Oh, My!

Meanwhile, I kept trying to "get" something myself. All I felt was energy flowing through me. I had no visions, no inspirations. I felt embarrassed and inadequate because I had nothing to contribute in that way. Leslie didn't seem to mind!

The energy flowed for about forty-five minutes. When it was complete, we opened our eyes and looked at each other. "What was that?" we chimed in unison. Neither of us had had an experience quite like that before!

The groom told me later that during this time, several people were leaving and wanted to say goodbye to Leslie and me. As they approached us, they sensed a huge bubble of energy around us. Perceiving that something powerful was happening, they left us alone. The fact that others felt that something significant was happening between us was intriguing to me.

This sharing with Leslie was my first experience consciously bringing the dolphin energy through for another person. I didn't know what to make of it.

Apparently something really is going on between the dolphins and me!

SEVEN

David

Meanwhile, remember that guy I met in the acting class? David Rosenthal is a big part of this story.

Even though he took my phone number during that first class, David did not call me the following week. I thought about him off and on, which surprised me. I wasn't really looking for a relationship. I was quite happy with my life the way it was. I had acclimated to living alone, and I was really enjoying my own company. There was nothing about my life that I wanted to change or fix. I woke up every day in a state of wonder about what new adventures the day would bring.

My sense was that David was in no hurry to call, since he'd be seeing me in class again the next week. Once it was clear that I was moving to Hawaii, however, I decided not to go to the next class. What was the point? I called the instructor and told her my news. I suspected that I would hear from David on Thursday, after not showing up for class Wednesday night.

Sure enough, at 9 a.m. Thursday morning, the phone rang. A man's voice responded to my hello with, "Is it true? You're moving to Hawaii?" It was David.

"It's true!" I told him all about the psychic reading I received right after that first class, and all the events that transpired during the week. None of this seemed to faze him. He was very open. We talked a bit longer, and he asked me if I'd like to have dinner with him before I left for Hawaii. We seemed to have a nice connection, so I agreed. Both of our schedules were full, and we didn't have a mutually free evening until four nights before I was due to leave. We made the date.

The day of our date arrived, and I was surprised—again—to feel excited about seeing David. I knew this dinner wouldn't lead to anything, though. In a matter of days, I was moving an ocean away, after all.

> I knew this dinner wouldn't lead to anything, though. In a matter of days, I was moving an ocean away, after all.

Ten minutes before David was due to arrive, I sat down to meditate, to center myself. Rather than my energy calming and centering, I felt it spiral upward, beyond the confines of my body and out into space. My energy was spinning, and it felt very high.

David arrived on time, and we left immediately for our mutually favorite sushi restaurant. Once we were seated, we launched into a fun and easy conversation right away. The fact that I was about to move away took some pressure off. We were free to be ourselves, since we were clearly heading into the "just friends" category. We felt comfortable with each other and quickly discovered that we had a lot in common.

David shared with me the surprising reaction he had when the acting teacher mentioned that I was dropping the class and moving to Hawaii. He said an intense energy surged up through his body that caught him completely off guard. He was shocked and distressed to hear that I was moving away, and he had no idea why. We'd talked for only five minutes the week before, and he thought I was cute, but what was the big deal?

"It took me a good ten minutes before I was able to clear my mind and be present in the class," he told me.

I listened, curious, remembering my meditation experience just before he came to pick me up.

Meanwhile, the waiter kept approaching to take our order and we continually waved him away. We were so engrossed in each other's company we weren't even thinking about food. Finally, even though we weren't really hungry, we decided we should order something. We ordered miso soup, edamame (boiled soybeans), and one spicy tuna roll to share.

The sushi arrived, and as I took my first bite of the tuna roll, a funny look came over David and his face flushed. When I asked if something was wrong, his reply astonished me.

"I'm having all the physical sensations in my mouth as if I'm eating that piece of sushi myself—I can feel the textures and I can taste the tastes!"

The three hours we spent in that restaurant flew by. We talked, laughed, and occasionally nibbled on the delicious food. David assured me he'd leave the waiter a big tip.

We had such a good time that night that we decided to spend as much time together as we could before I left. We both had very busy days, so we spent our evenings together. At the end of our third date, I walked around my townhouse feeling that upward spiraling energy again. My whole energy field was expanding and spinning, way beyond what I was used to. *Something is happening here, and it seems to have to do with David!*

When the time came for me to leave for Hawaii, David offered to drive me to the airport in Phoenix to see me off. This is a two-hour trip each way—his offer touched me deeply. While waiting for my plane to board, we agreed to stay in touch with one another by phone. We didn't feel sad, necessarily, because we had just met. But we were both rather confused about the timing of what was feeling like a sweet and special connection.

When I arrived at the retreat center where I was staying on the Big Island, I noticed that the guest telephone was conveniently located in the hallway just outside my room. Thankfully, all the other rooms in that building were empty during my two-week stay. With the phone to myself every night, I spent hours sitting on a hard wooden chair at the tiny desk out in that hallway, talking to David.

♡

I'll never forget our talk that first night, when I was fresh from my incredible dolphin encounter. David answered the phone immediately, as if he'd been waiting for my call. "You had a big day today, didn't you?"

"How did you know?" I asked, brimming with excitement.

During the day, he told me, there were two specific moments when surges of energy rushed through his body. He knew, intuitively, that he was feeling my close encounters with the dolphins.

Every day, we talked and talked, and laughed and laughed. I shared my daily adventures, and he told me about his day. He read poetry to me—his favorite poet was E. E. Cummings. He played his piano for me. It was very romantic!

He even sent me flowers on Valentine's Day—the largest bouquet I'd ever seen. The arrangement overpowered my small bedroom, so I placed it on the desk in the hallway, for others to enjoy.

It got to the point that I didn't feel complete in an experience until I shared it with David over the phone at the end of the day. Every call took us deeper into relationship. We were reaching depths within ourselves, and between each other, that surpassed all my previous relationships.

I remember saying once that it was probably best that we were physically apart at this early stage. Had we been together, the physical connection might have consumed us and we may not have gone as deep with each other emotionally. I cherished those hours of dedicated time talking and getting to know one another. I knew how rare and precious that time was.

During my time on Maui, I stayed with Paula and David Green in their tiny 400-square-foot studio apartment. When it was time for my nightly call, the only privacy to be found was in their postage stamp-sized bathroom. I sat on that bathroom floor talking with David for hours, while Paula and David G. cuddled on their bed just on the other side of the door, watching TV with the volume turned up, so they couldn't hear me.

Once Paula and David G. saw the depth of what was happening between David and me, they did their best to include him in the pre-wedding festivities. Several times, we put David on the speakerphone and all talked. We laughed together and cried together. It was a magical time.

After the wedding, I flew to Kauai to continue my dolphin adventure. The first step was to find a place to live.

I arrived in the rain. For the next ten days, it rained. I hardly left my rented room. *Am I supposed to connect with the dolphins or not?* I kept wondering. I'd been in Hawaii for five weeks, and swam with the dolphins only those first two days. I was confused.

Frustrated, I sat in my room one gloomy day looking out at ... the rain. I was reviewing my options. *What options?* Things didn't seem to be flowing anymore. All the doors to the dolphins seemed closed now. Aside from those first two days with them, I was rained out from further physical contact. I still felt their presence around me—that high, fine frequency exciting every cell of my body and saturating my energy field. I knew they were connecting with me telepathically. But I thought I was there to establish a *physical* relationship with the dolphins. I thought I was supposed to live here, so that I could swim with them all the time. That didn't seem to be happening.

I didn't know what to do next, and I wasn't getting the kind of guidance that I did in the early part of the trip. My inner voice had become silent and still.

The only door that seemed open to me now was the growing relationship with David. I didn't understand it, but that was the reality. There didn't seem to be anything more for me to do, or anywhere else for me to go, on the islands. I felt lonely and confused.

During one of our calls, I shared with David about these thoughts and feelings. I suggested the possibility of me returning to Sedona so that we could explore, in person, what was happening between us. David was open to the idea; but I needed to know that returning to Sedona was for *my* highest good—our relationship aside.

David waited as I went inside myself and asked, *Is it for my highest and greatest good to return to Sedona to be with David?*

My attention was immediately drawn to my heart space, in the center of my chest. It pulsed open and became huge. I felt an overflowing energy of warm, liquid golden amber pouring out of my heart space. I told David what I was feeling, and then said, "I'd say that's a YES!"

We each took a deep breath. For better or worse, we had just made the decision to take our relationship to the next level.

At the crack of dawn the next morning, I called my travel agent and told her to book me a flight back home ... to Sedona ... *today*. I wrote a "mahalo and aloha" note to the owner of the room I was renting, and left Kauai within the hour.

On the flight home, I pondered how odd it was that my trip to Hawaii ended the way it did. It started out auspiciously, but then my adventure with the dolphins seemed to fizzle out. I didn't know if I'd ever see them again. I wasn't attached, as the idea of a connection to the dolphins was an enigma to me anyway. But the whole thing felt unsettled, incomplete. I had to admit that I felt some sadness about leaving Hawaii, and the dolphins. I had no idea what to do about it. I just let it be and lost myself in my imaginings about the new life I was going home to.

I didn't realize it yet, but I did, indeed, receive exactly what the dolphins intended for me to receive during that trip. I only needed that one moment, on that one day, with that one dolphin. That encounter, and those clicking sounds, marked the beginning of an extraordinary relationship between the dolphins and me.

With a glad heart, I returned to Sedona to explore a life with David.

EIGHT

Dolphin Heart World is Born

Shortly after returning to Sedona, I accompanied David to the local Unity Church one Sunday, where he played piano during the morning service. At the social following the service, a lovely woman named Fanny introduced herself to us, and thanked David for his beautiful music.

Then she and I began to talk. Within moments, we were talking about dolphins. My head got all tingly, and she got goose bumps all over. I knew the dolphins wanted me to share their energy with her, but I was too shy to tell her. It just seemed too weird! I opted to stay safely ensconced in my comfort zone, and said nothing. Eventually, we both moved on to talk to other people.

I wasn't able to get the thought out of my mind that Fanny was to receive a transmission of energy from the dolphins. It felt like the dolphins were nudging me. They were relentless in my head. I felt bad that I didn't say anything to her. Finally, I promised the dolphins that if I bumped into Fanny again, I would invite her to receive their energy.

David and I continued socializing and ended up being among the last to leave. As we walked toward our car in the nearly empty parking lot, one lone woman was headed our way, walking from the opposite direction. It was Fanny.

We rushed to each other, simultaneously blurting out that there was something we needed to do together. When I told Fanny what I had in mind, she got really excited. She definitely wanted to receive dolphin energy!

Fanny followed us home in her car. During the drive, I was inspired to transmit the energy to her outdoors, in our backyard. Ours was a corner lot, so there was some exposure to street traffic. But an abundance of beautiful, mature trees gave us shelter from the sun, and enough privacy from cars passing by. A multitude of songbirds flew around us, singing boisterously throughout her session. They enjoyed the dolphin energy too!

Fanny's experience was different than Leslie's. There were no visions, no past life memories. It was a pure transmission of dolphin healing energy. I felt the energy flow through me, and Fanny felt the energy move into, and through, her. She felt peaceful, deeply refreshed, and relaxed at the end of the session. We both felt joyful and grateful for the opportunity to be immersed in dolphin energy ... in the desert!

Over the following weeks, I had similar experiences two or three times a week, with friends and strangers. We'd be talking, the subject of dolphins would come up, my head would get tingly, and they'd get goose bumps. I began giving dolphin energy healing sessions to anyone who was willing to receive one.

Each session was unique. During the session, I'd have no idea what, if anything, people were experiencing, as I transmitted the energy in silence. At the end, the receiver described what happened, and we were always amazed. Every experience was fascinating and perfect for that person.

There I was, a former banker, fresh from my first swim with wild dolphins, transmitting dolphin energy to humans on land, in the desert! Since leaving the corporate world in search of a life that was more personally and spiritually fulfilling, I was being led on quite a journey! My life became stranger every day. I must admit, I loved the magic and mystery of it. I loved the adventure.

Now that I was settling down in Sedona again, living with David, I needed to decide what to do to make a living. I had done some massage when I lived here before, but my heart wasn't in it anymore.

I hiked onto the land one day, pondering this dolphin phenomenon, wondering what it had to do with my life. A big, smooth red rock beckoned me to sit. I sat for a while, and then decided to meditate on this question, and ask for guidance.

Since the dolphins had begun working with me, entering into the silence and stillness during meditation had become remarkably quick and easy. It just happened naturally. As soon as I closed my eyes, my mind was silent and my body was peaceful. On this day, within minutes of resting in the silence, I sensed a subtle energy approaching me from the right. I recognized the dolphin frequency; it was a group of spirit dolphins. They sent me a pulse of energy—a communication. I heard these words clearly in my mind: *"Will you be one of our ambassadors on land, and do dolphin energy healing as your career?"*

In a state of deep inner peace, I received this love-filled invitation into my body. I did not feel the need to reply immediately. I remained in the silence with these spirit dolphins for a while longer, basking in their radiant love and light. Gradually I felt their energy retreat.

I came out of the meditation feeling honored ... and uncertain. As much as I loved the dolphin energy, and was just beginning to discover how amazing the dolphins are, the idea of putting myself out there in the world as a dolphin ambassador was too far out for me—even in Sedona, where anything goes! I wasn't at all sure I wanted to do that. When I returned home, I talked to David about it, and he agreed it seemed pretty strange. Still, I couldn't ignore what was happening naturally. I decided to at least consider it.

As the universe does so well, I was immediately presented with opportunities to test the waters of credibility in the community.

We had just moved into a new home (with a rich turquoise carpet ... the ocean!), and our doorbell rang one day. A retired couple introduced themselves as our neighbors. They had come to welcome us to the neighborhood. During our conversation, they asked what I did for a living.

David and I looked at one another. *What do I say?* I told them what I used to be—a banker and a massage therapist . And then, I giggled, took a deep breath, and out popped, "And now I work with dolphin energy!"

They didn't flinch. They were genuinely curious and asked a couple of questions about how I came to be doing that. Then the woman said, "Well, when you live in Sedona, you have to go with the flow! Everything happens for a reason."

David and I each breathed a sigh of relief. *That wasn't so bad!*

A few days later, while walking through the neighborhood, we bumped into David's former landlord. He worked in construction; he was a kind, ordinary guy. David introduced us, and the question I had come to dread was asked of me, "What do you do?" I followed the same course as before. Once I said the words "dolphin energy," David and I both noticed a shift in this man's energy. Instantly, he opened up to us. The conversation took on a whole new level of intimacy and connection. He spoke to us of things happening in his life that he had not shared with anyone. It was quite profound.

As we walked away, David and I looked at one another and shook our heads in wonder. "That was so beautiful! There really *is* something to this dolphin energy," I said. And then I thought out loud, "If simply *talking* about dolphins has this effect on people, what else can their energy do?"

 "If simply *talking* about dolphins has this effect on people, what else can their energy do?"

In these encounters, I was being shown that by simply opening my mouth and talking about dolphins, their energy flows and creates a pure space of unconditional love, where there is no judgment. A door opens that creates a safe space for all present to be more authentic.

I knew then that I couldn't walk away from this opportunity ... this gift. Inside myself, I took a deep breath and proclaimed to the universe—to the dolphins—*"Yes, I'll do it!"* I didn't even know what "it" was. I was now committed to this dolphin path, wherever it might lead. It felt *so right.*

♡

I began thinking about creating a business and promoting myself as a dolphin energy healer and dolphin ambassador. *How does one do that?*

Dolphin Heart World is Born

First, I needed a business name. A friend suggested, "Dolphin Heart ... something." That felt right, as many of the sessions so far did seem to be focused on the heart. *Dolphin Heart what?* I stewed over it for days. I made lists of possible names and none of them stuck.

One day while showering (I seem to get my best inspiration when I'm showering or doing dishes ... must be the water), I went through the alphabet, one letter at time, thinking of words that might work. I was approaching the end of the alphabet and nothing was clicking. *I'm not getting it.*

Then I came to W. *World. Dolphin Heart World.* Energy, a flood of energy, poured through my body. I had a vision of all the dolphins on the planet leaping out of the water at the same time. "*She got it! She got it!*" they all eek-eeked in unison.

WOW!! Dolphin Heart *World.* World. *That feels so huge.* "*Are you sure?*" I asked my unseen friends. Shivers and chills up and down my body. *Yup ... World!*

I got out of the shower, dressed hurriedly, and went to David. "Dolphin Heart *World*," I announced.

He closed his eyes and shivered. I felt him feel it. With his eyes still closed, he smiled a big smile and nodded, "YES."

I sat with those words, *Dolphin Heart World.* My imagination went wild. I had visions of traveling around the world doing my work. My ego had it all worked out. I was going to be famous!

Well, it's been seven years. I haven't traveled around the world yet, and I'm not even close to being famous!*

But what did happen was, the world came to me ... right here where I live in Sedona, Arizona. In this popular tourist town, this haven for spiritual seekers, travelers from around the world found me.

Dolphins in the desert? You bet!

---

* Patience, Grasshopper! When I wrote these words, back in 2002, the beginning of world travel was right around the corner ...

— NINE —

Dolphin Energy Healing

And so my life as a dolphin ambassador, and a dolphin energy healer, began. The dolphins immediately took the lead in helping me create a brand new life—a brand new livelihood. They masterfully choreographed my daily experiences, in the desert of Sedona, leading me into a wide variety of human interactions that were ripe opportunities to share.

I didn't have to "do" much. I simply remained open, went about my business, and when an opportunity arose to share about the dolphins, I shared. When I felt prompted to offer the gift of a dolphin energy healing, I offered the gift. That was all I had to "do." The dolphins took care of everything else.

Granted, I often had to step outside of my comfort zone, because nobody had ever heard of dolphin energy healing before. I never knew how someone would react. Time after time, I watched people open up right before my eyes and become genuinely curious and interested. They drew my story out of me. I found myself talking about dolphin energy healing in a different way with each person. The dolphins guided me to describe my work in a way that each specific person could hear, understand, and be touched by.

Over the following years, I shared the beautiful healing frequencies of the dolphins with anyone who was willing to receive—sometimes in the form of a session, and sometimes in the form of a casual conversation. I observed, and learned, so much by simply following my instincts and intuition, and speaking up when I was nudged.

Many people feel deeply attracted to dolphins, and sense that the dolphins have a gift for them. But not everyone has the means or opportunity to swim with dolphins physically. By activating people like me to transmit dolphin energy on land, the dolphins expand their capacity to touch people.

The dolphins particularly enjoy a tangible presence in Sedona—the desert. Their work through me is a clear demonstration that their healing abilities transcend the limitations of space and physicality.

I facilitate dolphin energy healing sessions both in-person and remotely. The remote sessions are as powerful, and often even more powerful, than in-person sessions, further demonstrating that dolphin energy completely transcends physicality.

In my sessions, I act as a bridge between my client and the dolphins. At the beginning of each session, I invite my client to express what she would like to receive. "What issue is present in your life that you'd like support with, or clarity about? Are there physical symptoms you'd like to have addressed? Emotional issues? Relationship issues? Life circumstances?" Sometimes people come with very specific issues. Others come just because they love dolphins and they're curious about this unique form of energy healing. They are open to whatever comes and trust that the dolphins will bring them what they most need to receive in the moment.

When clients come for an in-person session, they lie on my massage table, and I transmit the dolphin energy hands on. When I do a remote session, we initiate the session on the phone. My client shares her intentions for the session. Then it's up to her whether we hang up for the rest of the session or stay on the phone. It depends on what she's most comfortable with. Either way, my client sits or lies down in a place that's comfortable and free of distractions. All she needs to do is relax and receive.

To begin the session, I close my eyes and enter into the silence and stillness. I have no attachment to the outcome of the session, and I do not manage or manipulate the energies in any way. I simply open myself to the dolphins. I am in a state of *being*. The dolphins "do" the healing, in cooperation and cocreation with the higher self of my client. The session may be for healing, personal transformation, or both. I simply allow the love energy of the dolphins to flow through me, and I trust. At the end of the session, we share our experiences.

It's really fun, and amazing, to witness the wide array of experiences people receive in dolphin energy healing sessions. Here are some examples.

I received a call one day from an Israeli woman who was traveling through Sedona. She saw my brochure and knew she had to have a session. She said she had a strong connection to dolphins, but hadn't yet had the opportunity to swim with them.

During the session, I didn't feel energy moving through me at all, which happens sometimes. I'd done enough sessions to know that this was okay. My job was to surrender and trust. I would know soon enough what my client experienced.

After the session, I left the room to get her some water. When I returned, her long, lean body was lounged in the chair, and she was laughing. I waited, curious to hear what was so funny.

Finally, she said, "Who knew I would have my first dolphin encounter in the desert?!"

She sat upright in her chair, leaned toward me with wide eyes, and was quite animated as she described the amazing journey the dolphins took her on. "It was like they took me on a tour of all of my soul's lifetimes, on many different planets, in many different dimensions of reality. But it was different than watching a movie of my life. I relived these lives, one right after the other."

And then they took her out into space, where she experienced the vastness of who she really is. She was thrilled. The session was profoundly healing and transformative for her.

Dolphin Love

A friend and her new husband were planning a trip to Hawaii for their honeymoon. They wanted to swim with the dolphins there.

A few days before their trip, Jill scheduled an energy session with me to prepare for her encounter with the dolphins. The energy transmission was intense from beginning to end.

At one point, in my mind's eye, I saw a group of cartoonlike animated dolphins wearing brightly colored floral aloha shirts and leis around their "necks." They were putting on a Hawaiian luau! Some were playing musical instruments and others were dancing the hula. I told Jill what I was seeing and we cracked up!

In my mind, I asked these aloha dolphins to create some magic for my friend and her new husband during their visit to the islands. Particularly, I asked that my friends would enjoy successful and nourishing dolphin swim encounters. I felt the spirit dolphins dash away, excited about this assignment. They definitely had special plans in store for these two!

At the end of the session, Jill told me that most of the energy work was focused around her head area. A lot of shifting happened in her brain. It seemed as if the dolphins were creating new neural pathways between the left and right hemispheres of her brain, among other things. Her entire body and energy field buzzed and vibrated for quite a while after the session.

She left, excited about her upcoming trip, and curious about what the dolphins would create for her and her beloved.

When they returned home, Jill phoned me and excitedly shared that they had two wonderful encounters with the dolphins while on the Big Island. What fascinated her most was what she experienced *after* her swims, when she returned to their hotel room to rest and integrate the energies she received from the dolphins.

"On both occasions, the energy that saturated my field after my dolphin swims was identical to the energy I experienced during my session with you! The quality, the intensity, and even the focal point of energy around my head ... work on my brain ... was exactly the same as what I received in my session with you. Now I *know* that this is what you do. Not that I doubted you, but the experience was identical! Now there's no question."

David's friend Melissa called one day and told him about her efforts to become pregnant. "I've been trying for six months, I'm 37, my clock is ticking, and I'm impatient!" When David told her about my work with the dolphins, she felt intuitively that the dolphins could help her. I got on the phone with her. We talked briefly and scheduled a remote session for later that week.

During her session, Melissa could feel the dolphins working on her uterus, healing her. Two weeks later, we got the call. She was pregnant!

Several months later, we received an urgent call from Melissa. She had been in a minor car accident while vacationing on a remote island off the coast of France. She was having serious cramps and bleeding; her pregnancy was in distress. Melissa was terrified of losing the baby.

"I need your help. I need the dolphins' help!"

Immediately upon hanging up, I transmitted dolphin energy. Her distress symptoms disappeared. Melissa carried the baby to full term and gave birth to a beautiful baby boy.

Another woman who received a session cried afterward. She said that all of the fantasies she'd ever had about swimming with dolphins came true during her session.

She got to ride on the back of a dolphin. She swam by its side, cupping its dorsal fin, gliding through the water body-to-body with her magnificent dolphin mate. Two dolphins came up behind her, put their rostrums to her feet, and propelled her through the water. It was quite a ride! They gave her everything. Every dolphin interaction her heart desired was realized right there, in the privacy of her own apartment.

Are these experiences real? Are they figments of an active imagination? Who's to say? They were real for her. She felt worthy and loved. Her dolphin dreams came true. Her heart overflowed with joy.

Sometimes people are activated into an experience just by talking with me about dolphins. They don't need to have a session.

I met a man on a trail while climbing Cathedral Rock one day. It was early in the morning and we were the only ones there. As I approached him, I noticed he was wearing a dolphin T-shirt. I chuckled to myself. *There are no accidents!*

We introduced ourselves, and I asked him about his connection to dolphins.

He told me, rather emphatically, "I'm *not* connected to them. This shirt was a gift from my cousin. I'm just wearing it because I have it."

I smiled and told him, very briefly, about my work with the dolphins, and then offered to hike with him to the end of the trail. He had gotten stuck at the tricky part and didn't know how to proceed from there. We chatted the rest of the way, and then parted company at the top.

A few days later, I got a phone call pretty late at night from this man. He was back home in Ohio. I was surprised to hear from him and asked how he got my number.

He responded, "What did you do to me?!"

I asked him what he meant.

He went on to tell me that when he was visiting the various new age stores the afternoon of the day we met, people at the shops put my brochure into his hands twice, unsolicited. That was curious to me because I didn't even know those shops had my brochure.

What really got him, though, was the experience he had at a place called Rachel's Knoll. He was sitting on a rock looking out over the valley, when the valley began to fill up with water. It became an ocean. He saw this with his eyes open!

Then he saw dolphins materialize. They swam in, around, and through the red rocks. He was under the water, but was able to breathe.

He said that experience lasted for about twenty minutes. He'd never had anything like that happen to him before. (Nothing like that ever happened to me!) He assured me that when he returned to Sedona, he'd be sure to have a session with me. My feeling was that he didn't need one. After our brief conversation on the trail, he received his experience directly from the dolphins!

A friend came to me for a dolphin session with a soft-tissue injury in her midback.

Kathy is clairvoyant, and it was fascinating to hear her describe what she saw during her session. She watched a team of spirit dolphins superimpose healthy tissue over her injured tissue, and intricately weave the two together. She saw the tears in her damaged tissue begin to heal. By the end of the session, her healing was well under way. She got off the table feeling strong again.

We spoke several days later, and she was very pleased. "The repairs are holding and I'm pain-free!"

Mark was the publisher of a local spiritual magazine. When he learned about my work with the dolphins, he became quite curious. He had already experienced a wide range of energy healings. The idea of dolphin energy healing was intriguing to him. He couldn't wait to experience a session!

This was one of my early sessions, when I was transmitting the energy sitting face-to-face with my clients, holding hands. Mark and I sat comfortably in our chairs, held hands, closed our eyes, and opened ourselves to the dolphins.

From the moment we held hands, I felt energy flowing strongly through me. Immediately, Mark began stroking my hands with intensity. I could feel a yearning in him, and it was directed toward me. As the energy flowed, he kept grasping and squeezing and stroking my hands. Clearly, he was having a highly sensual experience, and this was pushing my buttons! I had no idea what was going on for him, but it was potent, and I was becoming more than a little uncomfortable. I kept breathing and surrendering. *We're only holding hands.*

"As soon as we touched, your skin was dolphin skin instead of human skin. Where our legs touched, your skin was dolphin skin."

After an hour of strong energy running through me, the flow came to a completion. We disconnected our hands and sat in silence. The atmosphere was thick with dolphin energy. It was a while before Mark was able to speak.

Curious to hear what happened for him, I waited. Finally, with his eyes still closed, he spoke: "As soon as we touched, your skin was dolphin skin instead of human skin. Where our legs touched, your skin was dolphin skin."

What?

He continued, "Ancient memories from someplace deep inside came up. Memories from another lifetime ... another era. It was a deeply satisfying and fulfilling lifetime."

After another long pause, he opened his eyes and looked at me with pure wanting. "I long for that time and that place ... for that way of being." Emotion poured through his eyes. "I held back. Every ounce of my being wanted to embrace you, to merge with you. But I felt your resistance. I sensed you wouldn't be open to that. It was all I could do to stop myself from going there."

He looked away and was silent. I was stunned. I didn't know what to do or say. When he resumed eye contact, his eyes bored into me. "I feel cheated. If you could have fully surrendered to the energy, it could have been amazing."

I sat there, looking back at him, speechless.

We sat in silence while our energies and emotions swirled. He sighed a big sigh and continued. "I've always been very tactile. I'm not surprised that this experience was so sensual."

Leaning forward and looking deeply into my eyes, he said, "Your buttons will be pushed in this work, particularly in the area of physical sensuality. Let go," he urged. "Allow the full magic to unfold." Inside myself, I thought, *I'm not sure I'm ready for that!*

I left that little studio, in the heart of red rock country, shaken by what had just transpired. *I became a dolphin in that room. What is happening here?*

I bumped into Mark a few days later. He said that a surreal quality surrounded his memories of that hour we spent together, as he returned to the routine of his daily life. It caused him to wonder if what had happened between us was real, or if it was just a dream.

Which is the dream and which is real? I wondered.

Another button-pushing session came my way, this time with a woman. Darlene came to the session loaded with questions she wanted to ask the dolphins. Even though I told her, "I don't do messages," her questions poured forth.

Darlene was most focused on relationship at that point in her life. She said that she sensed that her soul mate was actually a dolphin currently alive on the planet and asked if that was true. A very large, strong energy began pouring into my body. It kept coming and coming and coming. This was a huge energy! I described what I was experiencing and told her, "I think that's a YES!"

I felt the presence of a huge male dolphin inside of me. My body felt expanded well beyond the boundaries of my human form. I'd never felt a whole dolphin inside of me before. I sensed him asking me to lie down with Darlene in the spooning position—a full-body embrace, with me behind her. *"No, I'm not comfortable with that,"* was my immediate response.

The dolphin honored my decision, but I could feel his disappointment. I felt sorry to have denied him—them—that opportunity, but it just felt too weird to me. I wasn't ready for that.

Dolphin Love

After the session, I told Darlene what her dolphin soul mate had asked me to do. She, too, was extremely disappointed that I said no. She said that if that ever happened again, to please know that I had her full permission.

Oh, dear, here I was again, limiting a client's experience due to my own inhibitions. I felt bad that I didn't follow the energy all the way to its completion ... to its fulfillment. The dolphins were shining light on a place within me that was closed. *Apparently I have some blocks in the area of physical contact with my fellow humans.* I was being gently confronted here.

Quite a while later, fresh from my May 1998 Hawaii dolphin swim, a close friend came by for a visit.

Jeanne took one look at me and said, "I want what you have, Linda! I want that glow!"

She booked a series of three sessions.

By now, I was having clients lie on my massage table, as the energy was too strong to transmit just through the hands. Two clients in a row told me, during their sessions, that their hands were hurting from the energy. That's when I knew that my body's energy channels had opened significantly, and more energy was flowing through me than in the beginning. It was time to change how I was facilitating the sessions.

During Jeanne's first session, I felt the dolphin energy emanating from my whole body, not just from my hands and heart space like before. When I noticed that, I sensed a suggestion to lie with her on the table—in the spooning position—so that her whole body could receive the energy that was emanating from my whole body. *Not again.* But I also was aware that I was only mildly uncomfortable with the idea this time.

The prompting kept coming, and gradually I let myself open to the idea. The moment came when I felt ready to take the risk, probably because she was a close and trusted friend. I took a deep breath and told Jeanne what was being suggested. She was open to it.

I climbed onto the table and we assumed the spooning position—I've also heard it called "nurturing pose." We lay on our sides, both facing the same direction, with me behind her. I focused on matching her breath. Gently, her body's energy came into harmony and resonance with mine. The dolphin energy flowed fluidly between us. It was a blissful experience! We were both deeply nourished by that intimate sharing.

This request was repeated during her second session, and we complied again. The results were the same. Both Jeanne and I were deeply nourished, on all levels, by sharing the energy in that way.

A woman came for an in-person session. For me, this session was like all the others. I opened myself to allow dolphin energy to flow through, and remained empty in the silence and stillness throughout the session. When the session was over, this woman didn't say much, and she seemed to be in a hurry to leave. She didn't look me in the eyes as she left, either, which seemed odd.

A couple of days later, she phoned me to say that she felt that the energy that came in during the session "wasn't of the light."

"Really?" I replied.

I'd never had anyone say anything like that before. I asked her to describe her experience in more detail, and she just said that she felt that the energy wasn't pure, and it wasn't of the light. She couldn't say any more than that. I thanked her, sincerely, for having the courage to tell me this, instead of not communicating with me at all. The only thing I could think to do was to give her money back. She accepted the refund.

When we hung up, I was puzzled and curious. The energy of the session felt pure to me—it was the same energy that always comes through. I replayed the session in my mind to see if I'd done anything differently, or if my personal energy was off balance in any way. I was not able to identify anything that would have given this woman that impression.

There was nothing more for me to do. I trust the dolphins deeply, and I was satisfied that I hadn't done anything "wrong." I let it go.

Eighteen months later, I was very surprised to receive an e-mail from this woman. The first words of her message were "I owe you an apology." She had just returned from swimming with wild dolphins. "The energy that I felt in the presence of the dolphins was the same energy I felt during the session with you. But it was unfamiliar to me then, because it's an *impersonal* love. I'd never experienced that before. I wanted to let you know."

I thanked her for sharing her discovery with me, and I completely understood how she could have had that experience. Most of us humans think of love as the human emotion. The love the dolphins bring is a higher love—Divine Love. It may evoke emotion, but the love itself is beyond emotion, beyond the personality. It's a state, a frequency—a space. And it's not personal. It's all-encompassing. It just *is*. This love can indeed feel strange and foreign when we first encounter it. It's not what we're used to—and it may not be what we thought we were looking for.

I was happy that the matter resolved for her in such a beautiful way. And I acknowledged myself for staying in 100% trust of the dolphins, and myself, in the face of her earlier response to the session!

A handsome, distinguished gentleman phoned me for a session one day. I had just recently met Ulf and his wife, Beverly. They're a lovely couple, and were both fascinated to hear my dolphin story. When I arrived at their home for Ulf's session, I asked if he had a specific intention.

"I want to feel the Presence of God," he said.

Okay. I swallowed, and continued to listen.

"I've followed *A Course in Miracles* for over twenty years now. I've done all of the practices diligently. I've read the book over and over. I've read about God. I know that God exists, and I know other people who have experienced God. But I never have. More than anything, I want to know—to *feel*—God."

I was profoundly touched by this man's honesty, openness, and vulnerability. I'd had the extraordinary privilege of witnessing precisely that—the Presence of God entering into a session—a couple of times. So I knew that what he was asking for was possible.

I began the session at Ulf's head. I went inside, entered into the silence and stillness, and opened myself to be the vehicle for whatever was for this man's highest and greatest good. I consciously let go of any ideas or expectations that I may have been holding for Ulf's session. I became empty.

> We basked in the afterglow of God's Presence, each immersed in our own thoughts and feelings.

The energy streamed through me, and this precious man on my table began to talk ... and talk ... and talk. His arms and hands were flying through the air. I didn't know what to do. Usually my sessions are conducted in silence. I let him talk, but I had to keep my eyes open, and keep my own hands moving, to avoid a midair collision!

Five minutes pass, he's still talking. Ten minutes pass, he's still talking. *I'll move down to his feet—leave the close proximity of his head and face area—perhaps then he'll stop talking.*

I moved to the foot of the massage table and gently held his feet. I remained silent. He kept talking ... until he stopped. When all fell silent, the room was full ... of Presence ... the Presence of God. He cried. I cried. What we shared together, in that moment, cannot be described in words. It was a holy moment.

When the session was over, we sat together in silence. We basked in the afterglow of God's Presence, each immersed in our own thoughts and feelings. Neither of us wished to break the spell by speaking.

I was feeling deep intimacy and sacredness in our connection as we said our goodbyes. Ulf expressed his immense gratitude as best he could in words. The words were one thing, but the eye contact that passed between us as he held me before him, placed his hands on my arms, and squeezed, as if he didn't want to let go, was altogether something else.

When I got into my car to drive home, I burst into intense tears. I cried most of the way home. I kept thinking to myself, *I am so incredibly blessed to bear witness to such events in people's lives. Thank you, dolphins, for coming into my life. I can't imagine doing anything else with my life than sharing your profound love with my fellow humans.*

After this session, I didn't hear from Ulf for years. And then just recently, I learned that this beautiful man had passed away, which brought Beverly and me into e-mail communication again. I shared this story with her, and she sent me this message:

> Linda,
>
> What a lovely, blessed experience! I'm so grateful that you shared it with me. The strange thing is, Ulf was usually more reserved. The fact that he was talking so expressively was unusual. It tells me he how much he wanted to connect with God, but not sure how. Interestingly enough, this was a peek into his last years that I wrote about. Maybe you started something!! Being verbose, then silent, provided that wonderful contrast that amplified the experience.
>
> By the way, instead of older gentleman, you might say 'distinguished' :-}} After all, Ulf was a Swedish Count! He had very formal training in boarding schools. It would suggest that anyone, even nobility, can benefit from your sessions! :-}}} Coming to Sedona, and meeting folks like you, opened him up to these unusual experiences. Ulf loved nature and animals more than anything. That's why he was comfortable with you.

The dolphins never cease to amaze me—their generosity of spirit, their wisdom and grace, and their profound love, compassion, and healing.

This kind of healing work is perfect for me. I need adventure and diversity in my life, or I get restless and bored. I have never gotten bored sharing dolphin energy! So much happens in these sessions, I'm fascinated by each person's experiences. I've learned so much about the nature of energy, and how quickly and easily energy transmutes and transforms. When a person is truly open to receive, and able to let go of preconceived ideas and limiting beliefs about what's possible, beautiful, amazing things happen.

And I made a great discovery early on. When I facilitate a session for someone else, I receive increased dolphin energy for my own healing too! More dolphin energy flows through me during a session than I receive on my own in meditation. Facilitating sessions for others opens my own energy channels, clears stagnant energy blocks from my system, and expands me so that progressively more and more dolphin energy can flow through. I am really grateful that my clients receive so much during their sessions, because I do too!

Dolphin Love

In the course of sharing the energy of the dolphins, I was often at a loss when someone asked me, "What is dolphin energy?" One day, in a channeling session with my friend Ann Albers, the dolphins gave me these words to describe their beautiful healing frequencies.

Dolphin Energy is ...

the frequency of *Joy*

of *Movement*

of *Creating Flow* ...

flow of Love

flow of **Abundance**

an *Opening of the Heart*

... as never before!

I tell people they can't really understand what dolphin energy is until they experience it. There's nothing else quite like it!

TEN

The Human Pod

Within a month of hanging my shingle as a dolphin ambassador, I was invited to give a talk about my dolphin adventure at a local networking meeting. The meeting was in the evening, and I woke up that morning planning to spend the day preparing. The day filled up, and I ended up with no time to prepare at all—which I knew was perfect! I giggled to myself. *The dolphins know me so well.* I knew they wanted me to speak spontaneously, from my heart.

I could feel the dolphins' energy building throughout the day. My energy field around my body filled and filled with sparkly, bubbly energy. *The dolphins sure are excited about this*, I thought to myself as I drove to the event. I had butterflies in my belly, but I wasn't nervous—I was excited. I had no idea what to expect!

When I arrived at the New Earth Lodge, I was surprised to find the place already packed with people. And more kept coming and coming. I was overhearing comments about people's excitement about the evening's program—my talk! Many said they'd heard about it from a friend. Word of mouth can spread quickly through the Sedona community. Soon the room was filled to capacity.

When it was time to begin, the host gathered us into a seated circle. We went around and all gave our names, and spoke briefly about what we do. Then I was introduced as the guest speaker.

I was told that I had about twenty minutes. I spoke for thirty, telling my story of how the dolphins came into my life and sharing some of my experiences. When I was done, the room was still. It was a pregnant pause ... the air was thick with expectation and anticipation ... and dolphin energy! Somehow I knew that we weren't done. I heard myself ask the group, "Would you like to have a direct experience of the dolphin energy now?"

There was a resounding "Yes!"

I'd never transmitted dolphin energy to a group before. I had only transmitted their energy to individuals. I had no idea what, if anything, would happen in this kind of setting.

I told everyone, "This is going to be an experiment."

We dimmed the lights and closed our eyes. I immediately felt dolphin energy flowing through me, filling up the room. I was in that empty, silent space the dolphins take me to when I do a healing, but the emptiness and silence seemed fuller—bigger—in this room with the large group of people. I spoke the words that flowed into my mind—a guided visualization the dolphins gave me in the moment—to support the group in opening to receive their love.

And then I was silent. I could feel the dolphins taking us all into a deep, deep space. It felt as if we were floating together, silently, in the depths of the ocean. I sensed the soft, sweet, tender love and nurturing energy of the dolphins swimming around us, and through us. We were all in the same energy, but each person was receiving a gift of love that was personal and unique. The silence and stillness grew and grew as the dolphins took us deeper and deeper ...

We stayed in the silence for perhaps ten timeless minutes. And then I felt a subtle shift. My awareness gently returned to the room, and words began to form in my mind. I spoke the words softly and gently, guiding everyone to breathe deeply, and to return to present time and space.

Bodies slowly began to move and stretch. Eyes began to open, but no one spoke. The silence in the room was palpable. The air was so thick, I could have reached out and touched it.

I remained silent, making soft, gentle eye contact with various people as they returned. The energy that passed between us was sublime. Volumes were communicated through our eyes, in the silence, across the room. We lingered in the connection.

It took the group awhile to come back fully into the present. The energy in the room was deep, soft, and warm. There was a sparkling quality to it ... it felt mystical and magical.

When enough of us felt able to speak, a few people shared what they experienced. One man spoke quietly of his meeting with the "mer" people—mermaids and mermen. He felt that to be one of his lineages. He was deeply moved that they appeared to him, that they allowed him to see them, feel them, and be with them again. One man saw Archangel Michael appear in the center of the circle, and watched his energy grow and grow, beyond the confines of the room. He watched as Michael placed his huge thumb on everyone's third eye, giving a blessing. Several saw and felt the dolphins or became dolphins themselves, swimming in the ocean. They felt exquisitely blessed by the experience.

We had far surpassed the twenty minutes allotted for my talk, but nobody seemed to mind! Finally, it was time to leave, and nobody wanted to go. We all wanted to stay in the nurturing, loving energy of the dolphins.

I stood at the door as everyone left, thanking them for coming. One woman thanked me for telling my story. She was reminded of all of the magical opportunities that had presented themselves to her, to which she said "no," because she didn't understand them, or they didn't make sense. She said that my story inspired her to say "yes" to life, and to be open to wherever the magic would lead her. Her sharing touched my heart.

As I got into my car and prepared to drive home, I felt a large pod of spirit dolphins jumping for joy all around me! They were so very pleased with how the evening went. Their ebullient appreciation and acknowledgment for a job well done made me giggle. I, too, felt deeply fulfilled and nourished. The dolphins touched everyone deeply. And that touched *me* deeply. I was happy and relieved. The evening was a success!

Dolphin Love

In my meditation the next day, I felt an entourage of spirit dolphins enter into my energy field. I tuned in to them, feeling a smile dawn in my heart and on my face. I received a communication from them: *"We would like you to lead group dolphin energy meditations on a regular basis."*

Now that I knew that I could transmit dolphin energy to a group, I was excited to explore this new mode of sharing. Without hesitation, I said *"Yes!"* and began to facilitate weekly dolphin energy meditations in our home.

Sedona was the perfect place for this. I posted a few flyers around town, and locals who came spread the word to their friends. Within a few months, groups of 35-40 people were gathering in our house every Sunday night. People from all over the world found their way to these meditations! David and I were always surprised and delighted to meet our new guests who dropped by each week to share in the dolphin magic.

These evenings were very special to me. People entered our home and commented on the energy: "It feels like the ocean!"

We had a large room with no furniture. I'd always wanted such a room! This was pure open space, and the deep turquoise carpet was the ocean floor. I painted the walls soft purple and pink, and mounted little white Christmas lights around the perimeter of the ceiling for soft illumination. Candles were everywhere.

Come with me now, to a group dolphin energy meditation evening ...

Sedona at night is dark. Depending on the phase of the moon, it can be very dark. In the outlying and residential areas, there are no street lights. For people coming for the first time, just getting to our home is often an adventure! Some guests tell us they rely on their sonar to find us.

As you walk the winding walkway to our front door, the soft sound of music draws you closer. You can already feel the warm and welcoming energy of the gathering within.

You open the door and walk in. The gathering room is just ahead. Dancing is in progress. The music is fluid and gentle—dolphiny. You meander through the room, find your spot, close your eyes, and let the music move you. Thoughts and daily concerns of the outside world gently, softly dissolve away. Your body relaxes deeply ... you're letting go.

Your awareness is naturally and easily coming into the present moment, attuning to this time and this place. You enter into harmony with the others dancing around you. You are safe and at peace here.

The music comes to a close. You feel warm, open, and receptive to the gifts the rest of the evening will bring. You look around at your fellow journeyers with openness and curiosity, taking it all in.

We arrange the meditation chairs into a circle surrounding the altar cloth that I've placed in the center of the room. You select your place, and gather pillows and a blanket from a pile in the corner. You'll lie down on these later, for the meditation.

A hush comes over the room as I place the guest of honor in the center of the altar ... a magnificent dolphin skull that was gifted to me by a local healer early in my dolphin journey. This skull pulsates with life force and consciousness. All who come into contact with him are awed by his powerful and benevolent presence. I set three candles around him, and then arrange various other artifacts I've gathered over the years ... a shell from the "road of Atlantis" that I retrieved from 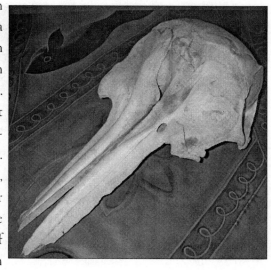 the ocean floor off the coast of Bimini in the Bahamas, a dolphin vertebrae, a sand dollar, special crystals, and photos of friends and family members in need of love and healing. I light the candles, and take my place in the circle.

Dolphin Love

I invite everyone to adorn Skull, and the altar, with any jewelry, crystals, or sacred objects they wish to have charged with dolphin energy throughout the night. Skull loves being honored and made beautiful in this way. I sense that he appreciates making contact with the various earth energies that are laid upon him. There are nights that he has so many jewels and crystals on him, I have to take a picture. He is an awesome sight.

Once all are seated again, I welcome you into our home, into this sacred space. Accompanied by Matisha's dolphin love song, "The Eyes of Home," I go around the circle, anointing each guest with a drop of Dolphin Heart Essence. This is an essential oil blend the dolphins helped me create. It carries the frequency of the dolphin heart.

I describe this evening as an energetic group dolphin swim. We will all be immersed in the same energy, but each of us will have our own unique experience. Some of you may have vivid visual or psychic experiences. Some will receive a healing. And a few may fall asleep! It's all okay.

It's time for the meditation to begin. I invite you to lie down, if you'd like.

I close my eyes. Instantly, and with ease, I enter into the silence and stillness. I am one with the dolphin energy and consciousness. Dolphin energy enters into my crown chakra and fills me up. It flows through me, passing out of my body through my heart space and hands, filling up the room.

As words float into my consciousness, I speak them softly. The words that come are different on each occasion. They're unique to each group. The words come from the dolphins, and are intended to prepare you to deeply receive the gifts the dolphins have to share with you this night.

Now we enter into the silence. The spirit dolphins that have gathered, and other spiritual beings present at the dolphins' invitation, interact with the group as a whole and with each of you individually. We remain in silence and stillness for 20-40 minutes. I am in a state of deep peace and relaxation. I have no thoughts. I'm experiencing no emotions. I am simply *being*.

At a certain moment, the dolphins let me know that it's time for me to go around the room and gently place my hand on each person's heart space for a few breaths. I love the feeling of the dolphin love flowing through me, out my hand, and entering into your heart. I can feel subtle variances in the quality of receiving. Some of you receive the energy in a soft, gentle, and subtle way. For others, the energy *pours* in—your whole being absorbs it like a sponge. I sense those who already have a strong connection with the dolphins, and make a mental note to share that with them when we talk after the meditation.

After the last person, I return to my seat and resume the state of just being. After a while, slowly, gently, my awareness returns to the room. I notice that my upper body's swaying in a figure-eight pattern—the infinity symbol. This is my cue that the meditation is complete. Quietly and gently, I speak the words the dolphins give me to bring the meditation to a close.

> I love the feeling of the dolphin love flowing through me, out my hand, and entering into your heart.

The energy in the room is soft, warm, and so deeply loving. Some need more time to fully return to their bodies. While they're "coming back," I invite people to share their experiences.

One man shares that this meditation was the most profound experience he's ever had in his life. Another says he feels inspired now about the vast possibilities of life. Many feel that their consciousness has expanded, and their heart is more open. Some have received profound healings. One woman arrived with a hurting heart, and feels connected to God again. One who came out of curiosity doesn't feel much at all—he's just relaxed. I thank him for being open and willing to explore something new.

Many comment on the moment when I placed my hand on their heart. Some experienced a heart healing. One woman shares that, after she heard me leave her and move on to the next person, she could still feel my hand on her heart. Most are in agreement that the hand-on-heart physical touch deepened their experience of the meditation in a beautiful and profound way.

We come to a natural completion, and I lead a closing circle. We hold hands, connecting our energies, and invite the energy of Mother Earth into the center of our circle. We create a pillar of light in our center, and invite all of the love and healing that we received from the dolphins this night to be sent to Mother Earth, for her healing. We feel our request being fulfilled, and a pulse of gratitude returned to us by Mother Earth. We are complete.

Everyone in the room is glowing. Our hearts are full. Love and appreciation is flowing. All is well in the world. *Thank you, dolphins.*

We share snacks that taste particularly yummy—you notice that your sense of taste is heightened. You enjoy socializing and connecting. This goes on until very late in the evening. No one seems to want to leave ...

For two-and-a-half years I led these meditations in our home. It was a magical time. I was continually impressed by how the simplicity of these evenings touched so many, so deeply. The gentleness of the dolphins' love touched us at our core.

Here are a few memorable stories from these meditation evenings:

One woman told me privately, after the closing circle, that during the meditation she began to experience curious sensations in her belly. "It was as if I was pregnant!" she told me, looking deeply into my eyes. She said that she felt a lot of energy and movement in her womb space during the meditation, and that she felt something growing inside. "I could feel my belly growing bigger and bigger. I kept putting my hands on my belly, and I was so surprised that it was flat. Energetically, my belly grew really large!"

Toward the end of the meditation, she felt a release inside, and a baby dolphin spontaneously appeared in her mind's eye, swimming in her energy field. "When we all stood up at the end for the closing circle, I felt physical pain in my body, as if I had actually given birth to a child! I had a hard time standing up."

I called this woman the next morning to see how she was doing. She was very matter-of-fact about it all, and she was joyful! She could still feel the baby dolphin around her energetically.

"What happened last night was real," I told her.

"I know!" she responded.

She also shared that her feelings were mixed. Alongside the joy, she felt deep grief, because she couldn't physically be this baby dolphin's mother in its home, the ocean.

One day a man appeared at our door who had come to a meditation two years prior. Warren was in Sedona for just a few days, and he said I was the first person he wanted to connect with upon his return. He wanted to receive a dolphin energy healing session.

I told him I was writing a book, and he insisted that I include the experience he had during his first meditation with me two years earlier. In that meditation, he found himself hovering in space, looking down at a gigantic shimmering dolphin form. The dolphin was made of light. "The entire Milky Way was contained inside the dolphin's body. It was the most exquisite vision I've ever seen!"

Several people made the unexpected discovery during these meditations that the dolphins are a big part of their spiritual path. Until this meditation experience, they had no idea the dolphins had such an important gift to share with them. A few of my regulars eventually moved to the Big Island of Hawaii, where they now swim with the dolphins as often as they wish.

One of these is Merlyn. He comes into my story again later, so I'll introduce him here. Merlyn is a wonderful, ageless hippie, with wispy, thinning, long white hair. He was a fixture in Sedona in the "good old days." He planted the first organic orchards here, and sold the harvest from a small roadside natural foods market. The moment I met Merlyn, I sensed something special about him. He had a unique perspective on things, and his voracious curiosity about life was deliciously refreshing. I quickly came to adore him.

Once Merlyn started coming to these meditations, he never missed a night. Merlyn is highly sensual. He soaked up the dolphin love energy like a sponge. At some point during each meditation, he would moan and groan with pleasure, making me giggle. His sound effects were a precious part of the evenings!

One evening, I found myself in California with four people who *really* wanted to do a dolphin meditation, but we had nowhere to do it. We were standing in a shopping center parking lot in Encinitas, north of San Diego, right on the Pacific Coast Highway (PCH). One woman suggested we do the meditation in the Starbucks coffee shop, on the corner.

"No. We can't meditate in Starbucks!" I replied. "We can talk there ... tell story ... but we can't meditate there."

Another woman thought a neighborhood church might be open that we could use. She left and drove around the neighborhood, checking to see if any of the churches were open. No luck, they were all dark and locked up.

Someone suggested doing the meditation in a car. *This group is tenacious. They're not giving up.* A car seemed to be the only option available, so we chose the biggest one, a mom's station wagon. I watched with amusement as this mom cleaned out her car for a bunch of strangers to pile into for a dolphin energy meditation. *This is a trip!*

All five of us climbed into her car. It was chilly out, so we kept the windows up. They fogged up in no time, which made us laugh. I was the middle of three adults scrunched together in the back seat. It was 7:30 at night and the PCH traffic was noisily zooming by. I couldn't believe we were doing this.

I started the meditation by stating that all the sounds that surrounded us during the meditation were perfect ... they carried frequencies that we needed in each moment. I spoke the guided visualization that came in the moment, to start the energies flowing, and then we entered into the silence, such as it was.

That was one of the most powerful, profound meditations I have ever experienced. The dolphins took us deep, deep, deep.

At one point, I sat forward from my spot in the center of the back seat so that I could reach everyone to do a few moments of hands-on healing on their heart space. By shifting my position, I entered the center of the circle. I had never been in the center of the meditation circle before. I felt energies swirling all around me, as if I was in the center of a powerful vortex of energy. A knowing came to me that the four humans around me were fully merged with their dolphin selves; but their humanness did not dissolve, it was included. It was a merging of human and dolphin, in a state of oneness, like I'd never experienced before.

Being in the center of this circle, I received these unified human-dolphin energies. It was extraordinary.

When the meditation was over, it took a long time for everyone to come back. We sat together in silence, our bodies vibrating, still immersed in the energy field that filled every inch of space inside that car. When they were finally able to speak, all four of these adventurers implored me to please keep doing these meditations.

I asked if the traffic sounds bothered anyone. They all said, "No, we didn't hear a thing." There had been sirens at one point! They all said that they had never, ever, gone so deep in meditation as they did that night.

> Being in the center of this circle, I received these unified human-dolphin energies. It was extraordinary.

I drove home chuckling to myself. So much for thinking I need the perfect space, the perfect music, the perfect altar, the Dolphin Heart Essence, etc., to facilitate a dolphin meditation event. The dolphins showed me that all I ever need is a gathering of people with open hearts and minds and a willingness to receive. The physical things create a lovely atmosphere, but that's not what brings in the energy. Intention, openness, love, and trust bring in the energy.

Dolphin Love

The dolphins have brought such magic into my life. I am completely devoted to sharing their energy with anyone who's willing to receive it. Countless people come to me to be touched by dolphin energy. In return, I am touched by all of them too.

Everyone's unique experience with the dolphin energy and consciousness reveals more about us all, and the nature of this world in which we live. It is as if all of us ... the dolphins, my clients, and I ... are weaving an exquisite tapestry. We each weave our own colorful thread into the fabric of the glorious whole.

ELEVEN

Inner Dolphin Journeys

I was getting my flippers wet as a dolphin ambassador, transmitting dolphin energy in private sessions and group meditations. Meanwhile, the dolphins were guiding me on a profound inner journey. From the comfort and privacy of my own home, the dolphins took me into their world, and accompanied me in mine. They heightened my inner senses and refined my perceptions, enabling me to journey with them on other planes of reality.

Living in Sedona, I couldn't be with the dolphins physically. I couldn't see them with my eyes or touch them or swim with them. I didn't have a dolphin living in a swimming pool in my back yard—so many people asked me that, even a newspaper reporter! But my interdimensional experiences with the dolphins were real—sometimes more real than the 3D reality I returned to.

All of life is precious, the seen and the unseen. Beauty and magic are all around us. The dolphins helped me to see this truth, to experience it, to know it in my bones. I'm so grateful!

Following are some highlights from my interdimensional journey with the dolphins. Welcome to my world ...

I went to bed early one night while David worked away at his computer. Sleeping on David's futon bothered my back, and our new bed hadn't come yet, so I was temporarily sleeping on the floor. I snuggled into my sleeping bag, lay down on my side, and closed my eyes.

In my mind's eye, I saw two spirit dolphins swim toward me—a mama and baby. They entered into me through my solar plexus, and my body began to undulate. I had no control over these rhythmic movements. Even when I tried to stop and be still, the movements immediately resumed. Finally I surrendered, and I became curious. *What are these dolphins teaching me?*

My awareness shifted. It felt like millions of tiny champagne bubbles were popping inside me, throughout my whole body. My body was in constant motion, and I noticed that I was exquisitely aware of every part of it. This awareness even encompassed my external environment. I knew precisely where I was, and where I was not.

I also noticed that I was in the present moment as never before. I had absolutely no concept of the past or the future ... they did not exist. All that existed was this moment in time. Every bit of my consciousness was present ... here ... now. I'd read about this state of "present moment awareness," but I had not yet fully experienced it, until now. I just *was* ... with complete awareness. I lay there undulating for a long time, being a dolphin.

When David entered the room to go to bed, he saw me lying on the floor undulating. Breathlessly, I uttered a few words to describe what I was experiencing.

"I can see," he responded nonchalantly.

David knelt down to kiss me goodnight. The next thing I knew, he was lying beside me, also undulating, nuzzling up against me! *Is this for real? Did they take over David's body too?*

Apparently they did! After a few minutes, though, David came out of it. He was exhausted and wanted to go to sleep. The dolphins let him go.

I was tired too. In my mind, I told the dolphins, *"This is really cool, and I'm grate-*

ful for the experience, but I want to go to sleep now!" They didn't leave my body. I kept asking them to leave, and I kept undulating. I was getting annoyed. Finally, I gave up.

When I stopped struggling, my attention returned to my body. Something was different inside. I only felt energy and activity in one side of my body; the other side of my body felt empty and still. *Oh! This is how dolphins sleep! They're giving me a direct experience of what sleep is like for them!*

Unlike us, dolphins are conscious breathers. They have to rise to the surface of the ocean to breathe air. Every single breath they take in their entire lifetime is a conscious choice. They can't fall asleep completely like we do—they would stop breathing and drown. They "sleep" by shutting down one half of their brain at a time. It would make sense that half of their body would shut down too, to rest.

> Every single breath they take in their entire lifetime is a conscious choice.

Once I got that, the dolphins released me to my human sleep. I was exhilarated and exhausted by the whole experience, and I fell asleep in a flash. Only we weren't done yet.

In a few short hours, I woke up ravenously hungry. I'd never woken up hungry in the middle of the night before. I tried to ignore the hunger and go back to sleep, but it was all-consuming. I had to get up and get something to eat.

I knew the dolphins were behind this. I fumbled for my slippers and traipsed through the dark living room toward the kitchen, scowling all the way. *This is ridiculous!*

I flicked on the lights and headed toward the fridge. The clock on the wall glared back at me ... 3 a.m. *What am I doing up at 3 a.m.?! What am I doing eating at 3 a.m.?!* I thought about turning right around and going back to bed. My stomach growled so loud I thought it would wake the cats! *Okay, okay!*

I scanned the fridge and the pantry, wondering what on earth I wanted to eat at this hour. I decided the easiest thing to fix was cereal. I poured a bowl, splashed some soymilk over it, and dug in for my first bite.

"How can you eat that dead food?!"

"What?" I exclaimed, out loud, in the empty kitchen.

"How can you eat that dead food?!!" A group of spirit dolphins bellowed at me from the atmosphere around me.

"It's 3 a.m. I'm a human. This is what I eat. Give me a break, okay?" I was exasperated.

I chowed down on that cereal like I hadn't eaten in days. Cereal never tasted so good! While I ate, I felt the dolphins hovering around, clucking their disapproval at my food choice. I laughed. *What an unusual life I'm leading. Now I have a bunch of spirit dolphins admonishing me on my diet!*

I returned to bed with a satisfied belly, and slept the rest of the night through. When I woke up the next morning, the dolphins were gone. I was left to my own wonderings about the course my life had taken since letting the dolphins into my life and my heart.

Shortly after that early morning feeding frenzy, I read that some dolphins are night feeders. I guess my lesson wasn't complete until I got to experience that aspect of their life too!

One day, David and I were enjoying some quiet time together. We were sitting on the sofa, cuddling and talking.

During a lull in our conversation, I saw (in my mind's eye) and felt a baby spirit dolphin enter my body, again through my solar plexus.

I became this baby dolphin, and I was swimming in heavily polluted waters. I described everything to David as I experienced it. I was sobbing. There was no escaping the poisons in the water. There was nowhere to go that wasn't polluted. This was my home, and the pollution had affected everything in my ocean world. It was excruciating.

I lay in David's arms and cried for a long time. I was devastated. It hurt so much to know how we humans have polluted the waters of our planet. I'd known pollution was a problem, but I didn't have a direct experience of its negative impact until this baby dolphin took me into its world. Now I knew it with my body, not just with my mind.

At first I thought the dolphins showed me that so that I would put energy into helping to heal the waters of our planet. But they said that wasn't my task. They just wanted me to know. I thanked baby dolphin for sharing its reality with me.

Bit by bit, they share their life with me. I am deeply honored.

The other side of this journey was that the dolphins were experiencing human life on land through me. I knew the dolphins were always with me. But it did not occur to me that they, too, were learning from our journey together until the summer of 1997.

I woke up one morning with an overwhelming urge to go to the mountains in Colorado to get my wildflower fix. David was more than ready for a vacation, so we took a road trip over the Fourth of July weekend. We looked forward to camping and hiking in the mountains.

When we reached southwest Colorado and were heading north along the Dolores River, we pulled off the highway and turned onto a back road to do some exploring and to find a picnic spot for lunch. We stopped at a pretty spot with lots of wildflowers. As soon as I got out of the car and stepped foot onto the land, I burst into tears. I didn't know why I was crying. I pulled myself together, and we had a leisurely picnic before getting back on the road.

An hour or two later, we stopped at a picturesque mountainside lake. The same thing happened. I got out of the car, stepped foot onto the land, took in the breathtakingly beautiful scenery, and started to cry. *What is going on?*

The next day, we headed up a crowded hiking trail in Telluride. At the beginning of the trail, we stepped to the side of the path to fully feel, and let in, the energy of the dense woods and mountains all around us. Gazing into the wildflower-laden forest, I burst into tears again.

This time I couldn't stop myself. My emotions were too strong. While streams of hikers passed by, I let myself cry until I was spent. David did what he does so well—he stood quietly by my side and held me until my tears subsided.

When the tears ebbed, I went inside myself and asked what was going on. I heard and felt spirit dolphins all around me. With profound love and tenderness, they said, **"You came here for all of us too! We are seeing the beauty of the earth through your eyes."**

I burst into tears again. I didn't care how many people saw me. I felt so much in that moment—my profound love for the land—these mountains, the forest, the wildflowers, all of it. I was overflowing with joy to be able to share the beauty of my world with my dolphin family, as they were sharing the beauty of their world with me. I felt that they really got it. They embraced everything I was seeing with my eyes and feeling with my heart.

Then, standing upon this mountain trail, immersed in intense feelings of love for the land, my love for the dolphins and the ocean arose within me. My heart ... my world ... was expanding in the most wondrous way. *Is my heart big enough to contain all of this love?*

This simple moment by the side of the trail was profoundly healing for me. I felt fulfilled in a way that I hadn't for a long time. It was as if I was drawn here to consciously embrace my love of the land, in the midst of my deepening journey with the dolphins.

The dolphins didn't leave me totally without a source of human guidance and wisdom. Early in the journey, a friend who came regularly to my weekly dolphin energy meditations shared that he had just started dating someone. Paul was glowing he was so excited. He wanted David and me to meet his new girlfriend, and asked if he could bring her over sometime. I was so happy to see my friend so happy. Of course we wanted to meet this woman!

We set a date, and a few days later, we opened the door to see Paul standing there, beaming, with a very pretty brunette at his side. He introduced us to her—her name was Summer Bacon. We welcomed Summer and Paul into our home. The four of us sat on the floor in meditation chairs, settling in for an afternoon of sharing and connecting.

Summer told us that she was a trance medium for a beautiful spirit by the name of Dr. James Martin Peebles. Without much background information about who this Dr. Peebles was and how she came to be channeling him, Summer asked, "Would you like to meet him?"

David and I grinned at one another, "Sure!"

Right then and there we watched, fascinated, as Summer, sitting cross-legged on the floor, went into trance. Her head jolted backward, and then forward. When she spoke, her gentle female voice had become a booming male voice with an accent that I couldn't place. And "he" talked very fast!

> When she spoke, her gentle female voice had become a booming male voice with an accent that I couldn't place.

Summer's head turned toward David. Her eyes were closed. I held my breath, mesmerized. Dr. Peebles spoke briefly to David. Then, with eyes still closed, he turned to me. *"A very special lady wants to speak to you. Is that all right, my dear?"*

"Yes," I replied, wondering.

My grandmother? I couldn't imagine who else on the other side might want to talk to me.

Summer's head thrust backward and forward again. I could feel a shift in the energy in the room. A different, softer female voice came through Summer, and said to me simply, *"Thank you."*

Summer's head thrust back and forth again, as Dr. Peebles' spirit re-entered her body. *"That was Mother Earth, my dear."*

Shivers went through my body. I was profoundly moved. *What is she thanking me for?* Later, I understood. At the end of each weekly dolphin energy meditation, we sent dolphin healing energy to Mother Earth. This was what she thanked me for. I was deeply touched.

We spent hours together that day. David and I were captivated by the story of how Summer met this special spirit, and came to channel him. She wasn't channeling Dr. Peebles professionally yet, but she felt that was coming.

The four of us became good friends. The next time we got together, Summer channeled Dr. Peebles for us again. This time he spoke to David and me together, about our relationship. He nailed us, right away, for ways that we were holding each other **"at arm's length."** His directness and accuracy was stunning and disconcerting. We were more than a bit uncomfortable with what he said to us, but we had to admit he spoke the truth. Over time, this message led to deep and positive changes in my relationship with David.

Dr. Peebles had our attention.

Shortly after this second get-together, Summer began hosting weekly open channeling sessions in her home. These sessions were a source of tremendous learning and support for me. Dr. Peebles brought through higher spiritual truths and awarenesses which perfectly complemented my inner dolphin journey. He was completely aware of what was happening between me and the dolphins, and he often gave me deep insights into the lessons that the dolphins were teaching me experientially. I was profoundly grateful for his guidance and wisdom.

Thank you, Dr. Peebles, for the gifts of love, truth, and inspiration you've brought into my life. And thank you, Summer, for surrendering totally and completely to Spirit, and allowing Dr. Peebles to speak through you!

I marvel at this journey. Here I am, intimately engaged in communion with highly intelligent beings of another species who reside in the waters of our planet. Yet most of our connecting occurs on land, in the subtle energy realms, beyond the scope of my five physical senses.

With the dolphins by my side, in spirit, I am a bridge between dolphin consciousness and human consciousness, and between their life in the ocean and human life on land. I am humbled and awed.

This exchange with the dolphins feels like the most real thing I have ever done. It has the deepest, most profound impact on myself and others that I have ever experienced.

As time passes, I surrender ever more deeply into the mystery of my relationship with these entrancing beings we call dolphins. I know they are always with me, even though I may not always feel them. While I still do not fully understand who they are, and how they do what they do, their presence enhances my life in the most wondrous and unusual ways.

I understand a bit more now why they've asked me to do this work on land. The dolphins want to help us humans heal, grow, and evolve. They are helping us in countless ways—in ways that we see, and in ways that we don't see—in ways that we understand, and in ways that we don't understand.

Through ambassadors like me, the dolphins are demonstrating that their energy and consciousness transcends time, space, and physicality. I'd never discourage anyone from swimming with dolphins—it's an incredible experience. But people don't have to travel to the oceans and meet with the dolphins physically to have a deep, profound, and complete relationship with them, and to receive their gifts.

When I did swim with the dolphins, often I felt both joy and disappointment at the end of my encounters. No matter how amazing the encounter, I almost always came away wanting more. I'd want them to swim with me longer, or to come closer. There was a yearning deep inside of me that was insatiable, a void that only they could fill. It was satisfied to a degree in the swim encounters, but not completely.

It seemed that the only thing that would truly satisfy me would be to fully and completely merge with the dolphins—to become one with them. That didn't make any sense to my mind. But I wanted it with all my heart.

Dr. Peebles told me countless times, "My dear, you are here to dissolve the illusion of separation between you and the dolphins. You are One!"

That does, indeed, seem to be my path!

— TWELVE —

Deep Dive

When this dolphin journey began, I didn't understand why it was happening to me. I was a land girl! I loved the earth, the mountains, and the wildflowers. The ocean was okay, but it didn't feed my soul like being out in nature ... on the land.

To me, there was nothing better than hiking a pine needle-strewn trail through the woods, breathing in the crisp mountain air. I'd look for the perfect spot. Lying gently on the soft earth, absorbing the rich sights, smells, and sounds of the woods around me, I'd gaze upward. The sky, peeking through the treetops, mesmerized me.

I never tired of watching the white, fluffy clouds shift and change shape overhead as they floated across the azure sky. I looked for faces and shapes in them, like I did as a kid for hours on end.

I loved walking outdoors on crisp autumn days, zigzagging my steps to crunch every crisp, fallen leaf in sight. And winter walks through silent snow-covered woods, hearing only the rhythmic crunch of snow beneath my footfalls.

Once, in a rather low moment, I was riding my bike along a forested road, seeking solace in my aloneness. I paused for a drink of water, looked up at the forest of tall trees all around me, and noticed something peculiar. The trees were moving and swaying—in pairs! One pair of side-by-side trees swayed in one direction, while surrounding pairs were swaying in completely different directions, and in different timing! *The wind can't be doing this.* I noticed the air, and there was just a hint of a breeze! I looked at the trees again, and every tree that I could see from my vantage point was paired up with another, swaying in perfect harmony and synchronicity. *These trees are dancing!* My melancholy mood dissolved in a heartbeat, as I was swept away by the tantalizing spectacle of this magical forest.

I'm a land girl! I was completely perplexed by this dolphin thing.

In the beginning, my work with the dolphin energy was a curiosity not only to me, but also to those who were drawn to me to receive the energy. During those first healing sessions, the dolphins often gave me messages through my clients. Numerous times, during a dolphin energy healing session, my client would say to me, "You are one!" They meant, "You are a dolphin."

I knew these words were from the dolphins, and that they were a message for me. But I didn't understand what they meant. I do know that, in truth, we are all made of the same stuff. We all come from the same source. We are all everything. So what were the dolphins trying to tell me?

One day, a woman who channels Archangel Michael came for a session. At the end of her session, she said, "Archangel Michael has a message for you, if you'd like to hear it."

"Of course!" I replied.

He spoke about my work with the dolphins, and as the message was coming to a close, he paused. Almost as an afterthought, he asked, **"Would you like to know about your lineage?"**

"Yes, please!" I replied.

He continued, **"A supreme concentration of your life experiences has been as a water mammal."**

As odd as that sounded, somehow it helped things make more sense. *So I've been a dolphin before, in physical form ... and not just once.* This revelation helped me to accept, a little bit more, what was occurring between the dolphins and me. It brought me some inner peace.

At the same time, that piece of the puzzle set into motion a subtle, and disturbing, undercurrent that quickly rose to the surface inside of me. I began to feel like my entire world, my entire identity, was in question. It felt like the rug was pulled out from under me. I didn't know who I was anymore. All that I knew myself to be was now in question.

It did not occur to me at the time that my self-knowledge was simply being expanded to include *more* of who I am. Rather than realizing that I am of the land *and* of the sea, my mind could only grasp one identity at a time. I began to perceive this journey with the dolphins as the dissolution of the Linda I knew. A brand new self-identity was being presented to me, and I had no frame of reference for it in my life. I felt lost, confused, and alone.

In the outer world, I shared my story and the dolphin energy with whomever came my way. Many people received inspiration, comfort, and healing from my work. Meanwhile, my inner world was rocking and rolling.

The dolphins became tour guides to my inner landscape, and my inner journey mirrored that first dolphin meditation (see Prologue), where we played at the surface for a while, and then dove deep. We returned to the surface to play and rest, and then we dove deep again.

The dolphins masterfully led me into the depths of my inner ocean. They took me into my darker spaces so that I could see, love, and heal those parts of myself that I had hidden, judged, and suppressed. The dolphins helped me to uncover and release pockets of emotion that I had spent my entire lifetime, perhaps lifetimes, suppressing.

As difficult and painful as that journey sometimes was, my dolphin spirit family was always with me. I was never alone. It was necessary for me to go into these spaces, to experience them fully, to learn to love these parts of me too. When I emerged on the other side of these deep dives, I was more whole, more integrated. I was lighter. More free.

Dolphin Love

A pivotal event occurred that intensified this identity crisis I was experiencing. David had begun to express his own mystical aspect during this time. He had developed a sort of spiritual friendship with Merlin the Wizard, and sometimes he channeled him. While I led dolphin energy meditations on Sunday evenings, on Tuesday nights David began facilitating evenings he called "Merlin's Magic Lessons." During these evenings, Merlin, through David, guided us through metaphysical experiences which were provocative and mind-altering.

> I was rendered completely vulnerable; there was no place to hide.

This particular evening, Merlin had us experiment with moving our consciousness at will, first within our own bodies, and then into the body of the person seated beside us. I was to move my consciousness into the body of the person on my left, and my body was to receive the consciousness of my friend Lori, who was seated to my right.

When it was time to move my consciousness into the person to my left, I was blocked from entering. Either that person wouldn't let me in, or I didn't want to go, I'm not sure which. My consciousness remained in my own body. I felt the moment Lori's consciousness entered me.

It was incredible feeling and witnessing another being's consciousness inside of me, exploring my inner recesses. I was rendered completely vulnerable; there was no place to hide. Probably for the first time in my life, all of me was revealed to another human being. It was intensely intimate. In that state of pure consciousness, there was no judgment; therefore, I felt completely safe. I was unconditionally loved and accepted for exactly who I was in that moment. It was an ecstatic experience!

Then I went somewhere far, far away. I did not know where I was, but my visceral experience was one of pure bliss. Wherever I was, I wanted to stay there forever.

After the meditation, we went around the circle and shared our experiences.

Lori, whose meditations are highly visual, described what she saw while her consciousness was inside of me. She saw us both at Seal Beach in La Jolla, California, observing in great detail the seals that were sunning themselves on the beach. Then she saw me lying at the water's edge, half in the water and half out, wiggling my body with great intensity. She watched as my human form faded in and out, revealing fleeting glimpses of my dolphin form. Finally, she saw my body change completely into a dolphin, enter the water, and swim out into the ocean.

So that's where I went when I left. I shape-shifted into my dolphin body and swam out to my dolphin family. No wonder I didn't want to come back.

The next day, I awoke in a state of longing and grief that penetrated to the core of my being. I was devastated about the conditions of my life. I was angry about being a human, about having to live my life away from the dolphins. I was crawling inside my skin, trying to get out.

None of this made any sense to my human mind, yet I couldn't make these thoughts and emotions go away. I couldn't shake the despair. My questions were unceasing. *Who am I, really? Am I a dolphin in a human body? What does that even mean? Why did I have to be a human in this lifetime? What is this all about?* I was angry and confused. Part of me wanted desperately to return to the dolphins, in my dolphin form. At the same time, I was terrified that if I became a dolphin again, even energetically, I might not be strong enough to come back.

The isolation was total. At that time, I knew of no other human who felt as I did. I knew a lot of people who loved dolphins, but I didn't know anyone else whose life was completely taken over by them. I felt utterly alone, and I thought I was going crazy.

Meanwhile, a portal had opened up inside me, through which dolphin consciousness began to bubble forth and permeate my being. I began to remember, and know, what it was like to live as a dolphin. In my dolphin lives, our interactions with each other and our environment were loving, joyous, and harmonious. We lived in a perpetual state of oneness, that elusive state of consciousness we humans spend entire lifetimes striving to attain. For dolphins, oneness is our natural state. As a dolphin, I was loved, loving, happy, deeply nourished, and fulfilled.

Dolphin Love

I became ultrasensitive to the cruelties and harshness we humans so casually inflict upon one another every day of our lives. With each infraction, large or small, I felt the pain of it in my body. *How can we be so cruel? How can we be so hurtful to people we love?* My desensitization to the human condition began to unravel. I frequently became so overwrought that I'd burst into tears. David would hear me, and he would come and hold me until I was empty inside. Neither of us knew what to do for me. There didn't seem to be an answer. For whatever reason, I needed to pass through these dark spaces. I needed to see what I was seeing, and feel what I was feeling.

I vacillated between struggling with the dark side of humanity and embracing the bliss of my awakening dolphin nature. *I preferred life as a dolphin.* I wasn't at all sure where this journey was leading, and if it was, for that matter, a good thing for me.

I often received phone calls from people who had heard about my work. Occasionally, in such a call, I would feel compelled to share the confusion, sadness, loneliness, and despair that I sometimes felt on my strange dolphin journey. Invariably, the other person would be silent for a moment, and then quietly reveal that they, too, felt more connected to dolphins than to humans. They, too, felt tremendous struggle being a human.

I believe that the dolphins brought these people to me. The dolphins nudged me to open up and share my deepest truths with these specific people ... because they were like me.

Each one of these conversations was a revelation to me. Until this time, I really felt like I was completely alone on this path—that no one else on the planet was experiencing what I was experiencing. I sometimes had an inner picture of myself floating in a life raft far out at sea, with no land in sight. It was an apt metaphor for the utter loneliness I felt much of the time.

But I wasn't alone. In these phone calls, I discovered that there were others, on a similar path, who truly understood what I was going through. We weren't crazy. These were healing connections. We were lifelines for one another.

Being that lifeline actually became a big part of my work. I spent a lot of time encouraging and supporting others in their unique journeys of self-discovery on this unusual dolphin path.

orca

THIRTEEN

Happy Birthday to Us!

Let's dive into the ocean again ... the physical, tropical, heavenly Hawaiian ocean!

In May 1998, I felt the pull to return to Hawaii to visit my dolphin family. I was in the midst of my identity crisis and despair about being a human. It wasn't good timing for us financially. We really did not have the money to spend on another Hawaii trip for me. But the urge persisted.

My friend Lori knew how important it was for me to go. She suggested that a small group of us could go together and share travel expenses. She was good friends with a couple, Sarah and Roy, who "would love to go with us!" Lori even offered to loan me my airfare.

I talked it over with David, and with his support I decided to accept Lori's generous offer and go to Hawaii. It seemed pretty clear that the dolphins were behind this. Who was I to argue with them?

I was beside myself with excitement. *I'm going to Hawaii!! I'm going to swim with my dolphin family again!!*

In the following days, I had conflicting thoughts and feelings about the trip. I felt shy about going with a couple I'd never met. What I really wanted, in my deepest heart, was to go alone. I wanted to re-create my first experience of being alone in the water with the dolphins for hours. This would be my second trip to swim with the Hawaiian spinner dolphins, and I was feeling a bit selfish. I didn't want to share my time, or my encounters, with anyone. I wanted to be alone with the dolphins!

At the same time, I was deeply grateful to Lori for the loan, and for her friendship. And, as soon as I met Sarah and Roy, my shyness toward them dissolved. They were pure, open hearts.

A couple of weeks before we were due to leave, I attended an open channeling session in Summer Bacon's home, to talk to Dr. Peebles about the upcoming trip. I wanted to know if there was anything I needed to know, or be aware of, before going.

"You will meet a very special dolphin on this trip, who you will channel one day. You'll meet him on his birthday! Oh, my dear, it's going to be a grand celebration—a big party! Just wait and see!"

Dolphins celebrate birthdays? I was surprised, delighted, and amused by that notion! It occurred to me that I should take this dolphin a present! *What kind of gift does one take to a dolphin?* I pondered this for days. No inspiration came. One day while meditating, I asked spirit what I could take to this dolphin as a gift.

"You! Just the fact that you are going to Hawaii to meet him is the greatest gift of all! He doesn't want anything else."

I smiled at that sweet response and let the gift idea go. Now I was able to simply enjoy every moment of the growing excitement I was feeling.

A week before we were due to leave, a curious intuition arose inside of me. I felt guided to put the tent up in our backyard and sleep outside under the stars every night before leaving for Hawaii. I wondered what that was about. *Perhaps the dolphins want to prepare me for this trip, and it will be easier for them if I'm sleeping outside, in nature.*

Trusting my intuition, I told David my plan to sleep outside. Nothing I do surprises him! He just accepted it as another part of my dolphin journey.

"I'll miss you!" He smiled.

"I'll miss you too! But we'll cuddle every night before I go out, and in the mornings when I come in, okay?"

Our house had a huge backyard. Grass lawns are rare in Sedona, the desert is just too dry. We had left the landscaping natural, and the native flora grew quickly and abundantly. When I glanced outside to see where to pitch my tent, I groaned. *Don't tell me I'm going to have to clear the ground to pitch my tent. That's going to be a lot of work!*

But in the back of the property, off to the left, I was relieved to see a large circular expanse of ground with no plant life growing on it. I walked over to that spot and saw a huge anthill at the periphery of the clearing. No ants were in sight, but I gave them complete credit for keeping this space clear. I counted my blessings and set off to prepare my campsite, silently thanking the ants for all their hard work!

I love camping and sleeping outdoors. It brings out my "nature girl" adventurous spirit. Even though I was camping out in my own backyard, the simple act of pitching my tent felt like a grand adventure. I was having so much fun!

I slept like a baby the first night, and woke up trying to remember if anything unusual happened. *Nope. Not that I'm aware of.*

I sat up, put my glasses on, and looked out the small mesh window at the rear of the tent. My eyes were drawn to something white lying in the red dirt. I was mildly curious, but I let it go, and went inside to start my day.

The second night, I entered into my tent. I lay down and connected to the dolphins. *"I'm open and available, if there's anything you have to share with me!"*

Nothing. I didn't feel any sort of response.

I closed my eyes and listened to the sounds of the desert night around me—crickets mostly, and the occasional howling of a distant pack of coyotes. Before long, I drifted gently off into a restful slumber.

I awoke the next morning feeling rested and refreshed. I tuned in to myself. *Anything different? Nope, everything feels pretty normal. Huh ...*

I sat up, curious about why I was guided to sleep outside. Glancing out my little back window, my eyes were drawn, again, to that white object embedded in the red earth.

My curiosity was piqued again, so I decided to check it out. I walked around to the back of the tent. What I saw took my breath away—a pure white seashell half buried in the Sedona red earth, and half exposed to the sun-drenched desert sky. *A seashell ... in my own backyard!* I couldn't believe my eyes!

Carefully, I dug the shell out of the ground and was stunned to see that it was perfectly intact. There was not a crack on it. The shell was gorgeous! It was delicately tapered at both ends, the tips deep maroon in color. The center bulb was pure white, and about four inches in diameter. I turned the shell over and over in my hands, touching it, admiring it, running my fingers along the symmetrical lines and nubby textures on its surface. *This is the most exquisite shell I have ever seen!*

Excitedly, I took the shell inside and washed it with soap and water. The half that had been buried in the red Sedona dirt was permanently stained red, and the half that was exposed to the sunlight was pure white. *This is it! This is the gift I'll take to my dolphin friend!* I couldn't take my eyes off of it. *It's so beautiful.* I felt a reluctance to let it go. *Maybe I should keep it. Maybe it's really meant for me.* But I knew better.

Then it dawned on me. I spoke to the dolphins inside myself. *"This shell symbolizes both our worlds! Seashells are from your world, but this one was buried in my world!"*

I shook my head in wonder. In all my years hiking the land in Sedona, never have I found a seashell—much less such an exquisite one, in pristine condition! This land was under the sea long, long ago ...: but still! And I never would have found this shell, had I not listened to my intuition and camped in my backyard.

How did I miss seeing it while I was putting up the tent? I wondered. *Did the dolphins do this? Did they manifest this shell just for me to find?* I laughed. The very special birthday gift that I had given up searching for was right there, awaiting my discovery—a half-buried treasure in my own backyard!

Stepping off the plane in Kona, our little group of four was greeted by the soft, warm, deliciously humid Hawaiian breeze. I breathed deeply, squinting and blinking to adjust to the bright sunlight. My whole being was singing. It felt so very good to be here.

We quickly went about the business of getting checked in to our condo in Kailua-Kona, the tourist area on this side of the Big Island. This whole trip revolved around swimming with the dolphins; but we spent our first night out on the town, exploring the shops and restaurants. It was lovely to see all the happy, colorfully dressed people on vacation. Joy was in the air.

We had booked a boat outing for the following day. Because it was just the four of us, the captain took us out on his little Zodiac, essentially a rubber raft with an outboard motor installed at the rear. We made the early morning trip to the harbor, met our captain, and boarded. I couldn't wait to get back out onto the ocean … in a boat.

This little Zodiac was so much fun. We skimmed along the water at high speed, our bodies mere inches away from the surface of the water zooming by. Our eyes were peeled for any sign of dolphins—fins, tails, spins, flips, or blows. We didn't have to wait long! After about thirty minutes, our captain spotted a small pod of Hawaiian spinner dolphins nearby. We headed in their direction, and then the captain stopped the boat. We waited to see if the dolphins would come to us. Our excitement overflowed when the dolphins headed our way. I was in tears. The dolphins came very close, made a connection with us, and then turned and swam away!

"What happened?" we all exclaimed in unison.

Our captain looked off into the distance, in the direction the dolphins were headed, and saw a big white boat about a half-mile away. "That's Joan Ocean's boat. She's got a big group with her this week. If she's here, I hate to say it, but you guys don't stand a chance."

We continued watching, and then were thrilled to see those sleek gray fins swimming back to us, at full speed! The dolphins were leaping and spinning, as if to say, *"We wouldn't abandon you! We just had to say 'hi' to them too!"*

Dolphin Love

"Get suited up and jump on in!" the captain shouted with urgency. He was amazed that the dolphins had come back!

I tucked my Sedona seashell into my lycra skin to keep it safe. I didn't know when I would meet my special birthday dolphin, and I wanted my hands free to swim!

We suited up, jumped into the water, and were immediately surrounded by a small pod of six beautiful Hawaiian spinner dolphins. My heart pulsed open. *"Hi, babies!!! It's me! I'm sooo happy to see you again!"*

Ohhhh ... it was a sweet encounter. The dolphins stayed right with us. They came close to us, and then swam a little way away. Came close again, and then swam a little way away again. For Lori, Sarah, and Roy, this was their first wild dolphin swim. I sensed that the dolphins were engaging us in this way to create safety and trust among us all. After a few such approaches, they stayed close, giving us each our own personal encounters.

One large dolphin approached me again and again. He felt like a male to me. Each time he came near, he came very, very near. When he was close to me, he looked so deeply into my eyes. After a succession of approaches by him, I asked, telepathically, *"Are you the one? Are you my special dolphin?"* I wasn't sure. Every time I thought about giving him the shell, I hesitated. *What if he's not the one?* I was surely enjoying our warm and wonderful connection, but I wasn't sure.

We swam and swam with these beautiful, friendly wild dolphins. My three travel companions were having exquisite encounters of their own. I was so grateful to the dolphins for staying with us for so long.

And then my attention was drawn to a sound. I stopped swimming to listen. A voice, a woman's voice ... singing! Hearing the familiar melody, my heart leapt with joy as I listened to the words, "You are my sunshine, my only sunshine. You make me happy, when skies are gray ..." *It's Joan! She's in the water now, and she's singing her greeting song to the dolphins!* I'd read about that in her book, *Dolphin Connection*, and now I got to hear her sing to the dolphins myself! That was very special!

I thought to myself, *Dr. Peebles, you were right! This is a grand celebration, indeed!*

Raising my head to scope out what was happening above the surface, I saw the big white boat floating just a short distance away. There were now loads of swimmers in the water. Joan's group had joined us.

The four of us in our little group came together, treading water, and decided that it was time for us to return to our boat. We'd had a wonderful swim. We'd leave the dolphins to swim with Joan's group now.

We climbed into the Zodiac, smiles beaming from ear-to-ear, dripping salty seawater onto everything. Our captain was beside himself with excitement. He was practically hyperventilating!

"The dolphins kept coming back to you guys! And they swam so close to you!"

He told us that when Joan's boat arrived, she instructed her group to stay onboard for a while, to give us some alone time with these dolphins. I was deeply impressed by that. That told me a lot about who Joan is.

We spent several minutes watching the dolphins play and interact with their new human playmates. What a sight to behold. Sheer grace, joy, beauty, and love.

In one moment, Lori turned and looked at me expectantly. "Did you give him the shell?"

"Who?"

"That large dolphin that kept swimming with you!"

"Do you think he was the one?"

"YES! Didn't you?"

"I wasn't sure!"

The look on her face told me everything I needed to know. I looked at the bulge at my thigh, where the seashell was still firmly nestled for safekeeping. Sigh. *I blew it.* I felt so silly to have doubted ... and disappointed that I didn't give that beautiful dolphin his gift.

It wasn't possible to feel bad for long. Our captain received a radio communication from another boat captain. There was a pod of pilot whales about five miles offshore—would we like to go see them? I'd never even heard of pilot whales, but we were up for wherever he wanted to take us!

♡

The little Zodiac accelerated to full speed. Sea spray splashed over us as we rode the waves. The ocean wind whipped through my hair. The water, the wind, the sun, this boat, wonderful companionship ... I needed nothing more! I was in bliss.

About four miles out, I felt a shift in the energy. Overcome by something, I burst into tears. I sobbed and sobbed. I had no idea why I was crying, but I couldn't stop. A large, intense stream of energy was passing through me; it seemed to touch my very soul. After several minutes, Roy became concerned and asked if I was okay. I couldn't speak; all I could do was nod yes, and cry.

And then we saw them ... the pilots. The sight of them took my breath away. For as far and wide as we could see, giant gray fins moved toward us. Unlike dolphins that travel in tight pods, these pilot whales were spaced far apart.

The silence ... The beauty ... The grace ... They were incredible.

The captain stopped the boat. No land was in sight. We floated in the midst of this vast expanse of big blue in silence, watching, witnessing, feeling. My tears continued to flow, but softly now.

The pilot whales occupied the entire expanse of ocean around us. In every direction, their large gray fins sliced silently through the water, rising and descending. They were in constant motion. Some swam at the surface for a while, and then dove; some surfaced only occasionally, preferring to remain below. A profound aura of peace, tranquility, and silence emanated from these magnificent beings. It was a sacred moment, a blessing to witness and receive. The only sounds were the water lapping softly against the boat, the occasional expulsion of air when a pilot surfaced to breathe, and the beating of my own heart.

> No land was in sight. We floated in the midst of this vast expanse of big blue in silence, watching, witnessing, feeling.

After spending time in silence together watching these exquisite beings, the captain invited any of us who wanted to, to go into the water, so long as we held on to the side of the boat. He suggested that if a pilot whale came close enough, we might be able to see what their whole bodies look like from under the water. Lori and I looked at one another tentatively, as if to say, "I'll go if you go!" We nodded a silent agreement, put on our masks and snorkels, and headed overboard. We were very happy to hold on to the boat! I'd never been in the ocean this far from land before.

Submerging my head to look around, deep blue was all I could see. No pilot whales yet. I wasn't relaxed, by any means. Visibility was poor. I had no idea who, or what, was swimming around just beyond my limited range of vision.

A juvenile pilot approached the front of the boat and began heaving himself out of the water and smacking against the surface, creating big splashes that drenched the front of the boat. The captain told us to get inside. He didn't have to tell us twice!

This juvenile continued this odd behavior even when Lori and I were safely back in the boat. Soon he was full-body breaching right in front of us. His behavior was clearly intentional. He was trying to tell us something!

The captain said he thought this juvenile was being territorial, that he wanted us to leave their waters. I had a different sense. My intuition was that he was protecting us. As I turned to face the rear of the boat to speak with the captain, I saw a different kind of fin steadily approaching the center rear of our boat. It was about 20 feet away when I spotted it.

Pointing to this ominous-looking, rapidly approaching fin, I asked the captain, "What's that!?"

He turned. "That's a white-tipped shark! Everyone stay inside the boat!"

Lori and I looked at each other, both aware that we were very, very lucky. I silently thanked the young pilot whale for his warning. He was gone now. *Message received.*

The shark hung around our boat for several minutes. The captain told us that it's common for white-tipped sharks to swim in the vicinity of pilot whales. "Pilot whales are messy eaters, and the sharks are opportunists. They eat up what the whales leave behind."

When the shark moved on, we breathed a collective sigh of relief, and returned our attention to the serene, benign pilot whales that still traveled silently and elegantly through the peaceful waters around us.

After about ten more minutes, the captain broke the silence and said it was time to leave. "You've had quite a day!"

Before he could start the engine, three pilot whales swam straight toward us, approaching the left side of our boat from directly behind. Two adults were sandwiching a young one in their center. They were in full-body contact, with the young one secured safely in the middle. This threesome swam toward us as one, undulating at the surface in perfect synchronicity. They swam up alongside our tiny boat, sustaining eye contact with us the whole time. Then, when they reached the midpoint of the boat, they dove. Mesmerized, we continued watching, waiting for them to surface. They did not. We looked around the expanse of ocean around us, and not a pilot whale was in sight.

We looked at one another in stunned silence. The captain said he'd never experienced anything like that with the pilots before.[*]

The next morning, we made the forty-five minute drive to the bay where I had my very first wild dolphin encounter that completely changed my life. During the drive, we each connected to the dolphins in our own way, inviting them to swim with us in the bay today. Forty-five minutes was a long time to wait to discover if our invitation would be accepted!

As we turned off the main highway to begin the descent to the bay, our excite-

---

[*] A few years later, I received an unexpected gift in the mail, a book called *Dolphins* by Chris Catton. There was a section on pilot whales. When I read the words, "Pilot whales, like orca whales, are of the dolphin species. They're actually really large dolphins," my whole being vibrated, letting this new information in. I remembered the extraordinary energy experience I had on the boat, just as we entered the pod's energy field, but before we spotted the pilots with our physical eyes. That's why I cried so much. The pilot whales are a part of my dolphin family—they're a part of who I am! I needed to fully receive, and integrate, their energy too! Crying intensely helped me move that vast amount of energy through my small human form.

ment and anticipation grew. We were giggling and talking, but underneath the surface of our banter, we were all wondering, *Will the dolphins be there?*

When we reached the end of the long, steep drive, the parking lot was filled with cars. A very good sign! We found a spot for our rental car, grabbed our snorkel gear out of the trunk, and headed for the bay. We could see many swimmers out in the bay, frolicking with the dolphins. Our hearts leapt with joy. "They're here!!"

We stood there for a few minutes, taking in the delightful scene. I became aware that my body was actually quite fatigued from all the swimming we had done the day before. I wondered to myself, *Can I even make that half-mile swim to the dolphins today?* I wasn't sure. On the other hand, I couldn't believe I even asked myself that question!

I dared to mention what I was feeling to the group, and they all felt pretty much the same way. As thrilling as it was to see the dolphins out there, we were really wondering if we had it in us to swim out to play with them!

As if in response to our indecision, a whole bunch of dolphins started leaping and spinning into the air. We whooped and hollered in response, but we were still very tired from the day before. I could not believe I was standing there, seeing the dolphins in the bay, and actually considering not swimming to them because I was tired. *Am I crazy?*

In my mind, I told the dolphins about our situation and suggested, *"If you come in a little bit closer, we'll come out and play with you!"*

Within moments, one dolphin appeared much closer to us, jumping and spinning into the air, joyfully enticing us to get our bodies into the water! That was all we needed. We looked at each other with ear-to-ear grins, suited up, and started swimming.

I chuckled to myself when I realized that the dolphin who had enticed us into the water had now returned to the pod. The little trickster! We would be swimming the entire distance to them after all! Once we were in the water, though, our energy and stamina was buoyed just knowing the dolphins were there, and that they wanted to swim with us too!

We paused frequently to check our bearings. Nearing the pod, I scanned the scene. There were quite a few kayaks with people in them watching the dolphins. I could only see one person in the water swimming with them.

I eagerly anticipated my first underwater sighting of those precious dark gray forms. My heart raced, as much from the excitement as the swimming. So much for being meditative! An image flashed through my mind: the dolphins encircling me, with me in their center.

And then I saw them ... dark gray shapes up ahead. *They're in serious play mode!* I'd never seen them like this before. Dolphins were everywhere—darting about at full speed, spiraling, spinning, charging to the depths, and then soaring back to the surface at dizzying speeds. It was exhilarating and exciting!

Then something happened ...

I must have blinked. When my eyes opened, a large group of dolphins was arrayed in front of me, swimming in the harmonious, synchronous style that I remembered so well from my first encounter. It didn't occur to me to question how they just appeared in front of me like that. It also didn't occur to me to question the instantaneous shift in their energy from supercharged play mode to elegant underwater ballet. They were here, I was here, and I was mesmerized.

No one else was around. It was just the dolphins and me. It didn't occur to me to question that, either.

The dolphins swam about ten feet beneath me while I swam at the surface, watching in awe. I took in every detail. I wanted to remember these precious moments forever.

There were mamas and babies. There was lovemaking. One by one, a few dolphins left their position in the pod to swim by my side for a while, making eye contact. Then they returned to their place in the array. *They're matching my pace,* I marveled. In previous encounters, the dolphins always swam just a little bit faster than me, so that our actual eye-to-eye time was brief. Now they swam at my speed, and our eye contact was prolonged.

People always want to know how many dolphins I swim with, so I began counting. I counted to thirty-five and wasn't even halfway, so I stopped. *They're here. I'm here. We're together. That's all that matters.*

My awareness expanded. I noticed that the dolphins were swimming in a semicircle in front of me and that the semicircle began immediately at my sides. *They're encircling me!* I sensed that they were focused on keeping me in their center. We made a large turn in unison. We had turned a few times by now. I lifted my head above water to get my bearings in the bay. I realized that we were swimming in a large figure-eight pattern ... the infinity symbol.

A knowing rose up inside me. *These dolphins are welcoming me into their family.* I was deeply moved.

It was amazing swimming with the dolphins in this way. I was ecstatic! I began wondering where my friends were. I wanted to share this with them! I looked up out of the water and saw no kayaks ... and no people.

How can that be?

I didn't know what was going on, but I was here now, and I wanted to stay in this experience. Wherever my friends are, dolphins are with them too, I assured myself. I didn't give it another thought. I continued swimming with my dolphin family.

> A knowing rose up inside of me. *These dolphins are welcoming me into their family.* I was deeply moved.

New understandings flowed through my consciousness. I experienced the divine perfection of me being in my human body and the dolphins being in their dolphin bodies. *It doesn't matter that I am in human form. We are the same. There is no separation; we are one. This is unity consciousness. The dolphins brought me here. I'm so grateful!*

Somehow I knew that the dolphins were healing my relationship with humanity—my own humanity, and humanity as a whole. Receiving this direct experience of the higher truth—that there is no separation between us—enabled me to make peace with my humanness. All the grief, anger, and confusion I'd been feeling about being a human in this lifetime dissolved. That was the most precious gift the dolphins could have given me. In that ocean, with those dolphins, I experienced grace.

Where are my friends? I want them to feel this! Again, I looked above the water and saw no people, no kayaks.

I swam with my beloved dolphin family in this cocoon of oneness for perhaps thirty minutes. It was timeless.

Then, in another blink of an eye, I saw a pair of human legs dangling in the water to my left. I recognized Lori's suit and swam over to her.

"Where were you? That was so amazing!" I exclaimed breathlessly once I reached her.

"Where was *I*? Where were *you*?" Lori told me that the dolphins and I just disappeared. She had treaded water and looked everywhere, and we were gone!

The realization came to both of us at the same time. "The dolphins took me into another dimension of reality!"

We'd both read about the dolphins doing that with Joan Ocean in one of her books. Joan wrote that sometimes people would see her and the dolphins just disappear and become invisible. I never dreamed that would happen to me.

Lori told me that as time passed, and the dolphins and I did not return, she became concerned. She thought to herself, *David will kill me if I come home without Linda!* Lori had made this trip possible for me, and she felt partially responsible for my well-being. "When I tuned in to you, I knew you were fine. But I feel a whole lot better now that you're back!"

We were exhilarated and relieved to be back together again.

After my disappearing act, the four of us reconvened, treading water, deciding whether to stay longer or swim to shore and get breakfast. We were hungry, and we felt complete, so we decided to head back in.

But the dolphins weren't done with us yet. They had one more gift for our little group.

Just before beginning our swim back, we felt a shift in the atmosphere around us. A hush fell over the bay. The water became silky and thick. The air was dense and charged with electricity—it felt as if I could reach out and touch it. We were enveloped in total silence. The only sound was our breath, and the gentle lapping of the water against our bodies.

The four of us looked at each other quizzically. My gaze was directed to a man in a kayak a short distance away. He was motionless, absolutely still. *That's odd.* Looking around the rest of the bay, I noticed there was no movement, anywhere. No kayaks moving, no people swimming, no dolphin fins slicing through the water. The only movement I was aware of was the four of us treading water.

After a minute or two, the atmosphere around us mysteriously shifted again. The movement resumed. There were splashes. Squeals of laughter and delight. Activity in the bay returned to normal. Looking around, it appeared as if nothing out of the ordinary had happened. Shrugging in bewilderment, we donned our masks, secured our snorkels, and started the swim back to shore.

Lori and I swam ahead, and Sarah and Roy followed a short distance behind. As we swam our final strokes in the shallow water, we heard one sustained high-pitched dolphin tone.

Breathlessly, we stood up, tore off our masks, and exclaimed in unison, "Did you hear that!? It was as if that sound was just for us! As if the dolphins were saying goodbye!"

I marveled at the mastery of the dolphins. They seemed to know exactly where Lori and I were on our swim, exactly when we were taking our last swim strokes. They took me into another dimension of reality! And whatever that moment was with the four of us together ...

These dolphins are amazing!!

♡

Six months later, back home in Sedona, I was grocery shopping one day in the local natural food store. Suddenly, the memory of that odd experience in the bay—when everyone and everything became still—surfaced in my mind. I stopped in my tracks. A knowing came over me. *They stopped time! The dolphins caused time to stand still in the world around us, while we remained fully conscious.* I couldn't wait to get home to tell David. Energy masters, indeed!

Dolphin Love

This is what my journey with the dolphins has been like. I have an experience that I don't understand. Later, sometimes much later, the understanding or realization comes.

The dolphins have taught me to dance with the mystery of life. I have come to feel comfortable with not knowing everything all the time. I've learned that when I need to know something, the information comes. Until then, I hang out in the mystery, and I trust. It's all right. Actually, it's pretty cool!

There were other swims, on other days. Every day, I swam with the Sedona seashell tucked safely into my lycra skin. I never had another deep, recurring close connection with one single dolphin like I had with the male dolphin on our first swim, from the boat. On my last day, floating alone in the middle of the bay, with no humans or dolphins around, I decided it was time. It was time to release my shell into the ocean home of my beloved dolphin family.

Because of my own silly doubt, I had missed my opportunity to give this gift to my special dolphin friend on his birthday. So, instead, I gifted the shell to this exquisite bay, and all the dolphins that swim there.

My heart was overflowing with love and gratitude for these amazing beings. From out of the blue, they swam into my life and swept me off my feet. With soft tears streaming, I spoke to the dolphins from my heart, *"I love you all so, so deeply. Thank you so very much for who you are, and for all that you do ... for me, for humanity, and for planet Earth. I give you this seashell, from my heart to yours, from my home to yours."* Extending my hand in front of me, I dropped the shell and watched it descend, out of sight, into the rich blue depths of the bay.

"Happy Birthday, precious one," I projected telepathically to my special dolphin friend. *"I love you."*

On the plane, homeward bound, I reflected on this extraordinary trip.

My deepest heart's desire for this trip was to be alone with the dolphins. More than anything, I had wanted to re-create my first encounter with them. When the dolphins took me into that other reality, when we "disappeared," they gave me that gift! They took me to a place where we were alone. There were no other humans there.

I relived that extraordinary experience. I marveled at how the dolphins shifted realities so quickly, so naturally, in the blink of an eye! The quality of our encounter was very much like my first encounter. It was peaceful, harmonious, an exquisite underwater ballet ... and so much more.

If I hadn't been with friends, I probably wouldn't have noticed that I was in another dimension of reality.** It wasn't until Lori and I were reunited, and she told me about her experience searching for me and the dolphins, that we realized that something truly remarkable had happened.

I smiled with the realization that the dolphins orchestrated my trip perfectly by arranging that I go with my three lovely friends.

The biggest gift of all was the healing of my grief about being a human. The dolphins gave me a direct, tangible, physical experience of the higher truth: *We are one. There is no separation.* All the heaviness I had been carrying simply lifted away and dissolved.

Making peace with my own humanness enabled me to make peace with humanity as a whole. Yes, we have a long way to go to learn how to live with one another peacefully, lovingly, and cooperatively; but, at the heart of it all, we're all connected. We're all the same. All of life is one. I know that now, in my bones.

Sitting in that plane, flying high over the Pacific Ocean, surrounded by strangers, pure joy flowed through me. I felt reborn to my human body, and this human experience. I felt pure love for every person on that plane, and inside myself I told them so. Most of all, I felt joyful about the life that lay before me at home, in the desert. I was excited to return home to David, my sweetie.

My new male dolphin friend's presence hovered before me. *"Hi, baby,"* I said

** Years later, our dolphin spirit guide, Archie, corrected my understanding. You'll meet Archie later. He said that what really happened was that the dolphins took me to a "parallel world." Archie's a stickler for correct physics! Although I'm not sure I know the difference between the two.

to him. *"I kind of had a birthday of my own in your beautiful waters."* A giggle erupted inside of me. *"Happy Birthday to us!"*

I was sporting an unstoppable ear-to-ear grin.

The healing I received from the dolphins on this trip had one notable result in my relationship with David. A few weeks after my return home, we were hiking together on a Sedona trail. I suddenly stopped David on the trail, turned to him, and answered the question he'd been asking me for almost as long as we'd been living together. With love and joy overflowing from my heart, I said, "Yes. Yes! Let's get married!"

FOURTEEN

Stranger Than Fiction

I am about to relate to you a compilation of events and circumstances that occurred over the course of my journey with the dolphins that are flat-out bizarre. This is weird stuff; and it's all true.

I am deeply grateful that David was by my side every step of the way during this journey. His witnessing of the events I am about to share validated that what was happening to me was real, and that I wasn't going crazy. His stable presence and support grounded me when I didn't know which end was up.

Way back in the beginning of my dolphin journey, about a month before my life-changing psychic reading with Antarah Rose, I began feeling compelled to take baths, long baths. I was never a bath person. But, suddenly, I had to take a bath almost every day, and I couldn't take one that was less than an hour-and-a-half long. In the bathtub, my body moved continuously, in an undulating motion. At first I didn't think anything of it, other than noticing that it kept the warm water circulating, and that felt good.

When I took my first bath after the psychic reading, with the message from the dolphins fresh in my mind, the undulating took on a whole new significance. *Dolphins ... undulations ... dolphins ... What is going on here?*

I consciously stopped my body's undulating movements and tried to remain motionless. But after only a moment or two of stillness, my body was undulating again. I could not stop it. My body seemed to have a life of its own; I was not in control. This went on for the duration of the bath.

I was mildly freaked. *This is definitely dolphinlike movement ... Am I turning into a dolphin?*

Around the same time, a childhood memory surfaced that seemed related to this dolphin connection that was revealing itself to me.

In my family, the four of us kids took swimming lessons when we were very young. As soon as we were able to swim our first lap, we were on the swim team. I was seven or eight when I accomplished that feat.

When I was around ten, part of our swim team practice was to swim underwater as far as we could on one breath. I remember practicing this frequently during open swim time later on in the day. I went under the water and held my breath for as long as I could. When I needed to breathe, I did something instinctively with my jaw that I swear enabled me to extract oxygen from the water, extending my underwater stay. And then my mind kicked in and told me that that was impossible, and I rushed to the surface, gasping for air.

Other dolphin people have shared stories with me of unusual experiences they had in the water as kids. Many remember playing in the water like dolphins, spinning and spinning, and moving their bodies in that undulating movement. Can it be that when we are children, memories of lifetimes as water mammals rise to the surface, and we play them out in our neighborhood swimming pools?

During that same time period, my vision changed. I had just had my contact lens prescription updated to 20/20, and one day I noticed that my vision was blurry. I waited a few days to see if it would clear up, and it did not. My intuition told me that I was experiencing a change in my body's vibrational frequency, and not to worry about it. But driving was becoming difficult, and I was beginning to get mild headaches.

I went back to my eye doctor, and he suggested I get tested for diabetes. The results came back negative, as I knew they would. My blurred vision remained a mystery until a week before my scheduled departure for Hawaii to swim with the dolphins for the first time.

I was hiking one day with my friend and gifted psychic, Andrea. We stopped at one point and stood together in silence, taking in the beauty of the red rocks towering all around us. My thoughts turned to my vision and what was happening with my eyes. I looked at the rocks, paying attention to my blurred vision. Then my head, seemingly on its own, turned to one side so that I was seeing the rocks through my peripheral vision. The rocks were crystal clear! My head turned to the other side, and the rocks were clear. I moved my head from side to side, noticing the exact points at which my vision blurred, looking forward, and then cleared, looking peripherally.

I told Andrea about it. She looked deeply into me, and then said, matter-of-factly, "Well, where are the dolphins' eyes?"

Gasp. *Oh, my God! This is really weird! What on earth is happening here?*

This phenomenon still comes and goes. I've learned to live with the fluctuation of my forward vision. On a practical note, the dolphins guided me to a very open-minded optometrist! I amuse him. My peripheral vision has remained crystal clear.

Andrea's conclusion was validated a couple of months later when I was back in Sedona after my first wild dolphin encounter. David was immersed in his work at his computer one day, and I was in the kitchen doing dishes. With my hands immersed in water, I felt an energetic "tapping on my head." The top of my head was tingling. I stopped what I was doing and tuned in. One of David's spiritual guides, the Archangel Metatron, had come to me with a message for David. He wanted-ed David to stop working and meditate. Metatron had something to share with him.

I told David, and he complied. In fact, Metatron's presence was so strong that we both stopped what we were doing and meditated, in separate rooms. After awhile, David called out to me and offered to channel Metatron if I wanted to ask any questions.

"Sure!" I never pass up an opportunity like that.

I asked Metatron about my work with the dolphins, and one thing he said was, **"Your parts aren't where they expect them to be!"**

No kidding! I thought to myself. *And I like my parts just the way they are, thank you very much!*

A few days later I was giving a dolphin energy healing session to a woman and my nose began to buzz and itch. The buzzing got stronger and stronger. I felt dolphins hovering all around me. In my mind, I exclaimed to them, *"Leave my nose alone, please! I like it just the way it is!"* The buzzing faded away. Whew! I don't even want to think about what might have happened there!

And then there was the blowhole phenomenon.

This story originates in 1995, after my telepathic communication with the Lanai dolphins, but well before I knew about my personal connection to dolphins.

I was in the process of moving back to the mainland after living for a brief time on Maui. I lived in the charming upcountry community of Kula, at 4,000-feet elevation, almost halfway up to the top of Haleakala, the dormant volcano that towers over the island. I chose Kula as my home because of its pristine energy.

During my last week, I stayed in my landlord's house, while packing and shipping my belongings to Sedona. Richard and his sons were early to bed and early to rise. Once the lights were out, the house was totally, and I mean totally, dark and silent. I did not recall being in a place so utterly dark and silent before. I liked it. It was deeply comforting somehow.

The first couple of nights, I wasn't sleepy that early, so I took advantage of the stillness and meditated. I sat in the bed, closed my eyes, and within moments felt a sensation at the top of my head. It felt like a finger was softly rubbing the top of my head in a clockwise circular motion, just to the left of center. I knew I was alone in the room, but I instinctively felt the top of my head with my hand, fully expecting to feel someone's finger there. There was no hand or finger there other than my own.

"Do you know how to open your blowhole?"

I removed my hand, and the sensation continued. I felt my head again, and nothing was there. I continued meditating. The next night I had the exact same experience. It wasn't uncomfortable, and I didn't feel afraid, I just had no idea what caused the sensation or why I was experiencing it.

Several months later, back in Sedona, I met Nickie, my acting class buddy, at a coffee shop. A friend of hers stopped by our table to say hello. During our conversation, I mentioned that I was going to Hawaii to swim with the dolphins.

This man responded, "Do you know how to open your blowhole?"

Only in Sedona! I chuckled to myself.

He continued, "Take your index finger and rub it softly on the top of your head in a one-and-a-quarter-inch diameter circle, over and over. That will open your blowhole."

It was amusing to hear this man share this information as casually as if he were telling us about a movie he'd just seen. I thanked him for the tip, and he went on to join his friends at another table. It didn't occur to me to ask him *why* I would want to open my blowhole.

On the drive home, I remembered that sensation I had while meditating on Maui. *That's what was happening. My blowhole was being opened!*

I had no idea what purpose that would serve. I supposed I'd find out soon enough. I always do!

Sure enough, months later, while giving a dolphin energy healing session to a friend, I noticed that I was practically hyperventilating. The energy coming through was so strong, my breathing became rapid and shallow in an effort to move the massive amount of energy through me.

I felt spirit dolphins all around me. In my mind, I heard them say: **"Breathe through your blowhole!"**

"How do I do that?"

They assisted me in shifting my awareness to the spot on the top of my head that I now knew to be my blowhole. **"Imagine breathing in and out through this space,"** the dolphins suggested.

As I did this, it tickled. I definitely felt something happening up there. I was simply imagining breathing through that spot, while still physically breathing through my nose, but my breathing pattern did, indeed, shift. It slowed and deepened. I felt the air circulating throughout my entire body, not just my respiratory system. My body energy calmed way down. I was no longer at risk of passing out.

At a later time, during a meditation, the idea popped into my mind to practice breathing through my blowhole again. While I was imagining breathing in that way, a momentary shift occurred. For just a few moments, a pronounced muscle reflex opened and closed, with tremendous strength and force, in the spot I knew was my blowhole. This muscle-spasm sensation penetrated through my skull and into my head about one-and-a-half inches. I experienced one forceful inhale and one exhale through this very real-feeling blowhole. The experience was shockingly real. That particular sensation hasn't happened again since.

I've since experimented with this phenomenon in my group meditations, guiding others to open their blowholes and breathe through them. It is a profound experience for many. I still get comments from people, years later, who remember this process and tell me they breathe through their blowholes in times of stress, with wonderful results.

A curious thing happened in Bimini, where I went to swim with the spotted dolphins.

I went snorkeling alone one morning just offshore and happened upon a school of brilliant cobalt blue fish. As we swam toward each other, the fish came very close. They swam past me, just inches from my body. I stopped and turned my head to watch them go by. My stopping altered their flow. The next thing I knew, they were swimming chaotically, in all different directions, until they wound up swimming in two distinct groups. The inner group swam in a tight circle around me clockwise, and the outer group swam in a circle around me counterclockwise. It was surreal to be in their center like this.

When I emerged from the water, and began the walk back to the cabin where David and I were staying, I realized I was in an altered state of consciousness. I walked into our cabin, went straight to the bed, and sat with my back against the headboard, so I could be fully present with this energetic experience.

My body felt like it was still in the water, swaying rhythmically with the gentle underwater current. My awareness was drawn to a peculiar sensation on the sides of my face. There was movement at the surface of my cheeks. *Gills! I have gills!* I could feel them opening and closing ... and I could feel air passing through them!

The moment I opened my mouth to tell David what I was experiencing, the sensation faded away. My body energy felt giddy inside, but my mind was saying that was just too weird!

The strangest phenomenon was when my skull began changing shape. I was going about my life, giving dolphin energy healings to people, when something strange began happening while I slept at night.

For a couple of months, I occasionally woke up in the middle of the night to discover that the hair on the back of my head and/or neck was soaking wet, as if I'd just showered. The rest of my body wasn't hot or uncomfortable in any way. The first few nights it happened I shrugged it off and went back to sleep. After several consecutive nights, I became curious and mentioned it to David as soon as we woke up one morning.

David reached out with his hand and explored the back of my head. His eyes popped open. "Do you remember these ridges and soft spots being there?" he asked, while guiding my hand to also explore my head.

"No!" I exclaimed, mildly freaked out.

We began examining my head every morning, and there were definite changes taking place in its physical structure. It also seemed intentional that I was being awakened during the night so that I would know that these changes were taking place.

I had no idea what was occurring, or why. I was so glad David was with me to validate that this was real. If I was alone and having this experience, I don't know how I would have handled it.

In 2003, when I went to Hawaii to swim with the dolphins, I donned my mask and snorkel and headed out into the bay bright and early my first morning there. About forty-five minutes into my swim, I noticed that my forehead was hurting—a lot! *The dolphins must be working on my third eye this trip!*

As I swam, I kept welcoming the discomfort. I breathed into the pain. I kept surrendering to whatever it was the dolphins were doing now. After awhile, I stopped. *This is ridiculous. This isn't right.* Treading water in the middle of the bay, I took off my mask and rubbed my forehead. The imprint from my mask in my forehead was very deep. My forehead actually felt bruised! *My mask is too tight!* I realized. I loosened the strap and put it back on. *Ahhh ... much better!!*

I resumed swimming, contemplating how long it had been since I'd last worn this mask, when it fit perfectly. About a year. The circumference of my head grew that much in a year!

♡

In 2004, I was questioned by a security agent at the Amsterdam airport. He looked at my ten-year-old passport photo, and then looked at me. He took my passport to his supervisor across the room, who did the same thing. They both kept looking—at my passport, at me, at my passport, at me—with puzzled expressions on their faces.

Finally, over the gathering of travelers awaiting their flight, the supervisor called out to me, "The structure of your face has completely changed!"

"I'm not a redhead anymore!" I replied meekly.

"That's not it. It's your whole jaw area, and your cheekbones—they're completely different now."

I didn't dare say, "The dolphins did it!" Thankfully, they decided that I was really me, and they let me on the plane. When we returned home, I got a new passport with an updated photo.

♡

This phenomenon is ongoing. Sometimes I look in the mirror and really look at my head and face. I do, indeed, see changes in their structure! I'm sometimes tempted to shave my head to see what my bare head looks like now! I used to have such a nicely shaped—normal-shaped—head. Now there's a defined ridge where a hat brim would rest, and the top of my head is pretty flat! The hairdresser I've had throughout these years has witnessed my head changes with amusement.

Sometimes I wonder if I should worry about what's happening, but I know that it's part of my spiritual journey with the dolphins. I trust them completely. I may not understand what they do, but their impact on my life is always benevolent.

Dolphin Love

In the midst of the skull shape-shifting process, there was a two-day period that I walked around our house feeling very spacey. I knew I was going through another process related to the dolphins, and to allow it.

Late in the afternoon of the second day, I felt my consciousness slip back into my body. I was "back." I had a sense that whatever was going on was complete. My inner voice told me that my consciousness had been expanded to include the cosmos, and it was done while I was in a waking state so that I'd be aware of the process.

Immediately afterwards, I went through a phase in my dolphin energy healing sessions where I began accessing a vast array of cosmic energies, and linking people to their galactic source. None of this was intentional on my part. It just happened. People came to me for a session, and during the session we were linked to the star or planet where their soul originated. Often I "saw," in my mind's eye, an elder from their "galactic home" come to them during the session to deliver a message, or gift them with an etheric crystal that would help them to remember their source. Most of the time, we did not know the names of these home stars or planets. They were places far, far away.

It was during this time that I gave the session to the woman who channeled Archangel Michael. In his message to me after her session, in addition to telling me about my past lives as water mammals, he also told me that my work with the dolphins involved "intergalactic communication."*

It was fascinating and exciting having these intergalactic visitors appear in my little healing room in Sedona! People were profoundly moved to have this reconnection to their source facilitated by the dolphins.

Is there any limit to what the dolphins can do to help us remember who we really are?

---

* The dolphins orchestrated one more confirmation of this cosmic link. Linda Dillon is a channel and spiritual teacher who used to give her Council of Love weekend workshop once a year in Sedona. That year, she invited me to give her group a dolphin energy experience. In return, I attended the whole workshop as her guest.

At one point in the weekend, Linda guided us all into a meditation, and then came around the room and, one by one, "hooked us up" to cosmic energies. When she came to me, and began to initiate the connecting process, she opened her eyes in surprise and whispered, "You're already hooked up!" She moved on to the next person.

Through these and similar experiences, I have come to understand that the dolphins and I are engaged in an experiment. The dolphins made changes to my energetic and physical structure, and to my consciousness, to improve my abilities to transmit their energy to humans on land.

Even though many of these experiences seemed really weird to me, I always felt safe. I have developed absolute trust in the dolphins. In moments of doubt or fear, I keep coming back to that trust.

The dolphins will never harm me. They will only lead me to a better future.

Chuckles

At the very beginning of my journey, just days before leaving Sedona to go to Hawaii to swim with the dolphins for the first time, I met a Peruvian tour guide. He was in Sedona gathering people to go on his next trip. When I told him I would soon be going to Hawaii to swim with the dolphins, he told me about the Amazon River dolphins, commonly referred to as pink dolphins. I was fascinated to hear about these freshwater dolphins swimming in the rivers that wind through the rainforests of Peru. *I have to meet these dolphins! I guess I'll be going to Peru!*

The next year, David and I were preparing for our annual Christmas visit with my family in Pittsburgh, Pennsylvania. Two weeks before our trip, my mother informed me over the phone, "The dolphin in the zoo just bit a woman."

Back up ... "*What* dolphin? *What* zoo?" I asked incredulously.

"The dolphin in the Pittsburgh Zoo," my mother replied.

"There's a dolphin there? It's alone?" I asked, distressed.

"It volunteered for this service," my mother answered matter-of-factly.

"Yes, of course," I replied.

Wait a minute ... my mother said that? How does she know about such things? My mind was reeling with questions.

We arrived in Pittsburgh and walked into the kitchen of my parents' home. Lying on the kitchen table was that day's newspaper. The headline story glared up at me. It was an article about the dolphin incident at the zoo. David and I leaned over the table to read the article together. The first sentence read, "The Amazon River dolphin in the Pittsburgh Zoo ..."

I stopped reading and looked at David, wide-eyed. "There's an Amazon River dolphin at the Pittsburgh zoo? Right here in my own backyard?" This was so unexpected! We both knew we'd be making a trip to the zoo while we were here. *I guess I won't have to go to Peru after all!*

With all the holiday festivities, it wasn't until our last day that time finally opened up for us to go to the zoo. We arrived at four in the afternoon, to find all the ticket booths closed! *How can the zoo be closed at four in the afternoon?* We could not believe we were this close to seeing the dolphin and we couldn't get in.

Dumbfounded, we wandered around in front of the ticket booths wondering how we possibly manifested this. Then a man came out the zoo exit gate. He told us that the zoo was closed and suggested that we come back tomorrow.

In a daze, I kept saying out loud, "We just came to see the dolphin!" over and over. It was like I was five years old.

David was coherent enough to talk rationally to this man. He told him we were visiting from Arizona, we loved dolphins, and we were leaving the next day. The man looked at us, and then turned around, opened the gate and let us in.

"Take your time. If the guard asks, tell him you have my permission."

We didn't know who this man was, but to me he was an angel! We didn't even have to pay!

When we passed the guard, we opened our mouths to explain, and he said with a smile, "I heard. Have fun!" He pointed us in the direction of the aquarium, and we were on our way.

We charged up the walkway, cuddled arm in arm, bracing ourselves against the bitter cold, quickly passing a breathtakingly beautiful snow leopard and other exotic creatures. *We're going to see an Amazon River dolphin ... in Pittsburgh!*

When we arrived at the aquarium building, we had the whole place to ourselves. We delighted in the divine perfection of our timing! Our excitement increased.

We wound around past all the tanks of fish and sea life, and passed through the penguin area. (Penguins are so cool!) When we came to the bigger tanks with the sharks, we knew we were getting close. Our hearts raced as we approached the dolphin tank.

We were not prepared for what we saw. There was a lone dolphin, swimming listlessly in circles in a small, austere concrete tank. It broke my heart. There was no life or spark in him that I could see. He was astonishing to look at, though. He looked prehistoric, very different in appearance than the ocean dolphins.

In subdued silence, we watched him swim around and around. We weren't quite sure what to do. David left my side, walked to the end of the tank, and disappeared around the corner. I approached the side of the tank and continued watching the dolphin, trying to make a connection. He didn't even seem to know I was there.

After a while, I noticed that the dolphin had stopped swimming. He was stopped at the end of the tank where David was. I walked down the corridor and looked around the corner to see what was going on.

I was astonished to see this dolphin hovering right in front of David, looking at him—connecting with him. His rostrum was touching the glass. He got as close to David as he could possibly get. Their faces were mere inches apart.

I backed off. Clearly, this was David's experience. It was so beautiful seeing them connect like this. My heart filled with wonder at what I was witnessing.

David sensed my presence and turned to look at me. Tears were streaming down his face. I felt his unspoken invitation to join him. I walked over and stood quietly by his side. The dolphin resumed its swim as David and I stood in silence, watching. Then David told me what had happened.

He said that when he knelt down to watch the dolphin, a strong, primal emotion came over him. It came from the depth of his being. David closed his eyes, surrendered to the emotion, and cried. When he opened his eyes, the dolphin was suspended motionless in front of him, looking right at him through the glass. It was a sacred moment ... a sacred connection.

I walked back to my spot around the corner to give David his space. Now the dolphin swam in smaller circles. He swam precisely between David and me, making conscious eye contact with each of us as he passed. He came as close to us as possible, often brushing against the glass with his body, as if trying to break through this barrier that was separating us. Now we were connected.

 He came as close to us as possible, often brushing against the glass with his body, as if trying to break through this barrier that was separating us.

David did some exploring and discovered a letter posted on the wall outside the tank. The letter was the zoo's response to a woman protesting the bleak conditions of this lone dolphin's tank. It explained that Amazon River dolphins are different from their ocean-dwelling cousins in many ways. For one, the river dolphins often travel alone, in shallow, narrow waterways. Also, the river dolphins' spines are not fused together the way the ocean dolphins' are, as they need the agility to navigate around tree trunks in the swamp waters of their natural habitat. Therefore, these dolphins are unable to perform the fantastic leaps and jumps that the ocean dolphins execute.

When David told me that this dolphin's name was Chuckles, I recoiled. "Chuckles?! What an undignified name for this magnificent being!" I was quite upset. Then I calmed down. *Oh, well. This is a zoo, after all, and zoos cater to kids.* I let my upset go.

David and I communed with Chuckles for about an hour. He made every minute count. Once we connected, he put on quite a show. He showed us every aspect of himself!

Chuckles was in his rutting (mating) season—and there were no female dolphins around. The newspaper article mentioned this as a possible contributing factor to his recent aggressive behavior. As we watched, Chuckles maneuvered his body so that he was floating, belly-forward, at a forty-five degree angle, right in front of us. His tail hovered just above the bottom of the tank, close to the glass in front of us, while his head extended to just below the surface of the water, pointing away from us. We watched in amazement as he extended his *really long* penis to a full erection, and held it out for our inspection! He stayed in that position for several minutes. He seemed quite proud of himself! We giggled at this intimate display.

We also got to observe his feeding time. The young man who came to feed Chuckles wasn't at all concerned that we were there. We watched Chuckles eat, and we noticed that he let a few little fishies escape so that he could play with them (and snack on them!) later.

After his meal, David and I were talking, wondering how Chuckles sleeps. I began to notice him repeating a peculiar sequence of behaviors. He closed his eyes, then opened his mouth wide, then closed his mouth, then opened his eyes and looked at us. He closed his eyes again, opened his mouth, closed his mouth, opened his eyes and looked at us, over and over.

"Hey! He's yawning!" I joked to David.

Sure enough, once we "got the message," Chuckles went into sleep mode right then and there. Hugging the bottom of the tank, he withdrew his energy into himself, and became very quiet and still. He was no longer actively connecting with us.

"Chuckles is sleeping! He's responding to our thoughts!"

David and I looked at one another, amazed. The way he did it was so clever. He mimicked the way we humans behave when we get sleepy—he "yawned"—and then we understood what he was going to show us next! He only slept for a few minutes; just long enough to demonstrate what sleep is like for him.

Several times, David and I began to leave. But each time we started to walk away, we were magnetically drawn back to Chuckles. We just couldn't leave him. He had captured our hearts.

The last thing he showed us was the most astonishing. Chuckles floated vertically in front of us, in the middle of the tank, belly forward. Maintaining eye contact with us, he began bending his body ever so slowly, sideways, as if from his "waist." He kept bending and bending (he has an unfused spine, remember?), until the tip of his tail and the top of his head touched! His body formed a perfect circle, and he sustained that position, hovering motionless about twelve inches above the floor of the tank, for a full minute! *Where is my camera?! Wow!* We were floored.

The circle represents oneness, unity. We certainly felt that with Chuckles by the time our visit drew to a close. David and I were both in tears. We felt deeply honored and blessed by the privilege of meeting this magnificent being. We felt so much love for him, our hearts swelled to overflowing.

When we finally peeled ourselves away, we thanked Chuckles for sharing himself with us so completely. We promised him we'd come to see him every time we came to Pittsburgh. It has been a privilege and a joy to keep that promise.

The next time we visited Chuckles, his tank had been renovated to better reflect his natural environment. It was still sad to see him there alone, a captive in our human world. And I remembered that he volunteered to be here in service to us. Perhaps he reminded me of that, telepathically. It just made me love him more, and long for the day when we humans no longer feel the need to take any beings into captivity.

During our Christmas 2001 visit, David and I made our annual trek to the zoo, full of excitement and anticipation. This was our fourth visit to see Chuckles. As we made our way down the ramp toward his tank, we saw Chuckles swimming quite enthusiastically! We looked at one another with surprise and delight.

"Chuckles looks happy, really happy!"

We sat with Chuckles and visited for an hour or so as zoo visitors strolled by, making their various comments about this unusual-looking dolphin. Many were surprised by his appearance. He didn't look anything like Flipper, which I suppose is what most people expect when they come to the zoo to see a dolphin. Several regular visitors walked by and commented on Chuckles' unusually high energy that day.

I began to wonder. *Did Chuckles know we were coming? Is that why he was so excited? Surely not.*

Just then, a zookeeper walked by and also commented on Chuckles' unusually happy behavior. "He must be responding to all the great attention you're giving him today!" *Hmmm ...*

As usual, it was difficult to leave when the time came. It was wonderful seeing

Chuckles so happy! Reluctantly, we said our goodbyes and left the zoo, our hearts filled up with Chuckles' love and joy.

♡

Two months later my mom called. Chuckles had died.

My first reaction was, "Good for him! He's free now!"

And then my human heart felt incredibly sad. I knew that I would not see Chuckles in the physical again, and that was so very sad. He lived in that zoo from the age of four until his late thirties. It was remarkable to me that this gracious being gave his entire life to us humans. I could not imagine living the life he lived.

I remembered how excited he was during our last visit, and then I thought, *Maybe Chuckles really did remember us, and knew we were coming. Maybe he knew that was going to be our last visit with him, and his excitement was about, "I'm going home soon! I'm going home!"*

It's not the same going home for Christmas and not having those visits with Chuckles to look forward to.

♡

I did go to the zoo a few years later with my mom and sister, to see the two baby elephants that had just been born there. After visiting those precious beings, we went to the aquarium. As we neared the tank that had been Chuckles' home for so many years, my heart started beating faster, and my emotions surged. I had such mixed feelings—I wasn't looking forward to seeing the aquarium tank with Chuckles not in it; but I was also curious to see what the zoo had done with that space.

I was taken by surprise by what I saw. There was a big school of really, really large fish swimming in that tank—fish I'd never seen before. My deaf sister Robin watched as I kneeled down close to the glass to connect with these fish. Every single one of those huge fish swam to the glass, their large bodies forming a tight group, facing towards me. They all seemed to be vying for my attention. I looked up at Robin and saw her wide eyes.

She signed, "What's happening?"

Chuckles
Our beloved Amazon River dolphin.
1970 to 2002

"I don't know!" I signed back.

When I felt complete with the fish, I stood and turned to look for my mom and my sister. My heart skipped a beat as my eyes fell upon the painting hanging on the wall opposite Chuckles' former tank. It was a painting of Chuckles. Seeing it brought tears to my eyes. I read the plaque displayed beneath the painting, "Chuckles—Our beloved Amazon River dolphin—1970-2002." In the middle of a steady stream of visitors passing by, I stood rooted to that spot, looking at that painting, and I cried and cried. My mom and sister came to stand on either side of me. They held space for me as my love and longing for my friend, Chuckles, flowed.

It pleased me enormously that the zoo memorialized Chuckles, and the extraordinary contribution he made to so many, for so long, in this way. Well done, Pittsburgh Zoo.

Chuckles, words cannot express how deeply you touched us. Thank you, dear one. We will always remember you. You are forever in our hearts.

SIXTEEN

Time Out of Mind

The dolphins gave me a profound gift when I first began sharing their energy. At the start of each dolphin energy healing session, they shifted my internal state to one of no thought. My mind instantly became empty, silent, and still. These sessions lasted up to an hour, and during the entire time, this state of no thought was sustained. I started calling this the Void space. I emerged from each session deeply relaxed, peaceful, and still inside myself ... and at the same time, energized.

After giving several sessions, I became aware that this state of no thought, of silence and stillness, was staying with me as I went about my daily life.

David and I took frequent walks through our lovely wooded residential neighborhood, or out on the Sedona trails. Sometimes we would talk, but often we would walk together in silence.

When we'd been silent for a while, David would sometimes ask me, "What are you thinking about?"

"Nothing," I replied, truthfully.

After we had this same exchange multiple times, I realized I was in an almost continual state of no thought. Instead of being absorbed in my thoughts during our walks, my awareness was drawn deeply into the natural surroundings. It was as if my energy field—my awareness—was extending itself outward to meet every sight, smell, color, and texture of nature and the various objects around me. I was simply being, and interacting deeply, with everything around me.

It got to the point that when David asked, "What are you thinking?"

I would laugh, roll my eyes, and exclaim, "Nothing! I have no thoughts!"

Eventually he stopped asking.

David marveled at this new development. He observed me to be in a quiet state of pure awareness. I didn't have an opinion about this state of being one way or another. It just was. I just was. But it did dawn on me that this state of no thought was not the ordinary human experience.

This gift from the dolphins has certainly led to a much calmer, more peaceful state of existence for me. And my ability to meditate, often for periods of time up to one-and-a-half hours, has been greatly enhanced. When I lead others in meditation, I have to remind myself that this is not the case for most people.

Over the course of facilitating many dolphin energy healings, I've noticed that the dolphins work a lot on my clients' brains. This seems to be one of their areas of expertise. I have no scientific proof except for my own personal experience, but I believe that the dolphins have the capacity to make adjustments to our human brains for the purpose of activating unused parts of our brains, and creating new neural pathways between the left and right hemispheres of the brain, enabling us to be more whole, and more balanced, in our functioning. During dolphin energy healing sessions, when the energy seems to be focused on my client's brain, I sometimes hear the term *"whole-brain functioning."*

The dolphins certainly facilitated a big shift in the functioning of my brain. I had a visual image one time of the dolphins unplugging my brain, and rewiring all of my circuitry. For a while, my internal computer (my brain) went "offline." When the dolphins rebooted my system, my heart was in the lead, and my head was in service to my heart.

I attended a Dr. Peebles open channeling at a time when one particular life issue was troubling me. When it was my turn, I asked Dr. Peebles my question.

He said, "My dear, what you really want is to be able to answer your own questions from within. What I want you to do is to go into your heart, and ask this question of your heart."

"Okay," I said, thinking that when I returned home, I would meditate, go into my heart, and ask my question.

"Well?" Dr. Peebles followed up. "What is your answer?"

"You want me to do that now? Here?" I felt embarrassed to be put on the spot like this in front of the group.

"Why not? Yes, my dear. Go into your heart now, and ask your question now!"

I know that Dr. Peebles helped me, because as soon as I closed my eyes, I was *in ... my ... heart ...* as never before! All that existed was my heart! I had no body; I only had a huge heart. I was my heart!

After getting my bearings inside this extraordinary altered perception, I remembered that I was supposed to ask a question. I wanted to ask my question, but I couldn't remember what the question was. *What's my question?* I asked over and over, inside myself. I had an image of a pinball bouncing around inside my body, in search of the question.

"Well, my dear? Do you have your answer?" Dr. Peebles inquired.

With my eyes still closed, I said, "I'm in my heart, and I can't remember my question!"

I opened my eyes and looked around me, feeling strange and perplexed.

"Yes, my dear! When you're truly in your heart, there are no questions, are there?"

Everyone in the room chuckled. I was amazed! Dr. Peebles moved on to the next person, who asked their question, while I sat with the implications of my heart-centered experience. *When I'm in my heart, there are no questions. Everything just is!*

♡

Thanks to the dolphins, I'm blessed to live from my heart most of the time. I graciously welcome the inner peace and quiet that comes from living from this place. It's deeply relaxing, freeing, and energizing to have a quiet mind, and to live from pure awareness.

I was surprised to discover that not everyone was ready and willing to embrace this head-to-heart shift, however ...

A local Sedona man was preparing to travel to Hawaii for his first wild dolphin encounter. He wanted to talk to me, to discuss how he could best prepare for this experience. I was soon talking to him about this heart-brain phenomenon.

I told him, "Don't be surprised if the dolphins unplug your brain for a while and rewire it. Your heart will take over, and your brain will enter into service to your heart."

He phoned me when he got back from his trip. That was, indeed, what was happening for him. He was distressed that his brain wasn't functioning the way it used to. It scared him, because he identified strongly with, and greatly enjoyed, his brain's talents and skills. He felt disoriented. He felt like he was losing his sense of self ... his identity. He didn't know where this shift was leading, and he wasn't at all sure that he wanted to make that journey.

I told him, "If you want the dolphins to stop this process, ask them to stop, and to put your brain back to how it was before."

Apparently that's what he did. We never spoke about it again.

Another outcome of this head-to-heart rewiring was that I was disconnected from the man-made construct of linear time. For quite a long time now, my being has stopped operating within that time structure. Dolphins live in present moment awareness, and most of the time, I do too.

My sense of time is that it's vertical. When I'm truly in the present moment, there is no past, and there is no future. All that exists is now.

It's a bit challenging functioning in the material world from this present moment state. I rely heavily on writing things down and recording commitments in my calendar. But even that is no guarantee that embarrassing moments won't happen.

On several occasions, I've recorded an appointment in my calendar, only to look at the calendar, sometimes more than once, and have my brain register an entirely different day or time for the appointment. This doesn't happen often, but it's happened often enough for me to realize that it's not just a coincidence.

Once I made an appointment with the community events coordinator of a local healing center. I was considering renting space for a dolphin energy playshop, and I wanted to see the space. Sheila suggested that we meet the following Wednesday at 3:00. While we were on the phone, I wrote the appointment in my calendar. Wednesday, 3:00.

My desk calendar displayed a week-at-a-glance. On Monday of the next week, I looked at my calendar to review the week's appointments and saw that appointment notation. Inside my head I affirmed, *My appointment with Sheila is Tuesday at 3:00.* I looked at my calendar several times on Monday. Each time, my mind registered the appointment as taking place on Tuesday.

I woke up Tuesday morning with the thought, *My appointment with Sheila is today at 3:00.* When I went to my desk later that morning, I looked at my calendar again to confirm this. *Yep. It's today at 3:00.*

I showed up at the healing center and announced myself to the receptionist. She phoned Sheila and asked me to take a seat in the reception area.

After a few minutes, Sheila came out looking somewhat confused. "I thought our appointment was for tomorrow."

"No, it's today!" I responded.

"Well, I do have some time now, so let me go ahead and show you around. As it turns out, I just found out this morning that I'll be going out of town tomorrow morning for an extended weekend. I was going to have to arrange for someone else to show you the space. Now I don't have to do that!"

We had our meeting, and while I was describing my work with the dolphins, tears welled up in Sheila's eyes. She shared with me a very touching story of how the dolphins came into her life. She felt a deep connection to them, and was moved to hear how the dolphins were working through me.

I returned home, and out of curiosity, looked again at my calendar. There it was, as plain as day. This appointment was in my book for Wednesday, not Tuesday! I shook my head in wonder. I knew that the dolphins reinterpreted this information every time I looked at my calendar and made a correction. The ideal time for Sheila's and my appointment was, indeed, Tuesday—otherwise, we wouldn't have met. It was important to the dolphins that Sheila and I had the opportunity to connect in person!

This phenomenon occurs sometimes when I book dolphin energy healing sessions for clients. We'll agree to a day and time, and I'll "see" an entirely different time when I look at my calendar. Thankfully, most of the people who are attracted to me for sessions are flexible and understanding. When we shift the session to the adjusted time I'm given by the dolphins, we almost always discover that there was a really good reason for the time shift. The dolphins knew better than we did, and their corrected session time worked out for the best!

Buddhist traditions talk about the "monkey mind" or "inner dialogue"—the constant deluge of thoughts that go round and round in our minds. When I hear people complaining about their monkey mind, I silently thank the dolphins for leading me, effortlessly, to a different way. Living from the place of present moment awareness and no thought has been incredibly freeing.

Time Out of Mind? It's a cool place to visit. It's a great place to live!

- SEVENTEEN -

Up Close and Personal

In November 1999, three-and-a-half years into my dolphin journey, I felt the call again to return to Hawaii and visit my dolphin family. This time, with some swim experiences under my belt, I went with a specific intention. At Dr. Peebles' counsel, the issue I was working on in my life was to open myself, in love and trust, to let *all of life* in. I no longer wished to hold any part of life at arm's length.

With this in mind, while preparing for the trip, I formed the intention to allow the dolphins to come closer to me. I held this intention in my heart. I didn't have any particular idea about how this intention might manifest; in my mind, I kept telling the dolphins, *"I give you full permission to come close to me on this upcoming trip."*

Typically, the spinner dolphins maintain some distance from swimmers, until a relationship is established. Since my trips were so sporadic, I certainly did not put myself into the "close relationship" category.

I arrived in Hawaii full of excitement and anticipation. It had been a year-and-a-half since my last visit. *Will they remember me?*

Upon my arrival, I learned from the locals that during the last month, the dolphins only came into the bay on two days. No one knew why.

Uh-oh. My heart sank. *Don't tell me I came all this way, only to find no dolphins.* There are never any guarantees when you travel to swim with wild dolphins.

Dolphin Love

This seems to happen every trip. I show up in Hawaii and discover that the dolphins haven't been around for a while. I go into a whole big drama, preparing myself for the possibility that I might not see them at all during my trip.

I would be disappointed, I say to myself—the truth is, I would be devastated—*but I'll make the best of it. I was guided to come at this time for a reason, and I just have to trust.*

On these trips, every sense and emotion inside of me is amplified. Whatever I'm feeling, I'm feeling it in a big way, with all of my being. It's intense.

Thankfully, as usual, my concerns were unnecessary. The dolphins did come. In fact, they appeared every day, which was a first for me. I swam with them five days, for a total of about ten hours. This was the most physical contact I'd ever had with the dolphins in one trip.

The first day I swam out into the bay, there was a whole pod of about seventy-five dolphins there. There was a nursery pod, with mamas and babies and escorts maintaining their distance from the surface activity, swimming at the ocean floor, about thirty feet below.

I cried when I first saw them under the water. Do you know how hard it is to cry in a face mask and snorkel? I laughed at myself for crying! If I had surrendered to the fullness of emotions I was feeling in that moment, I would have sobbed uncontrollably. But I was with my dolphin family again after a long absence. I put those emotions aside so I could be fully present with them, here and now. I didn't want to miss a thing.

There were many swimmers and a few kayaks in the bay that day. The interactions among us all were fluid and harmonious. Humans and dolphins swam gracefully in each other's energies. I was so very happy to be there!

Many dolphins beckoned to me for closer interaction. Once I chose a dolphin to connect with, I'd follow that dolphin, or group of dolphins, as they led me away from the crowd.

A group of four dolphins approached me most frequently. The first time they

approached, they rose toward me from below. As they neared, I stopped swimming to give them space to surface in front of me, and then we swam together for
a while, with me bringing up the rear. I held my breath in anticipation as they came
near, consciously giving them space. They kept glancing back at me, assuring me
that I was welcome among them.

After their third identical approach in this fashion, the thought popped into
my mind, *Oh! I wanted them to come close to me, and here I am giving them space.* I
think they reminded me, telepathically, of my intention, so I could choose to interact with them differently.

On their next approach, we made eye contact as they rose toward me from
directly below. This time, I projected the thought that I was going to maintain my
course and speed, so that they could choose where to surface in relation to me. I
knew they knew exactly where I was. I watched as they rose, coming closer and
closer, not veering away. I held my breath, still swimming, watching in fascination.

Soon they were directly beneath me, almost touching me. The instant before
contact, they spread out in all directions, and I was in their center. All four dolphins
were inches from my body. There was a dolphin in front of me, one to either side,
and I assume the fourth was behind me. My entire field of vision was filled with
dolphin bodies, up close and real personal. I was amazed that we could be this close
to one another and not touch! I so wanted to reach out and touch that skin, but I
dared not breach the trust we'd developed. I willed my arms to remain glued by my
sides. It was hard to do, but I managed.

I had learned that my first instinct, my very first day in the water with these
beautiful dolphins, was correct. It is inappropriate to reach out and touch dolphins
in the wild. If physical contact is to be made, the dolphins should be the ones to
initiate it.

In this minipod we created, the dolphins' eye contact was so direct; their intention was so clear. They knew exactly what they were doing. They were giving me
precisely what I had asked for, with my heart.

I felt our energies merge. We were one. I felt a fulfillment inside that was so
complete, the thought passed through my mind, *I could leave today, after this en-*

counter, and be totally fulfilled. This encounter, with these dolphins, fed me fully and completely. The love I felt from them, and for them, and the honoring we had for each other, was profound. I needed nothing more.

In fact, I swam with this same group of four dolphins every day of my trip! It was incredible. I was at home with these magnificent beings; they were so welcoming. They became my dear, dear friends.

On the third morning of my trip, I arrived to find the bay quiet and still. No dolphins.

I camped the first few nights at a nearby beach, in part to save money, and also because I loved camping on the beach and waking up with the ocean right outside my "door." After the third night, my back went out. I didn't have sufficient padding to soften the impact of the hard sand. Reluctantly, I got a motel room for the rest of the trip, but I hadn't yet broken down my campsite. Since the dolphins weren't in the usual bay this day, I decided to return to my campsite and pack everything up.

With this single point of focus, I parked the car, crossed the wide expanse of beach and headed directly to my tent. I didn't look at the water, I didn't look at the people, I simply got to work breaking down my campsite. It didn't even occur to me to look for the dolphins in this bay, even though I had heard that they sometimes swim here too.

Merlyn, my friend from Sedona who used to attend my meditations, was camping out on this beach in between housesitting jobs. He had moved to the Big Island, and this was the first we'd seen each other since he left Sedona. Merlyn is not an early riser, and there was no sign of movement from his tent.

While I was breaking camp, Danielle, a German woman I'd met a few days earlier, saw me and we talked for a while, catching up with each other's adventures. She was on holiday on the Big Island, and it was a dream of hers to swim with the dolphins there. As we talked, I felt a tap on my shoulder.

A voice whispered in my ear, "The dolphins are in the bay. I don't think you know that."

I turned to see Celeste, another woman I'd just met. Celeste had recently relocated to the Big Island. The moment we met, we felt an instant connection. We were dolphin sisters.

"What?! Where?!" I asked, completely taken aback.

She pointed, and there they were, a short swim away right in front of where we were standing. *Dolphins!* I couldn't believe my eyes.

"Thank you for telling me!"

They're here! I get to play with them today too! I've never played with them here before.

I ran to my car to gear up, calling to Merlyn as I ran past his tent, "Merlyn, wake up! The dolphins are here. Let's go play!" When I returned, Merlyn was out of his tent, scoping out the scene and preparing to come in with us.

Danielle was so excited. Even though we really didn't know one another well, she said, shyly, "It would be so special for me to swim with the dolphins with you!"

I was just thrilled the dolphins had come. We asked around on the beach, found snorkel gear for Danielle to borrow, and in we went!

We swam and played with the dolphins. Merlyn told me that since moving to the Big Island and swimming with the dolphins frequently, this was his best encounter yet. He was so excited, and I was so happy to share this with him! We shared so many Sunday night meditations in Sedona, swimming with spirit dolphins in the etheric ocean; it was extra special now to share this physical dolphin encounter with Merlyn in the gorgeous tropical waters of his new home—Hawaii.

It was another magical day. I was thrilled to recognize a few of the dolphins by their unique markings; these were the same dolphins I'd been swimming with all week! The dolphins were in a gentle mood this day. They engaged us frequently for close encounters. The connections went deep into our souls.

When swimming with dolphins, it's best to observe their behaviors and match their energy. When they're mellow, it's a sweet, gentle interaction. When they're playing, we give it all we've got.

During our swim that morning, I projected a request to the dolphins. I asked them to teach me about their sexuality.

Dolphin Love

Aside from humans, dolphins are the only other known species that makes love for pleasure. In fact, they make love often—every day!—with many partners. Dolphins are not monogamous. They are highly sensual and sexual beings. Their skin is supersensitive, not just to physical touch but also to each other's sonar and energy. Skin-to-skin contact is highly pleasurable for them. They nuzzle and rub up against each other a lot because it feels so good!

Dolphin lovemaking is quite something to watch. Here's the kind of loving I typically see when I swim with them ...

One dolphin approaches another, flips over and swims belly-to-belly beneath the desired partner. Both dolphins maintain their swim speed as the one on the bottom swerves its rostrum from side to side, manipulating its partner's energy field with its sonar, giving pleasure. I understand this to be their version of foreplay. Then their bellies connect, ever so briefly, penetration occurs, and it's done! They disconnect. All the while, they remain in motion.

I watched and waited for the dolphins to respond to my request, but their mellow behavior did not change. *Maybe they're not in the mood.* Oh, well. I certainly had no complaints.

Danielle, Merlyn, Celeste, and I swam until we tired, and then came in and shared snacks and stories on the beach. When we'd gotten enough sun, we parted ways and continued on with our day.

I returned to my campsite to finish breaking down my tent. Soon, I was standing at the water's edge again, looking out into the bay. My tent was collapsed on the ground but not yet folded and put away. The dolphins were still out there. There were no humans swimming with them now; they had the bay to themselves. I watched them with great love and affection.

Suddenly I felt a strong pull toward them. *They want me to swim with them again.* I hesitated, knowing I'd had enough sun for one day; but I felt absolutely compelled. I simply had to go back in. I said a quick prayer, knowing I'd pay for this dearly with a bad sunburn. (I did.) Into the water I went.

When I sighted the dolphins underwater, I was stunned by what I saw. They were having a veritable love fest! For as far as I could see, dolphins were spiraling

wildly around each other, plunging to the depths from the surface and emerging back up into the light of day, over and over, at tremendous speed. All the while making love, making love, making love!

I hovered in their periphery for a long time, spellbound by this astonishing display. Their athleticism was amazing. Their fluidity, agility, grace, and speed were awe-inspiring. I was watching true masters in sexual ecstasy! I felt a huge bubble of laughter fill my being. *I asked them to teach me about their sexuality. Class is in session!*

Once again, I found myself in the midst of my favorite foursome. Our energies merged, and for about twenty minutes, I was in the energy field of their small pod, watching them make love with one another over and over again. This all happened just a few feet in front of me. They showed me everything. At one point, a milky white substance floated inches past my face. *Dolphin semen?* I giggled to myself. *Be careful what you ask for. Now I don't think I've missed a thing. These dolphins are very thorough teachers!*

When the loving wound down, we all settled into a peaceful rhythm and swam and interacted with one another some more. One dolphin played the leaf

Dolphin Love

game with me, only this time he tricked me. I swam hard under the surface to fetch the leaf, holding my breath until my lungs burned. Just as I reached out for the leaf, he sped in front of me and retrieved it first, and swam a short ways away, where he released it again. All the while, he maintained intense eye contact with me; our eyes were glued to each other the whole time we played. I burst into giggles as this scenario played out over and over again. We were connecting deeply through play. It was great fun!

Then I noticed a lone dolphin swimming along the ocean floor, in the pod's periphery. I felt myself pulled toward him. I swam until I was right above him and then floated on the surface, connecting with him from my heart. He remained still below. I could feel him connecting with me too. My awareness of the rest of the pod dissolved. It was just this lone dolphin and me now.

He seemed sad to me. Or maybe he was reflecting a sadness I sometimes carry inside when I'm with a group of people I know and love, and yet I feel alone and separate. During those times, I get the feeling that something's missing in me. I don't fit in somehow. I don't know how to connect. That seemed to be the quality that was connecting us in this moment.

I opened my heart wide and let this dolphin in. I projected a thought to him: *"You are in my heart, now and forevermore."* I remained floating silently above him for quite a while, feeling great affinity for him. He remained motionless below me, receiving my love.

Several times I left to go play with the others, and then I'd feel a tug in my heart and I'd return to this loner. He kept his distance from me, but in a way I felt even closer to him than the others.

Later, upon reflection, I realized that his gift to me was emotional closeness. I had been so focused on being physically close with the dolphins; this gentle soul taught me that true intimacy occurs at the level of emotion. We had a profound, timeless heart connection, even though he kept his distance from me physically. *Thank you for that, my friend.*

♡

I was ecstatic to see the dolphins in the bay on my last day. This last encounter was as wonderful as the previous ones. By this time, I truly felt like I belonged to this unique interspecies community. My heart expanded with love.

When it was time to leave, I treaded water, absorbing every detail of my surroundings: the bay, the dolphins, the land, the sky. I gathered it all into my heart for safekeeping, knowing that I could draw upon this memory, and these connections, anytime, anywhere.

Emotions tumbled through me. I was ecstatic, sad, grateful, and already homesick for my dolphin family. I marveled at how I could experience so many different emotions simultaneously. My mind sought a way to understand this cacophony of feelings. Then it came. I felt like I was leaving a precious lover for an unknown period of time. In this case, more than a hundred precious lovers.

Floating in a quiet spot alone, I let my emotions flow. I cried and cried until there were no more tears and I was empty. I swam to the dolphins one more time and thanked them, with all of my being, for their love, their magnificent gifts and teachings. With mixed emotions, I embarked upon my last long swim to shore.

I got out of the water and could not leave. I sat on a rock, looking out at the bay. Allowing myself to sit and be, I let all the experiences of the trip wash over me. My love and respect for these dolphins deepened profoundly during this trip. I felt everything there was to feel. I felt deeply grateful to be alive.

EIGHTEEN

Ocean Connection

When I was a baby, I took my first steps on a deep, soft sandy beach in New Jersey!

You know how you grow up with some memories, and as an adult, you wonder if they're really true? This memory is like that for me. I have a mental image of myself as a baby taking steps in deep sand on a beach; and I remember being told, as a child, that that's where I took my very first steps. But sometimes, as an adult, I've wondered if that was really true. How could it be that I took my very first steps on the most unstable of surfaces, in deep sand that slips and slides and gives way under foot?

During a trip back home to visit my family over the holidays, the conversation around the dinner table on Christmas Eve wound its way to that exact moment of my life. My dad was recalling the man who invited us to stay in their cottage at Long Island Beach, New Jersey, when we were kids.

My older brother, Paul, turned to me and said, "Yeah, Lin, you just popped up and took off walking there."

So it's true!

"Well, I'm a dolphin. I was going home," popped out of my mouth.

"Well, there you go," he answered.

Aside from a few vacations at the shore, I didn't have much exposure to the ocean while growing up.

When I was 21, I took my first plane trip and moved to Southern California. I landed in Laguna Beach, just one short block from the Pacific Ocean. The tropical climate and lush foliage was a feast for my senses. I spent hours in the water body-surfing. I enjoyed the ocean because it was there, but I didn't seek it out like I did wildflowers in the mountains!

What a surprise it was, so many years later, to find myself desperately yearning for the ocean, and grieving intensely whenever I left it.

There was a time when David and I attended a weekly healing circle in Sedona. One night, I was a week away from leaving for one of my Hawaii trips. I was beside myself with excitement about going to swim with the dolphins and didn't feel a need for any healing that night. I sat quietly and enjoyed being able to support the others.

As the evening progressed, an emotion welled up inside me. When I tuned in to it, I felt overwhelming sadness and grief. *What is this?* I spoke up, and when the group turned their attention toward me, the dam broke and I burst into tears. I sobbed and sobbed and sobbed. It was so intense, and went on for so long, that almost everyone else in the circle caught it and was also crying.

Finally, when I could speak, what came out in between sobs was, "The ocean ... I have to leave it ... and I haven't even arrived yet!"

I was completely distraught. In my mind, I saw myself at the end of my trip, in the plane, flying *away* from Hawaii ... looking out the fuzzy airplane window at the ocean and the island below as it drifted farther and farther away. The grief I felt was primal.

Now that seemed extreme. But that was my reality. I had no control over these intense emotions. I had no idea where these feelings were coming from.

A pattern had emerged around my Hawaii trips. About every eighteen months to two years, I would feel a strong urge inside to go to Hawaii to be with the dolphins. I usually took these trips alone, in part because it was less expensive for just one of us to go, and in part because David wasn't an ocean guy. He enjoyed having the house to himself while I was gone.

The trips were always amazing, but it soon became harder and harder to leave the island and return home. Reentry into my land-based life was rough. I grieved for at least two weeks after I returned home from each trip.

You can imagine how that was for David. "Honey, I'm home ... damn it!"

In the summer of 1997, David and I went on an adventure together to the island of Bimini, in the Bahamas. We joined a group of people who were going there to swim with the spotted dolphins, as well as explore the powerful vortexes and the mysteries of Atlantis. This was a five-day trip. I didn't feel the same soul connection with the Bimini dolphins that I have with the Hawaiian spinners. But we were on a boat in the ocean every day, and I was in bliss!

After leaving Bimini, David and I took off on our own to tour the coast of Southern Florida and the Keys. I had never been to Florida, and I always love exploring new places. Part of our purpose for going there was to check the area out as a possible place to live. It was becoming harder and harder for me to live in the desert. I was searching for a place to live that was closer to the ocean, and the dolphins. Hawaii was not an option because of David's East Coast-based job. We had to stay on the mainland.

We had a great time in Florida. We were definitely in vacation mode. I even talked David into renting a bright red convertible for our road trip down the Keys.

We planned to spend a few nights in Key West, mainly because I knew that there would be opportunities to meet the wild bottlenose dolphins there. Arranging that was my top priority upon arrival. We settled into our room by 4:30 p.m., which was cutting it a bit close to get a boat trip lined up for the next day, but I was determined. Armed with a handful of dolphin swim trip brochures, I phoned every boat captain listed. I didn't reach anyone; all I could do was leave messages. Inside myself, I asked my dolphin spirit guides to help create a swim trip with the dolphins for the following day. Then I let it go, and we walked into town for dinner.

When we returned to our room at 8:30, the lodge manager was waving a telephone message slip in the air. "Hurry! Captain Samone has two seats for you on her boat tomorrow, but you must let her know within the next ten minutes if you want to go!"

I phoned Samone immediately and told her to hold those seats! I scribbled the directions to the harbor and exclaimed to David upon hanging up, "We're booked for an 8 a.m. departure tomorrow morning!" *Yes! Good job, dolphins. Thank you!* I don't know what excited me more, the opportunity to meet new dolphins, or just the chance to be out on the ocean on a boat one more time!

We had a great time the next day. Even though the bottlenose dolphins were elusive when we jumped into the water, and we did not have close encounters with them, we were able to watch them swimming nearby. We felt their energy.

When I told Samone about the work I was doing with dolphin energy, she got very excited and invited me to join a group of women she was taking out the next day, as her guest. I was thrilled. She didn't have to ask twice. I was there!

While I was out with the women, David took the opportunity to fulfill a dream he'd had for a long time. He flew an ultralight plane! We bubbled over with enthusiasm at dinner that night, sharing our adventures with each other.

We talked about the possibility of living in the Keys. It had the ocean and dolphins, but it felt too isolated from the rest of the world. We agreed that it was a fun place to visit, but we did not see ourselves living there.

We left the Keys happy tourists. Next!

We drove north along the Gulf Coast to Naples. I had a client in Naples, who assured me dolphins were there. Perhaps this would be the place.

We fell in love with Naples immediately. It was charming and sophisticated. It looked promising. But in talking with shopkeepers and waiters, we discovered that this was off-season. The way they described the throngs of crowds during high season, we realized this wasn't a place for us to live.

After two nights in Naples, we continued north to visit a dear friend in

Sarasota. This would be the last stop on our trip. The night we arrived, David's friend Jill invited me to lead a dolphin meditation for a group of her friends. I jumped at the opportunity. Everyone was warm, receptive, and open. They all loved dolphins, but it hadn't occurred to them to connect with the dolphins through meditation. Many of them had deep and moving experiences. I love opening people's minds and hearts to new possibilities.

There is a large spiritual community in Sarasota, which made it an attractive possibility as a place to live; and we already knew some people there. As I drifted off to sleep that night, still softly buzzing from the evening's meditation, I wondered, *Is this the place?*

David and I woke up early the next morning for a final swim in the ocean before returning home. We were just a few blocks from the beach, and the walk through the quaint beach community was sweet. As we walked, I imagined what it would be like to live there.

When we got out of the water and walked to our towels, I felt my body become heavy and dense with each step I took away from the shore.

In the water, we frolicked in the surf like kids. I felt like a dolphin, jumping and diving into the waves over and over again ... spinning, splashing, and playing. I'd never had so much fun playing in the ocean!

When we got out of the water and walked to our towels, I felt my body become heavy and dense with each step I took away from the shore. *My life force is draining away!* My energy was so light and playful and joyful in the water just moments ago. *What's happening?* I was really scared. I didn't say a word to David.

When we returned to our room, David turned to me and said, "We need to talk."

Uh-oh. By the look on his face, and the tone of his voice, I knew that whatever he was about to say was probably something I didn't want to hear.

We sat on the bed and looked into each other's eyes. David took a deep breath. "We can't move yet. My job is way too demanding right now, and I just can't afford the distraction of a big move at this time."

My heart pounded in my chest. I swallowed hard. I felt fear rise up inside me.

Dolphin Love

My mind was spinning. I truly did not know how I could manage living in the desert any longer. My functional time frame there was down to about two months now before I needed to escape and get an ocean fix. Now David was telling me that it is still not time to get my body to the ocean to live?

David was still talking, but I wasn't hearing his words. Instead, I prayed. Inside myself, I implored, *"God, if it is not for me to live by the ocean yet, I need to know how to function in the desert. I don't know how to do it. I need help."*

I said nothing of this to David. He was already in agony. He always wants me to be happy, as I do him. He's done so much to support me in this strange, wonderful, perplexing journey. I couldn't put any more pressure on him. It was true that his job, at that time, was overwhelmingly demanding and stressful.

During that trip, I was on a boat, in the ocean, almost every day. David kept commenting on how vital and alive I looked. He'd never seen me so happy. He was happy that I was happy, but it also scared him. Our life is in the desert. How could he compete with the ocean?

We got through that day and spent our last night there. I felt sad that our vacation, which had filled us up with newness and possibilities, was ending on such a down note. I woke up our last morning feeling distant and withdrawn. I didn't know what to do.

Then, as I was showering, I heard a voice inside. *"Call forth your inner ocean to sustain you."*

Of course! Why didn't I think of that? Everything is inside of me, including the ocean! Suffering comes from the illusion of separation from all that we already are. It's so simple! Truth is always simple. I knew this was God's answer to my prayer.

I got out of the shower energized and excited. I dried off and quickly dressed. I told David the message I'd received and tears welled up in his eyes.

I went to the bed, sat with my back against the headboard, and closed my eyes. After taking a few deep breaths, I stated my intention, firmly and passionately, inside my mind: *I call forth my inner ocean to sustain me.* And then, as always, I relaxed and let go, and allowed my internal experience to unfold naturally.

Energy flooded into me. I knew I was feeling the energy of the ocean. It penetrated every cell and space of my being, both inside my body and in the energy field around my body. My entire being vibrated in resonance with the ocean. It was profoundly healing.

When the tingling and vibrating subsided, I opened my eyes and knew that it was done. In that moment, I felt complete with the trip. I actually felt eager to return to our desert home in spectacular Sedona, Arizona. This time, as I left the ocean and got on the plane, I did not grieve.

Upon my return home to Sedona, Dr. Peebles told me, *"My dear, your inner energy is like no other! It is the ocean!"*

Indeed, from this time forward, my healing sessions changed. Instead of feeling the dolphin energy flow through me in the form of a pulse, I felt the energy flow in waves, like the ocean, and in figure eights, like the infinity symbol.

Perhaps the most precious gift I received from this trip to Bimini and Florida was the awakening of my love for the ocean. When I embarked upon this adventure, I had no awareness that the ocean was so important to me. My soul was nourished by these ocean excursions in a way that I had not experienced before.

A big part of me came to life during this trip. It was as if I began the trip as a rosebud. With each passing moment on the various boats, as I sat dangling my legs overboard, gazing out at the sea, the bud opened ever so gently. I opened gladly to receive the sun, the water, and the ocean air. The ocean courted me. Her energy danced on the wind, enlivening my mind, body, and soul. By the end of the trip, I was completely, utterly in love with her. The flower of me was in full, glorious bloom. I felt positively radiant.

In June 2000, we finally extricated ourselves from Sedona and moved to Southern California to get me some good, solid ocean time.

On our weekend scouting trip to find a place to live there, my goal was to live as close to the ocean as possible. Really, I wanted to live *in* the ocean.

I kept saying to David, "I want an apartment *in* the ocean!"

I wasn't joking. We'd look at a place that was nice, and the first thing I did upon returning to the car was look at the map and calculate the distance to the ocean. *What's the quickest access? Can I walk there? Can I bike there?* If I couldn't walk or bike to it, it was too far away for me.

David was more attracted to the places a little farther inland, where we could get more for our money. Our divergent goals created stress and frustration. We were not having fun, and things were not flowing! We were down to the wire. We had one day left to find a place to live or we'd have to schedule another trip to come back again and look some more. We didn't want to have to do that; we wanted our next trip to be our move.

David woke up that last morning with the crystal clear awareness that what was most important to me was to be as close to the ocean as possible. He felt a let-go inside of his body, and he surrendered to that.

Now that our visions were in sync, we headed out with renewed commitment and enthusiasm, rental property guidebook in hand, to find our new home. We'd already decided to rent an apartment to start with. Once we moved there and got to know the area better, we could look for a house or a condo.

An apartment complex in Carlsbad looked promising, and they allowed pets. This was essential, because we had three cats—Tzu-Tzu, Tyler, and Cinnamon Girl—our own little feline pod! We agreed to start there.

We drove to Carlsbad, in North County San Diego. The directions took us along the Pacific Coast Highway. We were looking for Chestnut Avenue. The Pacific Ocean sparkled tauntingly at my right as we drove the few blocks on the PCH. When we reached Chestnut Avenue, we turned left, and began driving *away* from the ocean.

I watched as we passed the first house, and the next house, and the next. Reminiscent of my experience in Florida, as we drove away from the ocean, I felt my life force drain away. I got more depressed with each passing home. *We're going so far away!*

By the time we arrived at the apartment complex, it felt as if we had driven miles from the ocean. We met with the property manager and toured the complex. It had just been renovated, so all the apartment interiors were new. There were lovely gardens, a swimming pool, and even a dolphin water fountain in the passageway separating the two buildings. When I saw that, I knew this was the place.

We filled out the paperwork, submitted our deposit, and agreed on a move-in date. Mission accomplished! Now we could head home.

We returned to the car and David asked if I wanted to walk to the ocean before starting the eight-hour drive back to Sedona.

"THE
OCEAN!! It's
right there!!
It's just a block away!"

"It's so far. I'm tired. Let's just go."

I was pleased we found an apartment that we liked, but I was disappointed that it was so far from the ocean. I just wanted to go home and start packing up so that we could get here.

David asked one more time. "It would really feel good to me to walk a little bit before getting back in the car to drive home."

"Okay." I sighed, unenthusiastically.

We walked the gently sloping hill to its crest, a half-block away. When we reached the first intersection, I gasped as I took in the sight before me.

"THE OCEAN!! It's right there!! It's just a block away!" Tears streamed down my face as I jumped up and down on that street corner, squealing with delight. The ocean was literally a three-minute walk from our new apartment.

When we resumed our walk, I wondered aloud, "How is it possible that I felt like we were *miles* away, when we are really just over a block away!?" I marveled at how my mind totally skewed my time and space perception during that short drive away from the ocean.

David just beamed back at me. "I will never, ever, forget the look on your face back there." For him, that moment on the street corner was the highlight of the trip.

Dolphin Love

While living in Carlsbad, I was blessed to take long walks on the beach almost every day. Some days, the local bottlenose dolphins would make an appearance, and I'd point them out to everyone on the beach within shouting distance. I didn't want anyone to miss them!

But there were two instances when I walked the beach alone that I will never forget.

Both times, as I approached the shoreline, my knees went weak, that weak-kneed sensation that is associated with falling in love. That only happened to me once with a man, a long time ago. Here I was, having this "in love" reaction to the ocean.

I was in an altered state of consciousness. All that existed was the ocean and me, and I was in love. I walked ever so slowly, deeply feeling the presence of the ocean in my heart ... in my body. In this moment, the ocean was my world—my lover. More than anything, I wanted to fall at its feet, right there on the sand. I wanted to immerse myself in it fully and completely. I wanted to *become* the ocean.

It was all I could do to keep walking. This intense urge to merge with the ocean lasted for about half an hour, and then my awareness gradually shifted, and I reconnected with the larger world around me. My knees were solid and strong again, and I was able to walk normally.

I sometimes wonder if one of the reasons the dolphins came into my life was to reconnect me with the ocean. Sometimes it feels as if my love for the ocean is even deeper than my love for the dolphins. *How is that possible?*

NINETEEN

Surrender

When my journey with the dolphins began, I thought I was happy—I really did! I thought I was whole. I was not. Unbeknownst to me, I had some serious healing to do. I had no idea how much pain and suffering I had suppressed and repressed in this lifetime, and who knows how many other lifetimes. I had no idea how much anger—rage, even—was lurking deep inside that needed to be brought to the surface and loved, and then released.

There were periods of time when I felt great. I was in the world, being a dolphin ambassador and loving it. And then something would shift, and inexplicably, I'd find myself diving deeply within—into the darkness of my inner recesses. I cocooned myself in our home and willed the demands of the outside world to dissolve away. I wouldn't answer the phone. I wouldn't return my friends' calls. I wouldn't go out. I just wanted to stay home. I wanted to be alone. These were my "deep dive" periods.

The length of these deep dives varied. Sometimes they only lasted a few days; sometimes they lasted weeks. I rarely had conscious awareness or understanding of what was happening inside of me during these times. I vacillated between resisting—wanting to feel better, wanting to know what was going on inside of me, or just plain wanting things to be different—and surrendering, trusting that the dolphins were with me, that they were guiding my journey, and that I was exactly as I needed to be in that moment.

There was a period of time—my memory is that this period lasted about nine months, off and on—when I was stuck in intense internal struggle and resistance. I experienced long bouts of apathy and depression. I didn't know what was going on—what the dolphins were doing "to" me. Sometimes it seemed that nothing at all was happening, which frustrated me to no end.

During the really long deep dives, I thought something was really wrong with me. I got pretty good at beating myself up, thinking things should be different. When I was in these spaces, Time Out of Mind no longer applied—my brain was filled with internal dialogue, almost all of it negative. *It's not normal to feel this way for this long. I should be more responsible. I should get a real job. I should be more serious. What do you think you're doing? You're wasting your life.*

Dr. Peebles continually assured me during these times that much was happening below the surface of my awareness. **"These ventures into your darker spaces are you planting yourself in the fertile soil, where you will find and touch the face of God, my dear!"**

His love, compassion, and words of assurance were comforting. They kept me going—for a while. But then I'd find myself wondering, again, if there was any purpose to this dolphin journey at all.

There were times that I wanted the journey to stop. I wanted my life to return to "normal." Something inside of me was resisting this huge transformational experience the dolphins were leading me through.

Many years into my journey, I learned a pivotal lesson. I had finally surfaced from a particularly long deep dive, and I was totally loving being in the world again. Two days later, while enjoying a quiet moment at home, I felt myself going under again. It was like a dark gray cloud began rising from the earth to envelop me. *No! I just came out of this. It's too soon. I don't want this!* I panicked.

Determined to get hold of myself, and to stop this, I closed my eyes and went within. I saw myself walking down a steep staircase that was descending into a cold, damp, dark basement. With each step down, my body became colder. I did not want to continue walking down those stairs! In a moment of inspiration, a voice spoke in my mind, *"Well, then, just turn around and walk back UP the stairs!"*

So simple! In my vision, I turned my body around. In the split second it took for me to simply *look* up the stairs, into the light above, I was suddenly standing at the top of the stairs, bathed in light. I opened my eyes and felt great. My energy was fully back. I was overjoyed and relieved.

The dramatic shift in my energy from the descent into darkness, to the instantaneous return to the light, was a revelation. *I have choice! I can choose to descend into the darkness, or I can choose to be in the light!*

I realized then that at some point along the way, some of my deep dives had become escapes from the world. While this pattern of deep inner healing was under way, along with the healing, the deep dives were serving me in another way: I didn't have to engage with the world. Maybe I was afraid to step fully into my power. Maybe I had the idea that if I retreated, if I became small, invisible even, nothing bad would happen. I would be safe.

The realization dawned that I was behaving like a victim. It felt like the deep dives were happening "to" me, and I was helpless and powerless to avoid them, or to shift my experience. Now I knew the higher truth. Now I knew that I always have choice.

After this revelation, I still had deep dives, but the quality of my experience was completely different. When I journeyed into my darker spaces, I explored them with curiosity and fascination. *What new gifts will I uncover here? What wound is rising to the surface to be healed?* I was no longer a victim. Because I was surrendering to these experiences instead of resisting, I passed through these phases much more quickly, with greater ease and grace.

♡

Even after that discovery, I struggled. Many times, I thought of stopping this strange dolphin journey and doing something else. It was Dr. Peebles' gentle nudging, and David's steadfast support, that kept me moving forward. But there were three specific times during these seven years when I did, indeed, make the decision to quit this crazy dolphin thing. I'd had enough. It didn't seem to be going anywhere; I was making scarcely any money from my healing sessions; I felt like a failure; I was done. I went looking for something else to do with my life. When an appealing alternative path appeared, I jumped on it with great enthusiasm—only to have my life fall apart within weeks or months.

> There were three specific times during these seven years when I did, indeed, make the decision to quit this crazy dolphin thing.

The third, and last, time this happened was shortly after we arrived in California, in the fall of 2000, about four-and-a-half years into the journey. I got passionately involved with a new organization, and within two months it went out of business! I was so despondent that I knelt down on my knees in the middle of our living room, raised my head to the heavens and proclaimed out loud: "I need help! I can't do this by myself anymore. I don't know what to do. Please help!"

The next thing I knew, I was sitting at my computer, surfing the net, which I rarely do. I opened Google and typed in one word: dolphins. As various sites opened, and I read what people were doing with dolphins, my inner voice stirred. *I can do that ... I can do that ...*

I looked up from my screen and "saw the light." *I work with the dolphins. I share dolphin energy with humans on land. That's what I do! That's who I am.*

For the last time, with my heart and soul, I said *YES* to the dolphin path. Instantaneously, I felt amazing—turned-on, energized, passionate about life again. It was as if all of my energy centers came back online. My whole being was plugged in and connected to the source of my aliveness—the source of my joy—the dolphins. I was *back*.

A significant moment of surrender occurred for me when 9/11 happened. David was in New Jersey on a business trip. He was near the Jersey shore, thirty miles from the World Trade Center. I was home alone in California. With the time difference, it was 6 a.m., and I was still sound asleep when he called. Groggily, I picked up the phone and heard David's voice piercing through my fog, "We're at war."

"What?" I scrambled inside the sheets to sit up, now fully awake.

"We're at war. Turn on the TV. The World Trade Center has been attacked."

I turned on the TV and watched the horrifying scene unfold on the screen before me. We stayed on the phone together, watching the devastation in stunned silence. *How could this be happening?* David told me that all flights had been cancelled, and the airports were closed. He didn't know when he'd be able to fly home.

We didn't want to hang up. We didn't want to lose the precious voice connection we had with each other. Finally, we did hang up, and I went on watching the news until I couldn't bear any more. I turned off the TV and let my grief flow. I cried and cried.

Then I felt a stirring inside. Spontaneously, I closed my eyes and reached out to my spirit. *Take me to where I need to be right now.*

Instantly the grief fell away. Peace, silence, and stillness permeated my being. I was taken into the Void, where I remained for an indeterminate amount of time. When I emerged, my mood was subdued, but I was at peace.

Over the ensuing days, weeks, and months, as the 9/11 story saturated the media and our social consciousness, I saw the devastation, and heard the tragic personal accounts as they were reported in the media. I saw and felt the impact of this worldwide tragedy in our local neighborhood, and among our families and friends. I cherished every ray of light that broke through the clouds, as countless acts of generosity of the human spirit were also recounted.

While I did lapse into feelings of grief and despair, those periods were short-lived. Very shortly after surrendering to my intense emotions, I felt a stirring inside, a subtle movement—the dolphin consciousness within me. This stirring got my attention, which shifted my awareness away from my emotions. In a heartbeat, the emotions that consumed me just moments ago simply dropped away. I was now in observation. I was the sacred witness. From this elevated consciousness, I watched, and felt, what was happening inside of my body with loving allowance.

In the witness state, my emotions of fear and profound sorrow shifted to love and profound compassion for the human experience we are all living and sharing. The dolphin consciousness within me prevented me from getting sucked into a downward spiral of pain, fear, helplessness, and hopelessness.

In a matter of minutes, my inner state was returned to a state of deep peace, silence, and stillness. I was able to sustain this state for a substantial period of time.

The learning I took away from this experience was that it does not serve me, or the planet, to wallow in grief or despair, no matter what horrible devastation is going on in the world. This isn't about denying or repressing my feelings. The dolphins have helped me learn how to feel, and accept, my feelings as they arise. However, I'm not to get stuck in them. Rather, I'm to remain open, and allow my emotions to flow through me.

My job, with the help of the dolphins, is to maintain my frequency—my joy— no matter what is happening in the world. The only way I know how to do that is to surrender, surrender, and surrender again ... to "what is." It took me a very long time to realize, and admit, that all the time and energy I'd wasted over the years resisting, did not get me to where I wanted to go. One moment of true and complete surrender did. Surrender always does.

These pronounced experiences of contrast have proven to me, once and for all, that I am fully and completely nourished and sustained by the dolphin frequency. Ultimately I did, indeed, surrender completely to the dolphins, and this dolphin path. It was a huge relief to finally let go of the struggle.

I've come to have deep respect for the natural cycles of my life. I now welcome the wanderings into my depths without fear. I know, from experience, that I will emerge on the other side of the darkness, bearing unimagined gifts.

While I may feel alone during these explorations into my darker spaces, deep in my heart I know my dolphin spirit friends are with me. They hold the space of unconditional love and safety for me too, just as they do for my clients!

The dolphins want for me what they want for every human being on this planet. They want me to be happy—profoundly happy. They want me to experience the quality of joy that comes from within—that isn't dependent upon external circumstances. The dolphins want me to be free, in the truest sense of that word. They are helping me to heal my heart, so that I can grow in my ability to give and receive love among my fellow humans. They want to help me discover, and bring into reality, my deepest heart's desires.

Thank you, beautiful ones, for being there for me, in my light times and my dark times. Thank you for loving me unconditionally. I am grateful, beyond measure, for your companionship during these journeys into the depths of my soul.

TWENTY

Grandfather

In the fall of 2001, David and I were still living in Southern California. Bursting at the seams in the small apartment we were renting, we began searching for another place to live. We wanted to stay in the same general area, north of San Diego and close to the ocean; but we quickly discovered that the rental prices for condos, townhouses, and small houses were totally out of our reach. We were a one-income household—I was focused on my journey with the dolphins, so we lived on David's programming income. The places we looked at that were in our price range were in such bad condition, they were unlivable. There didn't seem to be a workable solution to our desire for a nicer home.

Discouraged, and at a loss about what to do next, we agreed to let go of the idea of moving for now. But we were restless. The idea of staying in that tiny apartment for another year or more seemed pretty grim.

In November, David suggested a road trip to Sedona over the Thanksgiving holiday, to see old friends and get out on the land. I immediately agreed—we needed to get away. I was feeling stuck with the whole house thing, and liked the idea of a road trip to get our energy moving, and to open us up to new perspectives and inspirations. We called friends, made travel plans, loaded up the car, and took off for our beloved Sedona.

The moment we crossed the border and entered Arizona, something shifted inside of me. I found myself taking slow, deep breaths. *I can breathe here.*

I tuned in to my body energy and felt a stirring inside. *Uh-oh.*

I started to cry. Silently. Tears of joy. I was driving; David was sleeping. I didn't want to wake him.

"What's wrong? What's happening?" David jerked awake and looked at me with concern.

"I was trying to be quiet. Did you hear me crying?"

"No. I felt it. The shift in your energy woke me up."

I took a deep breath and glanced sideways at this dear man who has listened to and honored my inner voice, sometimes more than I have. The words tumbled out through my tears.

"I think we're moving back to Sedona. We're going to find our next house during this trip. We're going to find it in Sedona."

David was silent. I kept glancing at him to see how he was reacting. His gaze was focused steadily forward. He took his time, slowly letting in my words.

Finally David spoke. "I'm allowing myself to feel cautiously optimistic—emphasis on 'cautious.' You know how much I love Sedona. I'd love to live there forever. It was never my idea to leave. I did it for you—so you could be by the ocean."

I was relieved, and my excitement about this new possibility began bubbling out of me. I talked and talked about how wonderful it was going to be to return to Sedona. I was already there—creating our future in my imagination. David listened, but remained quiet. He didn't want to get his hopes up.

We had a lovely time in Sedona. It was beautiful to be on the land again, and to see our friends. At some point during the weekend, David finally let it in that we would soon be returning home—to Sedona. He cried with joy.

And we did find a house that weekend—a perfect house! It wasn't available yet; the tenants were planning to move out very soon. We returned to California and waited patiently, and then impatiently, for that house to become available. It never did. Ultimately, I went back to Sedona and found another house for us. It wasn't until March of the following year that we finally moved back to Sedona.

During those final months in California, another life-altering, interdimensional adventure with the dolphins began.

♡

When we returned home from our Thanksgiving weekend in Sedona, there was an e-mail waiting for me. It was from Roberta Goodman, a dolphin researcher in Hawaii. Roberta had been hearing my name over the years and felt that it was time to connect.

We exchanged a few e-mails, getting to know one another. When I told Roberta that my work with the dolphins is primarily energetic, she asked me if I could communicate telepathically with a specific pod, or a specific dolphin. This was my response:

> I do get messages from different dolphins/pods from time to time ... The Bimini dolphins kept connecting with me prior to my trip to swim with them ... The Hawaiian spinner pod that activated me is my primary dolphin family, and I do connect with them. They are always with me ...
>
> When I saw my first pod of pilot whales (I didn't even know they existed at the time), my soul response was so intense ... I cried and cried and cried ... even before we saw them, but we had definitely entered their energy field.
>
> I haven't worked at honing telepathic communication, though. Word-message communications are sporadic and spontaneous, and are usually initiated by the dolphins.
>
> In my work, I bring their energy through rather than specific verbal communications, although that happens sometimes. People have experiences as a result of receiving the dolphin energy. Usually my sessions are done in silence, and frequently people have underwater dolphin experiences without any prompting or guiding by me. I just create the open space for dolphin energy to flow through,

and whatever that person most needs is what happens, be it a healing, an experience, or whatever ...

I've been content accessing their energy, rather than verbal
communications, because my sense is that when I work with people, if it's at the level of pure energy, they can receive that more
readily into their hearts and bodies.

When words are introduced, the tendency is for people to go
into their heads, and that can muddy the waters. This connection
with you may inspire me to develop the ability to communicate
telepathically at will, though. It will be fun to see what happens!

Roberta told me of a project she was considering, on the island of Bonaire, in
the South Caribbean. The project involved creating the world's first wild dolphin
sanctuary. She wanted some validation and assurance from the local dolphin pods
that her dolphin research would be welcome there. Specifically, were these dolphins willing to swim with humans?

I was impressed that she thought to ask them first, before showing up and
trying to make something happen. A lot was at stake for her. Moving her life and
her business to Bonaire was a very big deal. She asked if I'd be willing to tune in to
the Bonaire dolphins to ascertain if they were willing to work with her. Intrigued
by the idea of connecting with a new pod of physical dolphins in this way, I offered
to give it a try.

The next morning, I set myself up to meditate. I took the same approach with
this endeavor that I've taken with all my inner journeys. Even though I had never
attempted telepathy at will before, I knew that a larger aspect of me, my spirit, was
fully capable of this form of communication.

Sitting on the bed with my back against the wall, and my spine erect, I closed
my eyes and focused on my body and my breath. When I felt calm and still, I said
inside myself:

Spirit, it is my intention during this meditation to enter into telepathic communication with the physical dolphins that reside off the coast of Bonaire, in the South Caribbean. I don't know how to do this, but I know that you do. I surrender this meditation to you for this purpose. I give complete permission for my frequencies to be adjusted in any way to allow this communication to occur.

Then I relaxed, let go, and allowed the meditation to unfold naturally.

I sat in the silence and waited. My mind was quiet and clear. My attention was focused on my body and my breath. Sure enough, pretty soon I felt my body energy begin to shift. It was subtle at first—an ever-so-slight tingling sensation that permeated my body. Gradually the tingling got stronger. Then, all of the sudden, I sensed that I was in the presence of a young male dolphin.

I didn't have a vision of him. Rather, I felt his energy. It felt like he was swimming around me at a very high speed. He was energetic, enthusiastic, and very playful! I felt his excitement both inside my body and in the air around me.

Within myself, I told this young dolphin about Roberta and her dolphin research work. I told him that she was considering moving to Bonaire to participate in the wild dolphin sanctuary project. I asked him if his pod would be willing to work with Roberta. Would they be willing to swim with humans?

"Yes, yes, yes! Tell her to come!" I felt/heard him say. He was very excited about the idea of swimming with humans. I giggled. He was so cute!

I thanked him and felt his energy dissolve. I came out of my meditation, surprised and excited that the connection—the communication—happened so quickly. A tiny part of me doubted that it was real, but I knew that it was. I hadn't expected it to be that easy.

I was delighted to e-mail Roberta my first report. She wrote back that during her first trip to Bonaire, she swam along the beach with a juvenile dolphin and his pod. She wondered if this was the same dolphin.

She also shared that she had asked another friend to tune in to the Bonaire dolphins as well. This friend also connected with a juvenile who was exuberant and enthusiastic about the idea of swimming with humans. It was good for me to receive this independent validation of my first attempt at this kind of communication.

Next, Roberta asked me to make contact with an elder dolphin of this pod. She reasoned that this juvenile probably wasn't in a position to speak on behalf of the pod.

The next day, I entered into meditation in the same way. This time, I asked to be connected specifically to an elder of the pod. I gave permission for my frequencies to be adjusted, and then I relaxed, let go, and entered into the stillness.

> Up until now, the dolphins had always been very open and receptive toward me. It seemed this dolphin was protecting his pod.

After a short time, I sensed a presence. This presence seemed wary. This felt like a very large male dolphin, and he was keeping his distance. His energy felt cautious and protective. He seemed to be checking me out, to see if I was safe.

His wariness was new for me, and a little puzzling. Up until now, the dolphins had always been very open and receptive toward me. It seemed this dolphin was protecting his pod. I didn't know what kind of dolphin this was, but I certainly respected his caution. I simply remained open to contact. After a while, I felt him retreat, and my meditation came to a close.

I wrote Roberta about my experience. She said that she thought this was a pod of bottlenose dolphins. If that was true, this dolphin's wariness made sense. The bottlenose dolphins are the "show dolphins," the ones that are captured for display in aquariums and dolphinariums. Flipper was a bottlenose dolphin. If these dolphins were bottlenose, of course the pod elder would be wary. I respected his caution.

Over the course of the following days, this new dolphin began floating in and out of my consciousness. When I felt his presence, I asked his name. Nothing came. I thought up names to call him, but none of them fit.

One night, a few days after my first contact with this elder, David and I went out for dinner to a popular Thai restaurant in Del Mar. It was the first time we'd eaten there. The restaurant was packed and noisy; the energy was high and vibrant. It was fun to be there. After we placed our order, I felt a presence envelop me.

I looked at David and said, "I think this dolphin elder is here."

David closed his eyes and nodded. He felt the presence too.

I told David, "He wants to scan me. I need to give him permission to see all aspects of me."

I closed my eyes, connected with the energy of this dolphin, and gave him permission to see all of me. In the middle of this busy restaurant, the dolphin scanned me. I sensed him swimming through me and around me. He was looking deeply into me—into my now, into my history, and into my heart. There was nothing invasive about his explorations. He was observing me without judgment, with curiosity. It felt quite intimate to be seen so fully and completely. It also felt respectful and familiar.

When the scan was complete, the dolphin's energy gently withdrew and dissolved. The whole process lasted a matter of minutes.

I opened my eyes and was startled to find myself in a crowded, noisy restaurant. Without realizing it, I had entered into a whole other realm with this dolphin. Where we were, the restaurant didn't exist.

Now that I was back, our meals arrived. *Good timing*, I smiled to myself. The dolphin knew exactly when to show up, and when to leave.

David and I chuckled to ourselves. Our spirit friends visit us in the oddest places—they particularly like restaurants! Perhaps that's because when we're eating out, we're really relaxed and having fun together. We're more available to spirit when we're in this open, relaxed state.

Apparently the elder dolphin was satisfied by what he saw in me. The next morning, my telepathic communication with the Bonaire dolphins shifted to a whole new level.

♡

When I entered into meditation and gave permission for my frequencies to be adjusted for telepathy, I asked that this adjustment be fine-tuned so that I could receive the dolphins' messages in English words.

I let go of my intention, relaxed, and allowed my internal experience to unfold naturally. I focused on my body and my breath. Within a few minutes, my body energy began buzzing intensely. Then, in a moment, I was startled to find myself in the midst of an entire pod of Bonaire dolphins. I wasn't seeing it, I was sensing it—and knowing it.

There was tremendous excitement. The dolphins were having a grand celebration. One of the dolphins, I sensed it was an elder, had just died. The pod was ecstatic! A new dolphin was being elevated to the leadership role of the pod—the same dolphin that had been visiting me.

This is more than telepathy. I'm not just hearing words that tell me what's happening. I'm living this! Dolphin has transported my energy and consciousness through time and space. I am with this pod of dolphins—off the coast of Bonaire! I am feeling what they are feeling; experiencing what they are experiencing.

I marveled at these dolphins' perception of death—their celebration of it. I felt incredibly honored to be included in this rite of passage. The moment my consciousness appeared in their midst, they opened up and let me in. The whole pod accepted my presence without question.

They trust me. This was truly a profound moment for me. I was overcome with gratitude for their unconditional love and acceptance.

There was no sense of time while I was with these dolphins. At one point, I felt myself a distance away from the pod. Their new leader, and my new friend, was floating by my side. Inside myself, I heard him say, *"Call me Grandfather."*

Of course.

I communed in the silence and stillness with Grandfather for a period of time, relishing this connection and feeling his trust and his love. He really did feel like a grandfather to me. I felt utterly safe and protected in his presence. I think he took me on as one of his charges ... as a member of the pod.

While Grandfather floated by my side, I remembered that Roberta had given me a list of questions to ask him. In my mind, I thought the questions to Grandfather, and then relaxed and let go of any idea of how the answers would, or should, come.

Question: *"When we humans hear of terrible things happening to dolphins, we become distressed. What can we do for you? How can we best serve you?"*
Grandfather: "That is a small time to be in."

Question: *"What is your perception of planet Earth?"*
Rather than giving me an answer in words, Grandfather gave me an experience. Instantly, I found myself hovering with Grandfather in space. Together, we viewed planet Earth from the cosmos. I saw our lovely planet floating in space, beautiful and perfect, a shimmering jewel in the vast night sky.

What I perceived, in Grandfather's presence, was that planet Earth is one small, yet elegantly beautiful and perfect part of a magnificent whole. The "whole" was beyond my comprehension.

Question: *"What is your perception of humanity?"*
Again, this answer came in the form of an experience instead of words. My heart space immediately pulsed open. I felt myself seen as the dolphins see all of us—as a being of light. I felt that the dolphins saw my divinity, and brought that part of me to the surface, so that I, too, could feel, see, touch, and know the God that I am.

I sensed that this is the vision the dolphins hold of humanity, individually and collectively. They see our divine perfection, and hold that vision of us. By holding that vision, they support us in achieving self-actualization of our highest potential and our truest nature.

In addition to seeing our wholeness, the dolphins also see all the ways we separate ourselves—from self, from one another, from God, from our true nature. They see our weaknesses and vulnerabilities, our temper tantrums, our cries for love. Yet they do not judge us. They see us as a young species—as children who have much yet to learn.

♡

This experience with Grandfather and his pod was a breakthrough for me. I truly witnessed these dolphins living in an enlightened state of being. From the beginning of my journey with the dolphins, I had sensed this about them. Now I knew it.

Grandfather's "*That is a small time to be in*" response spoke volumes to me about who this being is, the state of consciousness he inhabits, and the Dolphin Consciousness he represents. From that state, the dramas that occur, in our lives and on the planet, happen in the blink of an eye. He was saying: "Don't dwell on such things. They're not what's important."

This is a consistent message I receive from the dolphins as I navigate the ups and downs of my own life. And it's the response I receive from them when people ask me questions such as: "What are the dolphins telling you about ... the recent beaching? ... what's going to happen in the year 2012? ... Atlantis? ... the recent earthquake? ... global warming? ... the economic crisis?"

The dolphins don't take me to these places. Their answer is always: "*Stay in your center. Stay in your joy. That is the best way you can be of service ... to yourself, to us, and to the planet.*"

♡

I reflected upon Grandfather's cosmic perspective of Earth, and compared it to my limited human one. When I thought about the planet, I thought of how we humans treat one another, and the various ways we attempt to control—our own lives, each other, and the natural world. I thought about the drama, trauma, and attachments we hold so dear. The loving and not-so-loving relationships we pour so much energy into. I realized that my view of Earth is a very limited one. Grandfather helped me to see there is so much more.

Pondering the cosmic perspective, I wondered how humanity fits into the big picture. As I viewed Earth from space, there was no visible sign of human existence to be seen. At the energetic level, I did not perceive the existence of humanity, separate and apart from the exquisite energy of Gaia herself—the spirit of planet Earth. This realization puzzled me.

With this thought, Grandfather popped back into my awareness. **"The human experience upon planet Earth is an essential part of the whole, but a smaller part than you realize."**

Every day for months, I entered into telepathy—more accurately, telempathy—with Grandfather, in service to the Bonaire project. Ready with a list of questions they'd sent me by e-mail, I connected with Grandfather and asked the questions. Much of the time, the questions went unanswered.

Grandfather always came, but when I asked the questions, he often remained silent, or he gave answers that I knew the project did not want to hear. I began to feel like the bearer of unwelcome news. I didn't enjoy that!

However, within the silence that followed the unanswered questions, I soon felt energy moving through my body. During our time together, Grandfather gave me a variety of interdimensional experiences. He gave me healings. He took me to places that were special to his pod. Pink Beach was one of those places. Our visit there left my whole body trembling with bliss. Much of the time, we floated together in a beautiful, divine state of oneness, silence, and stillness.

One day, after Grandfather met my questions, yet again, with silence, I asked him why. *"I'm connecting with you on behalf of the Bonaire project. My intention is to be in service to them. Why is it that most of the time, I'm the one who receives from you?"*

"You're the one who shows up," he replied.

Grandfather did make clear, very early on in our communications, that his pod has no interest in swimming with humans. That's not their purpose. They have a different mission.

Dolphin Love

Through the course of my experiences with Grandfather, I came to understand their mission. They are here to hold frequency for the planet. They do this by spending large amounts of time in deep meditation.

When I rest in the silence and stillness with Grandfather and his pod, I am joining them in their mission. They like it when I join them. For me, it's always a deeply nourishing and fulfilling experience.

I remember one of my first experiences entering into this deep space with Grandfather and his pod. As my energy began to shift at the beginning of my meditation, I felt myself diving into the depths of the ocean with the pod. We reached a particular spot and rested in the stillness. Our energies merged. We were one.

As we meditated in utter darkness, silence, and stillness, my awareness was drawn to my body. "*Notice*," I heard. I scanned my body with my consciousness and was surprised to discover that I felt nothing. No energy sensations, no tingles, no vibrations moving through me. My body, my whole being, was absolutely still.

This is the Void. I've been here before. I surrendered deeply into this space that contains both nothingness and All That Is. I felt the boundaries of my self, of Linda, dissolve. I was nothing, and everything, all at the same time.

I emerged from this meditation in awe. Roberta's out-of-the-blue e-mail, and my willingness to try something new, led me into this remarkable relationship with Grandfather and his pod of Bonaire dolphins. My heart swelled with wonder and gratitude.

It was only a matter of time before the richness of my inner life began to be reflected in my outer life.

♡

When David and I first moved to Southern California from the small town of Sedona, we were delighted by the multitude of shopping opportunities all around. We drove along the roads and freeways and gaped at shop upon shop upon shop. Sedona wasn't like this! It was mesmerizing to see restaurants, boutiques, and huge sprawling shopping centers everywhere.

But soon that honeymoon was over. Shopping became overwhelming to me.

There was too much of everything—too much traffic, too much noise, too many people, and too many choices. The proliferation of megastores was overwhelming; my energy drained when I went into them.

Under Grandfather's influence, these previously frustrating and exhausting shopping trips took on a wondrous and magical quality.

In the worst of traffic, I began relishing the opportunity of being on the road with so many people I would not otherwise have encountered. *I get to experience all of these new energies—the cars, the people, the road, the bridges, the street signs.* I began to feel positively abundant driving down the I-5 to go to Target, or wherever my destination took me on any given day.

In the midst of this fast-paced, diverse Southern California lifestyle, my inner silence and stillness stayed with me, serving as a nurturing and protective cocoon. And yet this cocoon did not separate me from the world. My serene inner state enabled me to immerse myself in the world, in all of life, as never before.

As I walked through huge stores, such as Target, Linens & Things, or Walmart, I felt the silence and stillness inside. At the same time, I felt my body energy expand and open to the delirious array of sensory experiences that surrounded me. Every cell of my body got to taste every unique frequency of energy that existed there, in the split second that it took to pass through me. It was exhilarating!

One day I took a walk on the beach, and I reached such an ecstatic state, I thought I was going to start walking on air! My body energy became so light, it felt like my next step couldn't possibly land on the earth.

The consistency of my meditation practice with Grandfather brought me into a sustained state of bliss. This had been a big goal of mine for a long time. I had so wanted to be able to remain in those high states of awareness, those higher frequencies, during my worldly life, when I wasn't meditating. Grandfather and his pod helped me to achieve that.

I experienced a wealth of growth and expansion during those last three months in California, thanks to Grandfather and the Bonaire dolphins.

TWENTY-ONE

Keiko

I'm so grateful for the people in my life who encourage me to go where I would not go on my own. At least, ultimately I'm grateful! Sometimes, in the moment, I resist, and I feel annoyed. And then I surrender. Even then, it's often not until after I do whatever was asked of me that I realize it turned out to be a really good idea.

The folks involved with the Bonaire project were like this for me.

On January 3, 2002, while my telepathic communications with Grandfather were in full flow, I received this e-mail from one of the Bonaire project members: "Another question. Can you communicate with Keiko (orca)?? We are thinking that Bonaire possibly, in the future, could adopt that orca."

You want me to communicate with Keiko—the Free Willy *whale?* Immediately my resistance came up. I did not want to do this. *It's one thing to talk to an unknown dolphin. It's a completely other thing to talk to a famous whale! It's like asking me to telepath with Tom Cruise, for heaven's sake!* I felt ridiculous even thinking about it.

At this stage in my journey, I knew very little about whales. I knew nothing about Keiko except that he was the orca whale that starred in the first *Free Willy* movie that was so popular in the 1990s. I was surprised to learn later that orca whales are actually the largest of the dolphin species. So, technically, Keiko was a really big dolphin!

In subsequent e-mails, I learned that Keiko was being rehabilitated, with the goal that he could be returned to the wild for the duration of his life. Keiko's handlers were looking for a new location for him to complete this process. This member of the Bonaire project wanted to explore the possibility of acquiring Keiko for the last phase of his rehabilitation. A part of the vision for their wild dolphin sanctuary was to rehabilitate captive dolphins and whales and then, if and when appropriate, release them in locations near to where they were caught, or as near as practical to their home waters.*

Nevertheless, my resistance to this request lingered. I procrastinated for two weeks, hoping that the issue would just go away. But this team member was persistent. Almost every day, I received an e-mail asking if I'd connected to Keiko yet. I hadn't, and I kept evading the question.

And then one day the universe stepped in and gave me a little nudge ...

Late one afternoon, I was at home in our apartment, feeling restless. I felt compelled to take a walk to the ocean to watch the sunset. It had been a while since I'd done that. I grabbed a book and walked along the boardwalk in search of an empty bench, where I could read until the sun set.

As usual at this time of day, the boardwalk was pretty crowded. I walked and walked, and all the benches were occupied. I didn't want to share a bench. I wanted to be alone. Just as I was about to give up, the people who were sitting on the bench I was approaching got up and left.

I was so happy to have found a bench! I sat down with my legs crossed under me, Indian-style, taking up as much space as my five-foot, two-and-a-half-inch frame would allow. I took a quick glance at the sun and the ocean; I had a little time before the sun would set. I opened my book—Marianne Williamson's *A Return to Love*—and began to read.

Within minutes, two men approached and sat down on my bench. *Hey!* I

---

* In preparation for publishing this book, I sent this chapter to dolphin researcher Roberta Goodman for her review and comments: "The location of Bonaire wasn't well thought out. More viable locations were sure to be found and considered, the infrequence of orca sightings around Bonaire, or any site, being one such measure of suitability."

looked over at them and tried not to smile, because I was annoyed. But it's almost impossible for me to pull off looking annoyed at total strangers. My benchmates were a man who appeared to be in his 70s, and a younger man who appeared to be in his late-40s.

They turned to me and flashed the biggest smiles, and said, "Do you realize that this is *our* bench?"

"No, I didn't know that," I replied, starting to feel territorial.

"Yep. A whole gang of us come to this bench every night to watch sunset." Bigger smiles.

"Really?" Not smiling.

Well, they don't own this bench. I have just as much a right to be here as they do. And I was here first.

I glanced around. Sunset was fast approaching. There was no way I was going to find another empty bench now. I stayed where I was, and felt my internal struggle. *I'm not going to have this time to myself after all.*

Two more people showed up, and then another. Pretty soon, I was sharing a nice, intimate sunset with a group of nine total strangers, mostly retirees. It was obvious that they knew one another quite well. And they were very happy to include me in their little sunset gathering.

I really want to be alone!

I kept to myself as much as I could, and tried to read while they joked and played around with one another. I had to admit, they were a fun group. It was clear that they truly cared for one another and enjoyed each other's company. I caught myself smiling from time to time in response to something someone said, and then stopped, remembering that I was still annoyed! From time to time they drew me into their conversation. Slowly but surely, they wore down my defenses.

The last to arrive was Irene, an 83-year-old woman whose claim to fame was that she used to dance in a vaudeville act in her younger days. She was quite a character! Irene's presence dissolved the last of my resistance. I let go, and allowed this group's joy to flow through me like a warm breeze. Soon I was really enjoying this lovely and gracious group of friends.

Shortly after Irene's arrival, the first two gentlemen asked what I did for a living. They already knew by this time that I was a local. I told them that I work with dolphins. I didn't say dolphin energy; I decided to keep it simple.

They lit up. "Well, you should talk to Irene then. That's right up her alley!"

That was all she needed to hear. She was on it. The first words out of her mouth were, "Guess what I have at home?"

"What?" I couldn't imagine.

She was grinning ear to ear; she was so pleased with herself. "I have a documentary video about Keiko's move from that awful place in Mexico to the aquarium in Oregon! You know who Keiko is, don't you? He's the *Free Willy* whale!"

I was shocked. "You have *what?*"

Oh, she was excited. She just couldn't stop talking about how she met the man who made the video and how he ended up giving her a copy of it. She decided right then and there that she should have all of us over to her house for a Keiko video party!

I couldn't believe my ears. *The one time I come out to watch the sunset ... the one time I end up mingling with a group of locals ... the topic of conversation is Keiko?*

Irene had no idea what she had just done. I was stunned. On my walk home after sunset, I yielded. *Okay, okay! I'll do it!* That was some trick my spirit friends pulled out of their fins to get me to take the Keiko telepathy request seriously.

I shook my head at myself. I was so sure I wanted to be alone ... I ended up having a really great time! My heart was full from all the love and fun that sunset group shared. Keiko had already given me a beautiful gift.

I look forward to meeting you, Keiko ... tomorrow!

The next morning, I prepared for my first meditation with Keiko. Sitting on the bed in our apartment, with my back erect against the wall, I closed my eyes and began taking slow, deep breaths. In just a few breaths, my mind was silent and still, and my body energy was relaxed and calm. Inside myself, I said:

Spirit, it is my intention during this meditation to enter into telepathic communication with Keiko, the Free Willy whale. I know that you know how to do this, so I surrender this meditation to you. I give you complete permission to make adjustments to my frequency that will enable me to have this experience.

I let go, relaxed, focused my attention on my breath and my body sensations, and allowed my experience to unfold naturally. My body and mind became even more quiet ... intensely quiet. I was going very deep. I sensed a presence ... a dim light far off in the distance. I knew I had located Keiko; however, this was not a strong connection, especially compared to the connections I'd been having with Grandfather. Keiko's energy felt weak and low. Thinking that this connection wasn't going to last very long, I got right to the point.

In my mind, I communicated the Bonaire project's interest in exploring the possibility of bringing Keiko to them to complete his release program. I brought in the energies of two of the people I knew would be involved, and asked Keiko if he would be willing to move to this new location.

There was silence, and then I heard, "I will be loved there."

I asked about any specific needs or requests that he had, and I did not get a response.

The connection ended, and my body energy slowly returned to my normal waking state. I felt sleepy. Keiko had taken me very deep.

While it seemed like I didn't get much from Keiko, I felt good that I was able to make contact. I e-mailed my report to Bonaire, and felt I was complete with Keiko.

The next day, I was looking forward to getting back to meditating without a specific intention or purpose. While the telepathic experiences were really wonderful, I also love meditating from a pure open space and letting spirit take the lead.

I was working through the *Course in Miracles Workbook* during this time, so I opened the workbook to the daily lesson. The entire two pages of text that lay before me were a blur. I couldn't read a word of it. I rubbed my eyes, looked again, and everything was still blurry.

Looking up from the book, I felt a strong energy around me. Something, or someone, wanted my attention. I closed my eyes and tuned in. *Keiko*.

> Something, or someone, wanted my attention. I closed my eyes and tuned in. *Keiko.*

I put the book down and opened to receive. I asked to be attuned to Keiko's frequency and gave permission for my frequencies to be adjusted so that I could merge with his mind, his body, and his emotions. *I've never asked to merge with the body and emotions before.* It just popped out.

I was immersed in Keiko's energy immediately. His energy was very strong. The first thing I felt was extreme anxiety ... panic, actually. My mind wandered to the thought of moving him, and I sensed that this was what I was feeling—his extreme anxiety about going through another move, and wondering if he would even survive it (don't know if that was my wondering or his).

Then I felt heartbreak. The grief and pain was so intense, so raw, it overcame me. I sat on my bed sobbing and sobbing. I'd never felt such intense, painful emotion. *These are Keiko's emotions.*

Through the pain and tears, beyond the heartbreak, I felt Keiko's immense love for humanity. I'd never felt such love before. It was huge. It was vast. And I knew that what I was feeling was just a fragment of the love Keiko feels for us. *His heart!*

I received energy impressions that my mind translated into thoughts.

Keiko realizes that our human efforts to free him are well-intentioned. It's what we think he wants—what we think is best for him. The reality is he doesn't want to return to the wild. The opportunity that came from being captured and trained to do the Free Willy movie enabled him to touch human hearts, by the millions. This became his mission, and his joy.

Keiko is in intense pain and grief that we're taking all of that away from him. On one level, he feels like we humans are rejecting him.

Oh, the tears. I was completely overwhelmed by the deluge of Keiko's emotions flowing through me.

♡

Slowly, gradually, the emotions quieted, and our connection dissolved. I returned to my waking state. It was 70 degrees outside, but my body was freezing cold, shivering, and shaking. As soon as I was able to move, I ran around the house in search of a blanket. Fraught with despair and sorrow about what we humans had done to Keiko, I wanted desperately to help him.

I immediately shared all of this with David. He held me while I cried. I wrote my e-mail report to the Bonaire folks, and then went online to learn more about Keiko's circumstances. I was still wrapped up in my blanket, shivering, freezing cold.

I found out that for ten years, beginning in 1985, Keiko's home was a very small tank in Mexico. The conditions there were terrible. By 1993, when *Free Willy* was filmed, his immune system was compromised, he was severely underweight, and he suffered from significant muscle atrophy because of his small tank.

In January 1995, Keiko was moved to a new rehabilitation facility at Oregon Coast Aquarium in Newport, Oregon. During his stay, Keiko's health, mental clarity, and socialization skills improved tremendously. As I read about this stage of his journey, I felt Keiko's excitement around me. *He liked it there. If he could have it his way, he'd go back.*

In 1998, Keiko was moved to a protected holding pen off the coast of Iceland, for the next phase in his release program. This is where he was when I tuned in to him. Apparently these were Keiko's native waters, and his handlers moved him there in the hope that the native orca pods would adopt him, and help him learn how to survive in the wild again.

Iceland! That's why I'm freezing. My merge with Keiko included merging with his physical body, and that water is freezing for my human form.

I read as much about Keiko as I was able before the cold became unbearable. I ran a hot bath and soaked in the tub for more than an hour before my body temperature finally, slowly, returned to normal.

The whole day, I couldn't get Keiko out of my mind. His pure, raw emotion stayed with me. I wanted to jump on a plane and go somewhere, anywhere, wherever I needed to go to do him some good.

The next morning, I woke up and tried to let the whole Keiko thing go. The idea that I could do something to help him seemed ludicrous. I took my time with my morning routine, and had a normal morning meditation. But Keiko kept sneaking into my mind.

When I completed my meditation, I decided to tune in to Keiko, just for a moment, to see how he was doing. I no sooner had that thought, than Keiko's energy ever so lovingly and gently took me over. His energy was completely different. What I felt in Keiko now was deep peace and acceptance.

The communication came as a series of impressions. Keiko had accepted his situation. While Iceland would not have been his first choice, he realized that he had gone too far forward in this release program to go back now. My feelings were mixed, but I was profoundly relieved that he was at peace.

Keiko stayed with me for a while, his energy completely merged with mine. We communed together in deep peacefulness, silence, and stillness. There was no sense of time. At one point, my awareness was brought gently back to my body, to my breath. I noticed that I was not breathing my body, this gentle giant was breathing my body for me!

That was a delicious, exquisite sensation. I felt my lungs fill up with air ever so gently, with absolutely no effort on my part. There was a sweetness to my breathing that I'd never known before. The in breath and out breath were so soft, so gentle, so full. It was a completely different experience from when I am breathing myself. I didn't want this to end!

Dr. Peebles teaches that surrendering one's breath to spirit is the first step in the channeling process. *Perhaps Keiko would like me to channel him!* That would be a way for him to continue to reach out and touch the hearts of humans. I told Keiko it would be an honor and a joy to channel him, if that was what he wanted. When the time was right ...

I felt a loving acknowledgment of my offer. Gently and softly, Keiko withdrew his energy from me, and returned my lungs to my own control. As our energies separated, I felt my whole body tingling from this sublime merging of our spirits. As my body energy returned to my normal self, I reflected back on this extraordinary experience.

It seemed to me that our second encounter was a healing one for Keiko. I witnessed and shared his intense emotions, and then Keiko was able to release them. The shift in his emotional state from one day to the next was profound—from pure, raw pain, to deep peace and acceptance.

Until these experiences with Keiko, I hadn't fully appreciated the vast range of emotions that dolphins and whales feel. Somehow, I had the idea that cetaceans were above feeling emotions. This was a big learning experience for me. They feel the whole range of emotions, as we humans do—they feel them deeply.

♡

Keiko was released into the wild from his Iceland holding pen in July 2002. His caretakers tracked his solitary journey along the coastline, where he didn't stop traveling until he arrived at a little village in Norway, 870 miles away.

Keiko used his newfound freedom to travel to, and live among, several villages that provided the eager and enthusiastic human companionship he longed for. He let humans pet and play with him, and even allowed some to crawl onto his back. Once released and free, it was his human family Keiko sought out, not his fellow orcas.

Keiko died of pneumonia on December 13, 2003. He was 27 years old.

Keiko's spirit and love carry on. He is a frequent visitor when I do my work with groups. His huge, sweet heart leaves a very large imprint on all who experience him.

Keiko means "Lucky One" in Japanese. It seems to me that we humans are the lucky ones—to have received the gift of Keiko's abundant love and exquisite presence.

Thank you, Keiko, for sharing yourself so thoroughly and completely with me. I am forever changed.

TWENTY-TWO

Grandfather in Sedona

Immediately upon moving back to the beautiful southwest desert of Sedona, far from the nearest ocean, I began receiving invitations to share dolphin energy with small groups in friends' homes. What was most present for me to share at that time was my relationship with Grandfather. Without fail, as soon as I mentioned Grandfather's name, everyone in the room felt his enormous, wise, loving presence.

These evenings became about Grandfather. I closed my eyes, opened my being to allow Grandfather's energy to flow through me, and he took over the energetic experience. It was fascinating to witness how Grandfather and his pod worked with each person in a totally unique way that was perfect for them.

It occurred to me that while Grandfather's pod may not be interested in swimming with humans physically, they were quite willing and eager to engage with humans energetically! Apparently this way of being in service to humanity is in alignment with their mission, whereas swimming with humans physically would be a distraction.

One night, I introduced Grandfather to a group of four women, hosted by my dear friend Nickie.

After a brief guided visualization, I welcomed Grandfather into the room. We entered into the silence together. I stayed tuned in to the energy of the group, so that I would know when to bring the meditation to a close.

As the meditation ended, I heard peculiar sounds coming from Nickie. I opened my eyes to see if she was laughing or crying. I couldn't tell. Her whole body was shaking with the effort of containing her emotions, so she wouldn't disturb the others.

One by one, as each guest returned to present time awareness, all eyes turned to Nickie. At last, she burst out laughing. Tears were streaming down her face. "My cheeks and forehead hurt from being stretched so far into the dolphin smile!" She laughed joyfully. Then she told us her experience.

> "Grandfather merged with me completely. I felt myself take on Grandfather's physical dolphin form—it was so amazing! In his powerful body, I swam through the water, slowly at first, and then with more speed. I felt the aerodynamic shape of my dolphin body move effortlessly and powerfully through the water. All of my senses were heightened. My skin was so sensitive ... the sensation of gliding effortlessly through the water was extraordinary. As I swam, I could smell the salt water and the crisp ocean air.
>
> "And then, in one moment, with a powerful flick of my tail—Grandfather's tail—I sped through the water at tremendous speed! I ... we (giggle!) leapt out of the water, spinning and ascending high into the air, and then crashed back onto the surface with a huge splash.
>
> "It was so real!"

We were all fascinated by Nickie's story. She looked around the room in wonder. Then she said she needed to sit quietly and integrate her experience.

Another woman, also a dear friend of mine, shared that she felt physical sensations on her body, as if a whole group of dolphins were all around her, nudging her gently with their rostrums. This nudging was interspersed with whole-body bumping. The contacts were all gentle, and they felt very real, very physical. She felt that the pattern of touch was conscious, not random, and that the contact was healing her. The dolphins told her they are with her always. She is not alone. All she has to do is reach out to them, and open to receive their love. This touched her deeply.

At the end of the evening, I felt Grandfather's energy surge up inside of me. I closed my eyes and connected. He asked me to thank Nickie for bringing her friends together for the purpose of receiving his love. We were all deeply moved by his gratitude.

♡

My friend Daniel Stief had such a special experience with Grandfather, I asked him to write about it:

Daniel Stief: A special experience with Grandfather

The two dolphin energy healing sessions I had with Linda were the most powerful of my life. The dolphin energy is just something that everyone should experience. It was so wonderful and powerful, on an elemental level.

The energy gave me a sense of the oneness we all are. It was uncluttered with emotions and beliefs ... it was just a sense of being. One of the most calming and energizing feelings I have ever experienced.

In both cases, I was able to merge with the leader, called Grandfather, of a dolphin pod. What an incredible being he is. He seems ageless and at the same time has the joy of being a child.

The first time we met, we both seemed to be checking each other out as I watched him in the water beside me. He was dark gray in color and had beautiful black-looking eyes. He seemed to be almost casually able to read me like an open book, and at the same time this happened without a feeling of unwelcome intrusion. He just "knew" me.

During the first session, we sort of did this "getting to know each other" energetic dance and energy exchange. Then, as we became more familiar and attuned to each other's energy, we merged. It was as if our bodies were horizontal in the water and we slid sidewise until we both were one.

How amazing that was, as I could feel his body and skin. And then, as we settled comfortably into each other, we began to swim, slowly at first. And what an incredible feeling it was, knowing I was sitting in a chair, and yet at the same time I could feel the gentle undulations as we swam.

Then we had some fun as we swam faster and took a dive down deeper. We navigated around some rocks, and through an opening, to come out on the other side into open water again. At this point, I know I was squealing with delight. Then, as we swam leisurely along, I heard Grandfather say, "What the heck, let's go for it!"

With an incredible burst of speed we went shooting through the water as if we were fired from a cannon! It was the most wonderful, exciting feeling. I tried to compare it to being on a roller coaster, but it was so much more exhilarating!

Next, I gulped as we shot through the surface of the water to soar high into the air and then plunge with total joy back into the water. I thought, how could this possibly get any better, when I suddenly found myself swimming on the surface, with a dolphin on either side, in perfect unison. The feeling was of having a wonderful family where we are in sync and as one. And we were, in fact, as one as we each exactly mirrored the movements of the others.

I was so happy and totally free of the weights of life WE put on ourselves. I asked Grandfather if we could go on like this for another hour. Sadly, but with total wisdom, he told me that this was enough for the first time. We came back gently to earth, so to speak.

And if this wasn't special enough, Linda told us that we could request healing on anything we wanted during the session. I made my choice as we began and felt ripples of energy flowing through my body, breaking up a block I knew I had.

When we finished the first short, introductory session (can you imagine this was just an introductory session!), I was so amazed and grateful that I immediately asked Linda when we could do another, full, session. (This is totally out of character for me. I just knew that I wanted more of this wonderful dolphin energy!)

Two nights later, we began the second session. I was so excited and so open to fully experiencing everything I could, and to totally eliminating the energetic block I worked on before.

As we began the session, I felt a little like we needed to be taking more time to allow me to sink deeper into a meditative state before the work began. And then I laughed inside and said just surrender, you know how. So I did, and the wonderful movement of energy through my body began to happen. Linda has a magical touch that is so light and gentle. I can only liken it to what I think it would feel like to have a fairy with beautiful flapping wings touching you. So light and gentle, while at the same time, perfectly in touch with what needs to be.

As Linda moved about my body, running the wonderful dolphin energy through me, I shuddered and shook in sync with the energy flow as it worked on me.

I totally surrendered and invited the fullest flow of the energy to work with me. I sensed Grandfather's presence with me and knew that he was watching over me and guiding the entire process. At times I became a dolphin and felt the rhythmic flapping of my flippers. I felt it physically in my body. My hands became flippers and beat perfect rhythms on the sides of the table.

As each wave of energy came through me, Grandfather was there at every step asking, without asking, if it was too much energy and should we tune it down a bit? Each time, I replied with love and gratitude for his concern with a resounding "NO!" The energy of the session grew and grew.

And as he honored my wishes, he also knew what was best for me. I would go through a very intense period of energy flow and then would feel it begin to soften and lessen in intensity. Then, as I began to wonder if we were done, it would begin to flow again and another part of my energetic system would be stimulated. This went on and on with wave after wave of this energy.

Finally, somewhat exhausted and yet exhilarated, I knew that the work was complete.

Sharing Grandfather with others has been an incredible gift for me. I did this work for six years before he came along. Since meeting and communing with Grandfather, I achieved a state of oneness with him and his pod that filled a deep yearning I'd had inside since my journey with the dolphins began. Having done that, I was now able to transmit that experience of merge, of oneness, to others who were ready and willing to receive it.

In light of these experiences with Grandfather, I've looked back over the years and observed the progression of my work. I saw that what came through me to be shared with others was a reflection of what I, myself, was open and willing to receive from the dolphins, and from life, at any given stage in my journey.

Grandfather's spirit is ever-present with me now. He is a primary guide and source of dolphin energy and wisdom in my work. I sometimes wonder if I'll ever meet him, in the physical, in this lifetime. Every time I ask him, he answers with an enigmatic, silent smile.

TWENTY-THREE

Waiting for You

Dr. Peebles suggested that I write a book about my dolphin journey. It wouldn't have occurred to me to do that. I resisted the idea for quite a while. But it stayed with me, and the energy around it grew. So one day I sat down and began writing my story.

I wrote a good chunk of the first draft, and then I needed to take a break. Months later, the book began calling to me, but I felt resistance inside. I kept procrastinating, and the stress around the project grew, increasing my resistance even more.

One day, the idea popped in to go somewhere for a writing retreat. This idea excited me! After considering a few possibilities, David came up with the brilliant suggestion that I go to Hawaii—both to write, and to reconnect and swim with my dolphin family again.

We both knew that that was the real source of my restlessness. It was time for me to return to Hawaii to swim with my dolphin family. Giving that trip a dual function eased our consciences about spending the money to send me to Hawaii again.

A friend of ours had recently relocated from Sedona to the Big Island, and generously invited me to stay with her. I gladly accepted! Sandy lived in Waikoloa, an hour's drive from the bay where I go to swim with the dolphins. I decided that this was a good thing, as it was important for me to focus on my book and not be swimming with the dolphins the whole time! If I were staying close to them, it might be difficult for me to get any writing done.

My first morning in Hawaii, I did drive to the bay, just to see ... I had to! There were no dolphins that morning. I had mixed feelings looking out into the stillness of the bay. Shaking away the sadness, I filled up with the dolphin energy that is always so strong there, whether the dolphins are physically present or not. My process of letting go of any and all expectations for this trip was under way.

When my energy field was fully saturated with dolphin love, I felt a nudge to drive to the other bay, the one where I had camped on the beach. I was eager to float, swim, and play in the delicious tropical waters of Hawaii. After a nice swim, I could settle in and do some writing. Play first! *And who knows? Maybe the dolphins are there!*

My Hawaii trips are typically quite spontaneous. I usually don't tell anyone I know there that I'm coming. I can be a bit shy that way. I prefer to just show up and let the island orchestrate my connections, synchronistically.

I was tickled with surprise and delight to see a familiar truck as I pulled into the dirt parking lot at the beach. *That looks like Merlyn's truck!*

I got my swim gear out of the car and stepped onto the sandy beach. Hopefully, I looked out into the bay. No dolphins.

While surveying the beach for a place to sit, I saw what looked like Merlyn's tent. There was no sign of life stirring around that campsite yet. Merlyn is not an early riser; I'd know soon enough if he was here. The dolphins always arrange for me to bump into Merlyn on my Hawaii trips. They know I adore him.

I sat on the beach for a while, soaking up the sun and the balmy Hawaii energy. Just being here soothed my soul. My whole being began to gently unwind and open to whatever adventures the dolphins, and the island, had in store for me.

A man was sitting a little way away and we struck up a conversation ... about dolphins, of course. He told me he was born and raised on the island, and I was surprised how little he knew about who the dolphins really are. He didn't even know that people could swim with them! *How can someone grow up here and not know that about the dolphins?*

He became quite intrigued as I shared some of my stories. He decided that he wanted to swim with them too, to experience their magic himself.

I excused myself and went for a nice long swim in the crystal clear bay. How I love the Hawaiian ocean! I feel so at home there. The swim was refreshing and restorative.

Emerging from the water, I saw Merlyn walking across the beach. A sarong was wrapped around his waist, and his shoulder-length wispy white hair blew in the breeze. He turned and saw me, stopped walking, and squinted in my direction. He hadn't fully registered that it was me yet.

I burst out laughing and ran up to him. "Aloha, Merlyn. It's me! I'm here!"

We hugged and giggled with delight. It's always a special gift when our paths cross. We have a sweet and special connection.

A lovely woman walked up to join us, whom he introduced as Zoë. I extended my hand, "Hi, Zoë, I'm Linda."

"I know," she replied.

"How do you know?" I asked, surprised.

Merlyn explained that they were awakened by a woman's laughter. He turned to Zoë and said, "That's Linda's laugh! I think she's here!"

I didn't know if I should be flattered or embarrassed. I've been told that my laugh is memorable.

Merlyn and Zoë invited me to join them for a breakfast of fresh mango, yogurt, and yerba maté. *Oh, yes, this is the Hawaii I love! Tropical fruit ... breakfast on the beach with friends ... the yummy ocean just footsteps away ...*

Merlyn and I talked as if we'd never been apart, and I felt completely relaxed and comfortable with Zoë. I adored her. We became instant sisters.

When I asked about the recent dolphin activity, they told me that the dolphins had been scarce the preceding weeks. I couldn't stop myself from going into doubt again. *Will they, or won't they, show up while I'm here?*

Dolphin Love

I forced myself to *let it go*. I had writing to do; that came first. I would not seek out the dolphins until my writing was complete.

♡

During the days, I wrote. Sandy worked, so I had her place all to myself. A cozy corner of her living room became my writing nook. Palm trees swayed outside the windows, a warm tropical breeze flowed through the room all day, and boisterous birdsong fed my spirit. What more could I ask for?

In the evenings, we had dinner together and caught up with one another's lives. We hadn't seen each other since she left Sedona and moved to the Big Island.

On the third night, I attended a channeling evening that Merlyn had told me about. It was being held in my friend Celeste's home. I was pleased with the progress I'd made on my book, and I seemed to be over that pesky shyness I'd been feeling about connecting with the people there. When I arrived, there were a few familiar faces, and many new ones. The few who remembered me welcomed me back with open arms and hearts.

During the evening, my attention kept being drawn to a Japanese woman seated toward the back of the room. *Is that Yurika?* I'd met Yurika in Sedona a few times. She guided groups of Japanese people through Sedona on spiritual journeys. Twice, she brought her groups to my dolphin meditation evenings.

This woman didn't speak until the end of the evening, when we were invited to ask questions. When she described herself as an author who wrote about dolphins for the Japanese people, I knew it was Yurika. I was excited to see her!

When the channeling was over, I walked over to her and said, "Yurika?"

"You from Sedona?" she replied.

"Yes!" I exclaimed, reaching out to hug her.

We talked for a while, and when I told her where I was staying, she invited me to stay in her apartment the following night, so I would be closer to the dolphins for an early morning swim. But I could only stay one night, because she had a houseguest coming after that.

"Wow! Thank you so much. I'd love to!" *Thank you, dolphins!* I mentally calculated that one more full day on my book was all I really needed. The timing of Yurika's invitation aligned perfectly with my first free day to swim with the dolphins!

When I showed up at her apartment the following night, Yurika looked down at my big suitcase and was visibly concerned. "I can only let you stay one night, yes?"

I laughed. I don't travel light! I assured her that I was only planning to stay one night, but that my intuition told me to bring everything. I sensed that another opportunity would open up for me to stay closer to the dolphins my last few nights. She was relieved!

Sometimes the dolphins come and sometimes they don't. This morning they did not. I felt deep, deep sadness.

We stayed up into the wee hours of the morning talking and getting to know one another. We were comfortable with one another right away, and we shared so much, so deeply. Even though we were from different countries with vastly different cultures, we had a lot in common, besides our love of dolphins. Issues of love, relationship, and motherhood are universal. I went to sleep feeling warm, loved, and very taken care of.

Early the next morning, we gathered our gear and drove down to the bay. We drove separately, as Yurika had promised to pick up a woman who was visiting from Japan.

Driving the winding road down to the bay, my heart pounded fiercely. *Will they be there?* I could feel them, but I wanted to *see* them. I wanted to *swim* with them!

I arrived at the bay first and got out of my car. The parking area was empty—never a good sign. With anticipation and trepidation, I walked up to the breaker wall and gazed out into the bay, looking closely for any sign of fins or spins signaling the dolphins' presence. There was only stillness. My heart sank. No dolphins.

People come here every morning hoping the dolphins will appear. It's a ritual. Sometimes the dolphins come and sometimes they don't. This morning they did not. I felt deep, deep sadness.

When Yurika and her friend arrived, we watched, waited, and hoped for a while longer. The dolphins did not come. We let the disappointment in, and then roused ourselves and decided to go to the other bay to swim and hang out.

We got into our cars and followed each other the twenty-minute drive to the beach. As soon as I got into my car, I burst into tears. *I've come all this way, and it's not going to happen. I'm not going to swim with the dolphins.* I felt so thoroughly sad, it was overwhelming.

I was crying so hard I had to keep clearing my eyes so that I could drive. At one point, I felt a shift in emotion from devastating sadness to overwhelming gratitude and love for the gift the dolphins have been in my life. I felt their love sweep through me so powerfully. Dolphin love is unlike anything I've ever felt. It is total and complete; it fills me up on all levels. Gratitude for all that they have been to me, and done for me, flowed through me. I was still sobbing, but now these were tears of immense love and joy.

In that moment, I was immersed in oneness with them.

I may not see you physically this trip, but I feel you so strongly. There is no loss here. There is only gain and expansion. There is only love and gratitude. There is only truth. We are one. I love you so much. Thank you for all you've given me.

In that moment, I knew that I no longer *needed* to be with the dolphins in the physical. *I am one with you always.*

I felt complete with this trip in that moment. I did what I had come here to do. I did my writing. I swam and played in the water. I reconnected with wonderful friends and made new ones. I really, truly, felt complete. I was ready to return home.

We arrived at the beach. No dolphins. Sigh. *All is as it should be.*

We claimed a shaded picnic table and each busied ourselves with an activity of choice. Yurika studied her massage school texts. Her friend borrowed some of my magazines, and I got out my knitting.

Zoë and Merlyn were still camping on the beach. Zoë walked by, and we chatted for a few minutes. I told her that I knew the dolphins would not come and that I was ready to return home. She looked sad, but accepting. She left, and I sat down and started to knit.

After five stitches, I looked up and saw the tail end of a splash. *What was that?* I stopped breathing, my heart skipped a beat, and my eyes stayed glued to that spot in the bay.

Moments later, a dolphin leapt out of the water and spun with joy.

"Dolphins!!!!" I yelled out for all to hear. My heart almost exploded in my chest.

Zoë walked by again and I pointed to the dolphins, speechless. She hugged me and I collapsed in tears in her arms.

We threw on our gear and headed into the water in record time.

Where it was shallow, close to shore, the water was crystal clear. There was no visual distortion as I observed my body swimming. I watched my hands and arms slice cleanly through the water with each stroke; it looked like they were moving through air.

In this bay, we don't have to swim far to meet the dolphins. That was a good thing! I noticed that my arms tired quickly and my legs felt heavy. *Uh-oh.* My recent inactivity at home had not served me. *Will I be able to make it out to them?* I was alarmed at my lack of strength and stamina in the water.

Pacing myself, I kept swimming. The buoyant water made the swim easier than it would have been in fresh water, and for that I was grateful. As I swam, I constantly scanned the underwater scene in all directions, awaiting that first sighting, which always takes my breath away.

All my senses were heightened. I never know where I will see them first. Sometimes I hear their sounds, but today they were silent. I always feel them before I see them.

Finally, my eyes made out their dark shapes gracefully skimming the ocean floor. The whole pod was beneath me now, swimming silently, elegantly. *I am home.*

We had an ecstatic swim that day. Even though it had been a year-and-a-half since my last visit, it was as though I'd never left.

One dolphin approached me immediately and beckoned to me to follow her. When I'm with the dolphins, I switch to swimming dolphin-style—I propel myself forward with strong dolphin kicks and keep my arms at my sides, or clasped behind my back. This dolphin and I swam and swam and swam and swam. *I'm so out of shape!* I swam until my lungs and muscles burned. I had to stop to rest. This dolphin—she felt like a "she"—waited a little bit ahead of me. She never took her eyes off of me. When I was ready, we swam some more. We swam and swam until I had to rest again. She waited for me again, and then we swam some more.

 This precious dolphin was busting my butt!

This routine of swimming and resting, swimming and resting, went on for quite a long time. During one of my rests, it dawned on me. What was my first concern when I entered the water? My lack of physical strength and stamina! *This beautiful dolphin has become my personal trainer for the day!* Oh, my goodness. I laughed! I was swimming harder for her than I ever would have done on my own. This precious dolphin was busting my butt!

Now, while I was swimming my guts out, I was also suppressing a giggle at this whole scene, and loving this dolphin so much. She stayed with me for a *really* long time to get me into condition to enjoy the rest of my time with the dolphins. She did a great job! Finally, she decided her job was done. She left me, and other dolphins appeared for close encounters. It was playtime!

The dolphins took turns giving me my favorite encounters. Sometimes two swam with me, sometimes three, sometimes four. First they swam by my side, slowing to match my pace. Gradually, our bodies intertwined and our energy fields merged. They let me into their energy field, and we swam together as one ...

♡

> I swim straight forward while two beautiful dolphins weave in and out, all around me. Our bodies are amazingly close, yet we do not touch. I feel them manipulating my energy field. It is pure pleasure. These sleek dolphin backs, bellies, and fins flicker and glide inches from my face and body.
>
> I am now one of the dancers in this exquisite underwater bal-

let. We dance and weave intricate patterns of light and love, merging our essences. We're creating something brand new.

This is the dance of life. This is the dance of love. This is the dance of unity … of Unity-Community. We dance together in timelessness. And then, ever so subtly, the energy shifts.

I sense another energy. Glancing to my right, I see a swimmer approaching from behind.

Ever so gently, my two dolphins separate. One veers to the right and one veers to the left. Which do I follow? Wrong-Way Shay follows the one to the right, where the other swimmer is approaching. The dolphins nudge me, telepathically, to the left. I switch directions and see that the dolphin to the left has stopped—he's waiting for me. When I catch up to him, he swims below me, a few feet in front, looking back frequently to make sure I am still with him.

We swim together awhile, and then he slows to a stop. I look up to see the main dolphin pod just up ahead. He has escorted me back to the main pod! *"It's time for us to swim with someone else now,"* he communicates, with great tenderness and love.

I watch him swim away to join his mate, ready to create magic with their new human playmate. What a lovely way to shift my experience.

A little while later, Zoë and I bumped into each other in the water. Full of love and ready for a rest, we decided to call it a day. As we swam back to shore, thoughts floated into my mind about camping on the beach for my last few nights. *That would be wonderful! But I don't have any camping gear.* So I tried to think of other places where I could stay close by, but none of the alternatives felt good.

Walking toward our beach mats, Zoë said, "The idea popped into my mind while we were swimming that you might enjoy camping with us for the rest of your stay."

Dolphin Love

Wow! "I'd love to! But I don't have any camping gear."

"A friend of mine has a tent she's not using, and I have an extra sleeping bag. Merlyn has an extra camp pad."

In no time, Zoë had gathered all the gear I needed to sleep right there on the beach. I couldn't get any closer to the dolphins than that! *Thank you, Zoë! Thank you, dolphins!* I was glad I followed my intuition and brought all my stuff with me.

I called Sandy and told her of my good fortune. I'd see her in a few days when I returned to clean up after myself and pack the few things I'd left at her house. For the next three nights, I was going to be camping on the beach!

Zoë helped me set up my tent, and we returned to our mats on the beach. Dolphin energy was still buzzing in our energy fields. It's a natural high unlike any other. I highly recommend it!

"I invite you to come and play with us again today. Of course, I will honor whatever choice you make."

That night, as I snuggled into my borrowed sleeping bag, I felt the dolphin energy buzzing all through, and around, my body. Listening to the sound of the surf rolling ceaselessly just outside my tent, I was intoxicated with the knowing that the dolphins were out there ... somewhere ... so close.

I tried to settle down and sleep. Back home, the silence of the desert lulls me to sleep. Here, I vacillated between desire for sleep and the excitement of being here and not wanting to miss a thing. Thankfully, sleep found me.

When I awoke, the predawn sky softly lit the quiet, still bay with a pink glow. The early morning energy was soft and gentle. I loved that I could crawl out from my tent and be right there at the ocean. No one was stirring. It was just the ocean and me. I was overcome with gratitude for the gift of being there, on that magical spot on the planet, in that moment.

The tide was low as I walked slowly along the shoreline. Prayers of gratitude spoke themselves in my mind. The rising sun ever so gently glorified the sky. I sat on the sand and closed my eyes in meditation. The spirit of the dolphins came to me and I basked in their love. I wondered if they would come again today. *Will I be lucky enough to swim with you two days in a row?*

I decided to play with my telepathy. I projected a question to the dolphins. *"Where are you in this moment?"* I paused, feeling my message being received. *"I invite you to come and play with us again today. Of course, I will honor whatever choice you make."*

I opened my eyes and looked far into the horizon. Way out there, a boat was making its way across the bay. I thought I saw something jump out of the water behind the boat. I waited and watched. *Could it be?* Sure enough, I saw it jump again.

I projected an invitation. *"Come closer! Come into the bay to play!"* With spiraling excitement, I watched and waited. In a matter of minutes, a lone dolphin jumped out of the water, at the dolphins' favorite hangout, just a short swim from shore.

"Thank you for coming! I love you so much!"

Still, not a single soul was stirring. I was thrilled to have this dolphin to myself at this early hour. I donned my snorkel gear and headed out into the bay. Each swim stroke felt strong and sure. I was incredibly grateful to be here, and to be welcomed so graciously into these waters.

I swam out to where I thought the dolphin was, but I didn't see him. I treaded water, watching and listening. Nothing. *Did he leave?*

I swam around, just for the pleasure of it, and soon a lone dolphin approached, staying deep below me. He stopped and looked at me, and then turned and swam in the direction from which he'd come. He looked back at me a few times as he swam away.

Silly me. I didn't realize that he had come to escort me to the pod! Since he didn't come close, I thought he didn't want to swim with me. I'm still learning their ways!

After awhile, I decided to swim back to shore. Lo and behold, during my swim in, I found the pod! They were in sleep mode. Their energy was soft, quiet, and *s l o w*. They swam languidly along the ocean floor, in a tight pod. In the time that I watched them—five, ten minutes?—they did not surface once to breathe. I decided to leave them alone. Soon enough, many humans would descend upon them. It felt right to not disturb their peace and quiet.

Anyway, it's not nearly as much fun being out here without a human playmate.

Hey wait a minute. Did I just think that? That's a shift!

In the past, my trips to the dolphins were so sacred, I didn't want to share them with anybody. It seems I've passed through that limitation ... now human companionship enhances my dolphin adventures!

I swam to shore and waited for Merlyn and Zoë to wake up. After a leisurely breakfast, we went in to play with the dolphins. By this time, many swimmers were in the water. It was great fun sharing these joyful encounters with my human friends!

The swim that day was very sweet. At one point, Zoë and I were bobbing at the surface together when a dolphin foursome approached us. They dove in unison, and Zoë and I dove after them. I decided, mid-dive, to let Zoë have this one. I backed off and floated at the surface and watched.

Zoë was beautiful. She is tall and lean and very graceful in the water. I watched her and the four dolphins hover several feet below the surface, communing in the silence of the underwater world. My heart pulsed open. What a joy to watch my friend in this loving encounter.

"The love and respect they feel for one another is extraordinary!"

Rising gracefully, Zoë broke through the surface, ecstatic and breathless. "We were one! That was so amazing! I get it now! We are the same!"

I was thrilled for my lovely new friend, and honored to witness her first moment of oneness with the dolphins.

A little while later, a foursome invited me to join them in a dive. We descended and hung upside down, gazing into each other's eyes. I felt a bubble of awareness enter me. Suddenly I knew all about their life as a family ... as a community. *The love and respect they feel for one another is extraordinary!*

We returned to surface (so I could breathe!), and the dolphins split off into two pairs ... and made love! I was positioned a little behind, and between them. From this perspective, their petite bodies looked huge! They coupled, belly-to-belly, and sustained their sexual connection for an unusually long time! The dolphin sexual act usually only lasts moments, and they're done. *This is dolphin*

tantra! My eyes were as wide as saucers, and I don't think I breathed until they separated!

Another bubble of awareness entered me as I received the dolphins' holographic message. They communicated that our dive, and my reception of their communication during our dive, was such an ecstatic experience for them that they had to express the energy that overflowed in them. They did that by making love.

These beings live ecstatic lives. Love and joy wells up inside them to the point of overflowing. In that ecstatic state, they reach out to one another and make love!

A little while later, I found myself alone in the bay. The dolphins and humans were spread out over a large area. I took the opportunity to tread water and rest, to let myself feel my emotions. Love welled up in me so strongly, I could not contain it. I was in tears again.

My body had to move. I had to move so that the intense love energy I was feeling could move through me. There was too much to release through my tiny little tear ducts.

I secured my mask, still crying softly, and swam at a leisurely pace. I heard myself speaking out loud through my snorkel, "I love you ... I love you ... I love you ..." to the dolphins. There were none nearby, but I was saying it to all of them nonetheless.

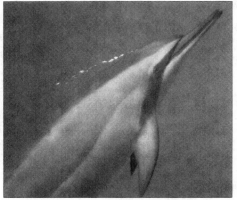

Suddenly, a dolphin appeared at my side. He matched my pace and swam beside me. I continued my verbal mantra, "I love you ... I love you ... I love you ...," gazing into his eye. My dolphin mate responded to each "I love you" with a whistle and a string of bubbles that looked like a string of pearls flowing out from his blowhole. Soon his whistle took the form of three short whistles. He's saying *"I love you" back!* We maintained eye contact as we swam and cooed to one another, "I love you ... I love you ... I love you ...," each in our own language, for as long as my stamina allowed.

On my last morning of this trip, I awoke to dense cloud cover and rain falling softly on my tent. I peeked out at the bay to find it quiet and still. The rain looked like it was just getting started, that it would last all day. I sighed with the realization that yesterday was it, that was the last I'd see of my dolphins, for this trip anyway. I tried to accept this. I'd received so many precious gifts! Still, I cried. The thought of leaving this place, "Bliss Bay," as I'd come to call it, was heart-wrenching.

An undercurrent of thought that had been with me throughout this trip rose to the surface.

Perhaps the dolphins will decide one day that they're done with this human-dolphin swim experiment. Maybe they'll choose to move on. As sad as that would be, it also feels right somehow. The day may come when they send us all out into the world with our dol-

phin school diplomas with the decree: *"Go forth into your world and create goodness by applying all that we have taught you."*

I may never see my dolphin family again. I may never swim with them again. Yesterday may have been the last time.

In a melancholic, pensive mood, I left my tent to walk up to the public restroom. No campers were moving yet. A lone car was parked in the parking lot with its engine running—doors open wide and radio blaring. A couple was standing in the rain, looking out at the bay.

As I walked up the pathway heading away from their car, I noticed that I was straining to hear the song that played on the radio.

"Wherever you go, whatever you do, I will be right here waiting for you ..." I burst into tears. The chorus repeated over and over, but I was no longer hearing the singer singing it. The dolphins were singing to me: *"Wherever you go, whatever you do, we will be right here waiting for you ..."*

Oh, did I cry. Yes, I'm leaving the island today, but the dolphins would not let me leave without assuring me that they will always be here, waiting for me to return.

I cry oceans of tears when I'm here. My inner ocean pours forth and joins the ocean that sustains and supports my dolphin family. I guess this is one way I leave some of my energy behind for them!

Thank you, dear ones. You have expanded my heart yet again. I leave you with renewed inspiration and hope.

I returned to my tent and wrote:

> I will do my best to love myself more, to treat myself and others with loving-kindness.
>
> I will bring more pleasure and play into my life.
>
> I will open myself more to my fellow humans and share your messages of love and life.
>
> Thank you for trusting me to be your ambassador to humans

on land. I will do my best. I know you are always by my side, guiding me and loving me. I love you too!

I am a better human because of you. Thank you from the bottom of my heart.

Merlyn, Zoë, and I shared breakfast that morning. I shed many tears of gratitude for the love, beauty, and magic of these timeless three days together.

As we took our last bites of mango and yogurt, and sipped our last sips of yerba maté, the light rainfall stopped and the sun broke through the clouds. I gazed out into the bay, taking a mental photograph. I did not want to forget a thing.

Leap ... Spin ... Splash ...

"Dolphins!!!" I squealed in excitement.

I could not believe my eyes. *They're here! I get one last swim with my beloveds before returning home to my magnificent red rock country!*

We jumped for joy, laughing like kids, and scurried to get into our suits.

This is meditation day. The dolphins stay below, hugging the bottom of their world. I am content to swim above, watching and feeling. Again, they move me so deeply.

From the moment of birth, these dolphins remain together as an extended family, every day of their lives. They live together, love together, play together, hunt together, sleep together, and meditate together. They do everything together! They truly enjoy each other's company.

As I watch them swim together, I see only love being expressed. *They love each other so much!*

I watch as two youngsters swim along the periphery of the pod, connecting pectoral fins, as if holding hands.

I watch as they gently bump up against each other, nuzzle each other, and glide against each other. *They love to give pleasure, one to the other.*

I watch the babies suckle as they swim. They play and test their boundaries, while mamas and aunties keep constant vigil. They venture out a little way on their own, and then they're reigned in when necessary, to teach them and to keep them safe.

I watch them make love. *Their lovemaking is a natural expression of the love they feel for the other. It overflows and they express it. It is beautiful. There is no shame.*

If everyone on this planet had the opportunity to witness what I've witnessed over the course of these three days, this planet would be a very different place.

Throughout time, dolphins have been called "angels of the sea" and "keepers of the light" for planet Earth. I've seen evidence of both.

By reaching out and touching those of us who are open, the dolphins are awakening the angels within us ... the light within us.

Thank you, beloveds, for reaching out and touching me. Thank you for loving me. Thank you for teaching me how to love.

TWENTY-FOUR

Drunk on Dolphin Love

A few months after David and I arrived back in Sedona, I began putting serious creative thought and attention to the next steps in my dolphin work. I designed and printed new business cards. I decided to begin offering weekly dolphin energy meditation evenings again. Our new home didn't have a room big enough for groups, so I researched and selected a gathering space I could rent.

When I gave these evenings in my home, I simply asked for a donation. Now that I needed to rent a space, I decided to charge a small fee for these evenings. I wanted to offer a discount for locals who would attend these dolphin energy evenings regularly. A moment of whimsical inspiration gave birth to the "Frequent Flipper Program!" When I told David about my idea and showed him the Frequent Flipper flyer I had created, he cracked up.

I printed a bunch of flyers and posted them around town, and placed a small ad in a local spiritual magazine. A few of my devoted regulars signed up as Frequent Flippers, but mostly the response was disappointing. Only a few people came to the evenings. And there were nights when no one came! This was utterly unlike my earlier years of offering dolphin meditation evenings in our home. I was perplexed and discouraged. *What am I doing wrong? Why aren't people coming?*

I knew enough about manifesting, self-responsibility, and the Law of Attraction to recognize that, somehow, my own frequency was creating this result. So I had to look inside. *Do I really want to give these weekly meditation evenings?* The truth was: *No. Been there, done that. I want to do something different.*

I realized that I had taken the easy path of doing what I knew—what worked in the past, what was comfortable for me—in an attempt to re-create the magic of those early years. The dolphins weren't letting me get away with it. It was time to grow and expand ... to step outside of my comfort zone ... again.

I want to go deeper.

Dolphin healing hearts ... dolphin healing hearts ... dolphin healing hearts ...

I woke up one morning with these words ringing in my head. *A new business name?* Throughout the day those words floated through my awareness. Finally, I sat down and wrote:

Dolphin Healing HeArts

The A in "Hearts" came out capitalized ... Dolphin Healing Hearts ... Dolphin Healing Arts

And then out came ...

... A Gateway to the New Paradigm

I knew what "new paradigm" meant, but I had no idea what this phrase had to do with what I would share in the world.

Dolphin Healing HeArts ... *A Gateway to the New Paradigm*

Okay! I'm curious. What's this about?

In sharing the dolphin energy with a wide range of people over the years, I was continually in awe of what the dolphins were able to accomplish in just a thirty-minute meditation, or a one-hour healing session.

Over and over again, I saw hearts touched and lives transformed in profound and wondrous ways. I often wondered, *If the dolphins can do such things for people in these brief encounters, what could they do if a group of people made the commitment to dive deeply into their consciousness, together, over time?*

In fact, a few years earlier, I added a "Deep Dive" program on my brochure that offered just that. Not one person asked about it. When I asked Dr. Peebles about it, he said, "*From what we can see here, my dear, you're a couple of years ahead of yourself. But go ahead and do it. Give it a try!*"

In receiving the message of this new name, I was excited! Now must be the time!

Thoughts and inspirations started to flow. An idea began to crystallize. For six-and-a-half years, ever since my first dolphin encounter, I'd given dolphin energy healing to individuals and groups. The dolphins had given me this gift directly. Now, for the first time, I began to envision passing this gift on to others.

I'd never thought of myself as a teacher, but why not? Teaching Dolphin Energy Healing would certainly be something new ... and deeper ... for me to share. This experience would surely expand and stretch me. Excitement bubbled up inside.

I came up with an initial structure for the training and wrote up a two-page information sheet. I wasn't comfortable using "A Gateway to the New Paradigm" in the name, because I didn't really understand it. So I referred to Dolphin Healing HeArts as "a Dolphin Energy Healing School." I printed a stack of flyers, posted them on bulletin boards around town, and placed a small ad in a local spiritual newspaper.

Weeks passed. No response. Again. *What is going on?*

♡

Meanwhile, in early October, I thought I was pregnant. The physical symptoms were all there. My breasts were swollen, my nipples were tender, and my sense of smell was supersensitive. When we fed our cats their wet food, I had to flee the kitchen because their food smelled so disgusting.

David and I were very open to having children. We both wanted at least one. I really wanted to experience the ultimate womanly journey of being pregnant, giving birth, and raising a child. I was so pleased to discover how great David was with kids! When I saw him in action with our precious goddaughter, Alana,* I knew he would be a really great dad.

There we were, both 47 years old, willing and hoping for a miracle. I believed it was still physically possible for me to have a child. I'd been pregnant twice already; both pregnancies ended in miscarriage. Would this third time be the charm?

My current symptoms completely matched my previous pregnancies. I'd been here before. So I waited impatiently to take a home pregnancy test, fully expecting a positive result. At the earliest possible moment, I took the test. It was negative! I waited a couple more unfathomably long days and took the test again. Negative again. I sure *felt* pregnant. *What's going on now?*

One night, I confided my suspicion and confusion to my good friend Susan Palmer. I first met Susan at Summer's open channeling sessions, and we became fast friends. The gang began affectionately calling Susan "SNN—Spirit News Network," because of her clear connection to spiritual sources and her ability to bring through accurate messages. Susan doesn't channel Dr. Peebles publicly, like Summer does, but I knew she sometimes connected with him in her meditations. I asked if she would be willing to ask him for some insight into what the heck was happening with my body.

When I opened my e-mail the next morning, Susan's message was waiting in my inbox:

---

* Alana is the daughter of Paula and David Green—remember the Maui wedding? My husband David and I assisted with Alana's home birth in 1999, and she's been an important and joyous part of our lives ever since.

Hi Linda,

Early this morning, I sat down and asked Dr. Peebles for a message for you in response to your question to me last night. I said, "Linda Shay has asked me to ask you a question on her behalf—she wants to know is she, or is she not, pregnant? She seems to be getting mixed messages on this."

Then I picked up my pen and paper and wrote down what "came through:"

"Dear Linda,

You are indeed 'pregnant,' my dear friend, but not pregnant with child. Rather, my dear, you are pregnant with 'Self.' At long last you are on the verge of 'birthing' your true nature into this physical reality—the 'birth of LINDA'— who SHE truly IS, the fullness of the expression of the Spirit of God that you are, now fully coming to the surface in the physical.

And this is no small feat of accomplishment, we assure you. If the truth be known, for most people, falling fully into LIFE is much more terrifying than the fear of death. But you have at long last now made a determination to step into the fire of your Soul and to bring YOURSELF fully to the surface. And this, my dear friend, is truly to be 'pregnant' with Self, and to 'birth' your own Spirit—which is why you were feeling that the 'child' within your womb was a 'girl'—and so it is, my dear, for it is the birth of YOU, fully expressed in human female form upon the Earth.

And so, while your physical pregnancy tests have always been 'negative,' i.e., no fetus developing in the womb of your physical body, your perceptions of the 'symptoms' of pregnancy have indeed been accurate. You are feeling this birthing of Self in your soul and spiritual body—a simultaneous awareness of yourself on different dimensions of your being. Although your physical body is not, and was not pregnant, your Soul certainly is!"

Hope this helps. Love, Susan

As I read Dr. Peebles' message, waves of confirmation shivers passed through my body. It was extraordinary to realize that my body was experiencing this spiritual birth in such a physical way! I was so grateful to Susan for bringing this profound message through for me. It helped me to surrender, fully and consciously, to this birthing of my Self that was occurring at the level of my soul.

About a week later, my dear friend Isaac George called to say he was coming through Sedona for a visit. Isaac channels Archangel Ariel, and he also has a profound dolphin connection. Years earlier he found his way to one of my dolphin meditation evenings. It was the first time Isaac felt safe enough to share the story of his own life-changing dolphin experience. We became instant friends. I adore him.

Isaac was planning a public event in Sedona for the evening of November 11. He wanted dolphin energy to be a part of the event, and he invited me to co-create the evening with him. I jumped at the chance!

We began exchanging ideas. Isaac came up with the event name: *11:11—The Eternal Wave.* I created the flyer. We sent e-mail announcements to our e-mail lists, and I posted the flyers around town.

The day before the event, Isaac and I met to finalize the program. He was planning to play his guitar for some of the program—music is one of his passions. He told me he was having a blast making dolphin and whale songs on his electric guitar. Then I heard myself say, "I can sing my dolphin song, and you can accompany me on guitar!"

What did I just say?

Dr. Peebles had been telling me for a while about my connection to sound. **"You have the sounds of creation and destruction inside of you, my dear. It's incredible! One day these sounds will come through in your healings."**

Every time Dr. Peebles encouraged me to explore expressing energies through sound, I resisted. *I don't think so! Bringing through dolphin energy for people is one thing. Making sounds is something else altogether. It's just too weird.*

But Dr. P was persistent. **"You have a very beautiful dolphin song inside of** you, my dear. It will be an ecstatic experience for you to surrender to the dolphin that you are, and sing your dolphin song!"

Once again, Dr. P had planted a seed. Sometimes, when I was meditating or facilitating a healing, a surge of energy would arise from deep within my belly. I knew that this energy wanted to be expressed through sound. But I was still too shy and self-conscious to open my mouth and let those who-knows-what-they-will-sound-like sounds come out of me.

My spontaneous outburst of volunteering to sing my dolphin song, in front of a room full of people, was pretty remarkable.

Whenever these urges occurred, I negotiated with my dolphin spirit friends inside myself: *"I will allow the 'frequency' of the sounds to come through me in the form of energy, but I'm not comfortable making the actual sounds."* This worked ... sort of. The dolphins honored my "no," but after these experiences, I always felt a bit yucky inside. I knew that I was holding back.

By the time of this 11:11 event, I had been holding back in this way for years. So my spontaneous outburst of volunteering to sing my dolphin song, in front of a room full of people, was pretty remarkable. I didn't feel any shyness or resistance at all. I felt excited and powerful!

November 11 arrived. Isaac and I met at the space in the afternoon to set up. When we opened the doors, half an hour before starting time, it was thrilling to see so many people already waiting outside. Soon the room was packed. More than sixty people came! Every seat was filled, and many sat on the floor or stood around the perimeter of the room. I was particularly relieved, given the dismal attendance record at my own events these past months! Clearly, Isaac and Ariel were the draw tonight. I was grateful to be a part of the program!

I began the evening with a dolphin meditation. I told the group that I wanted them to meet some of my friends. First I brought in the Hawaiian spinner dolphins, and we meditated in their high, fine frequency. Then I introduced Grandfather, who brought the group into his deep silence. The last special guest to grace the group was Keiko, who enveloped us all in his huge, pure heart.

When the meditation ended, everyone was glowing. I asked the group if they were able to discern a difference between the energies. The answer was an enthusiastic "Yes!"

Then Isaac channeled Archangel Ariel. The energy and message were beautiful and powerful. Starting the evening with the dolphin meditation was a lovely way to open everyone's field to deeply receive Ariel's love and wisdom. It was a beautiful blending of energy and experiences.

Then came the evening finale—our duet performance. Isaac and I joined one another in the front of the room and announced what we were going to do next. Isaac started playing cosmic instrumental weavings on his guitar. I stood at the microphone, closed my eyes, silently invoked my inner dolphin to come forth, and gave her complete permission to sing her song.

As soon as I heard Isaac's dolphin and whale sounds, my dolphin song emerged. A wide range of notes and tones came through me, some short and some sustained. I held nothing back. The sounds were clear, loud, and powerful.

Never before had I done such a thing. It hadn't occurred to us to practice. We just did it. Isaac kept playing. I kept singing. It was ecstasy.

David: I was standing in the back of the room during Linda and Isaac's duet. When they announced what they were going to do, I sensed some skepticism in the group. Even for Sedona, this seemed pretty bizarre. Then Linda's dolphin song began, with Isaac's beautiful music accompanying. I felt a shiver go through the whole room. **Whoa.** A gentle, loving dolphin was singing to us all. Her song wasn't just powerful, it was plaintive, poetic, and deeply moving. Everyone was transfixed.

After our musical performance, we invited everyone to dance. A woman came up to me and said, "You really *are* a dolphin, aren't you?"

"Yes! I am!"

"That took a lot of courage to get up there and show your authentic self like that!"

"Thank you!"

But it wasn't "courage" I felt. It was release, relief ... *freedom!*

We completed the evening with a beautiful closing circle. Our hearts were all wide open, and full of love and joy. The evening was a great success!

When we got into the car to drive home, David turned to me with wide eyes and said, "You were amazing! I looked around while you were singing and saw the looks on people's faces. Everyone was mesmerized. They were captivated by your sounds!"

A few teeny-tiny twinges of discomfort were sparking in my belly ... kind of like that "morning after" feeling of "What have I done?" But mostly, I was really proud of myself!

I was so high and energized. With a huge smile on my face, I said to my sweetie, "That was SO MUCH FUN!" We burst into loud laughter, joyously celebrating my breakthrough accomplishment.

Isaac and I talked the next day. We were both thrilled with the whole evening. Our only regret was that it hadn't occurred to us to record our unique musical performance!

♡

I had high hopes that that evening would be a launching pad for my new Dolphin Energy Healing School. I had updated the information sheet and handed out copies at the event. Days passed. Weeks passed. There was no response. None.

I honestly did not know what was happening. I had no idea what was missing in what I was trying to do.

♡

Ripples of fear began bubbling up inside of me. This fear wasn't ever-present; it came and went, like a sly stray cat who wanders the streets, allowing only the briefest of glimpses before retreating to a safe, dark, hidden place. As fall gave way to winter, shadowy tendrils of this fear began licking more boldly and insistently at my feet.

On the outside, I was doing everything I could possibly think of to expand my dolphin work into the world in new ways. But inside, something else was going on ... something I didn't understand. One day, an image came into my mind. I saw myself digging my heels into the earth—into sand, actually. I didn't just see it, I felt it. I heard myself pleading inside: *No, No, No!*

I felt a huge energy hovering just outside of my energy field, in front of me. Something big was coming. A new way to do my dolphin work in the world? Whatever it was, I was terrified.

And that didn't make any sense. I was already trying to do my work in a new way, without success. The latest idea of teaching Dolphin Energy Healing excited me! So why wasn't it happening? Why weren't people showing up? And why the fear?

Where is this coming from?

Meanwhile, my dolphin meditation evenings were leaking money. I was paying for the space every week, and attendance wasn't even covering my costs. There was one more evening scheduled, then I would have to decide whether to rent the space for another month. More than a little discouraged, I considered canceling the evening altogether. But, ever hopeful, I decided to give it one more chance. In the preceding days, I pleaded with the dolphins: *"If you want me to keep doing these evenings, bring the people—bring new people!"*

The day of the meditation arrived. Early in the day it became clear to me that the dolphins had something special in mind for this potentially last meditation. All through the day I felt their energy around me building and building. The potency and urgency in the air was palpable. I let my consciousness explore these new energies surrounding me, and a knowing flowed through me: *Tonight I need to dive deeply into the dolphin energy, as never before. I need to surrender to the dolphins completely. Tonight is going to be special—this meditation is for me.*

Only two people came for the evening—my two most loyal regulars, Joe and

Michael. *Perfect! There's no one new. It's just us.* My concerns about attendance were completely forgotten.

After hugging hello, I announced, "We're going to dispense with the dancing and opening circle tonight. The energy is so intense right now I'm feeling the need to dive right in."

Quickly, we created our spaces on the floor. I usually played a CD of dolphin sounds in the background during these meditations, but tonight I didn't even do that. We entered into this meditation in silence.

I lay down on the floor, and the very high, fine frequencies of the dolphins instantly engulfed me. I surrendered completely as their exquisite energy seeped deeply into my body. Deeper and deeper they went ... slowly ... deliberately.

Every cell and space of my being was loved, nurtured, and caressed by dolphin energy. I felt their energy penetrate all the way into me, all the way through *to the marrow of my bones*. It was extraordinary. In all my years of journeying with the dolphins, I'd never felt anything like this.

Slowly, gently, my senses returned to the room. Focusing on my body and breath, I eased out of the meditation experience. My whole body was buzzing intensely. Perhaps an hour had passed; I didn't know. I was breathless, barely able to sit up. When I did speak, I was panting as if I'd just run a race. Physically, I was completely spent. I felt as though the dolphins had made mad, passionate love to every single cell of my body!

I'd experienced many extraordinary dolphin meditations. I'd had exquisite and profound experiences swimming in the ocean with the physical dolphins. But something important happened this night—something brand new.

Joe and Michael shared their experiences, which were wonderful, but they did not experience what I did. We lingered in our small circle for a while, talking and sharing, until I was able to stand up. They helped me with clean up; we hugged our goodnights, and then we all left to drive home. Luckily, I didn't have far to drive!

All the while, this extravagant, beyond-orgasmic experience of joy and ecstasy continued. It was still going on when I went to sleep that night, and when I woke up the next morning ... and the next morning ... and the next.

For three days I was drunk on dolphin love. My body was in a perpetual state of buzz. I was giddy with joy. I felt like skipping instead of walking! Sparks of joy flew off me everywhere I went. My joy was contagious! Strangers I passed burst into huge smiles. Meaningful glances of joy and recognition passed between us, warming and lighting up our hearts. Ecstasy surrounded me.

Finally, on the fourth day, I mellowed out. I'm not sure if I came down, or if I just got used to living in this expanded state. I think it was a little bit of both.

I did cancel the weekly meditations after that night. It seemed they had served their purpose! I still wasn't sure what the next step was, but I was no longer worried about it.

TWENTY-FIVE

Awakening

A month after that momentous meditation, I flew back to Pittsburgh for my annual Christmas visit with my family. As my visit was winding down, I got sick. It seemed to be the flu. I was still sick when I boarded the plane to fly home. When I opened my mouth to speak to the flight attendant, no sound came out. *Ugh ... laryngitis.* The symptoms dragged on and on for five long weeks.

About two weeks in, every bone in my body ached. I'd never had bone pain before; it was intense. The pain seemed to radiate out *from the marrow of my bones.* For three days I couldn't sit, stand, or lie down without being in pain. I was crawling in my skin, trying to get out.

On the third day of excruciating bone pain I remembered my experience in that exquisite meditation, when the dolphin love energy penetrated all the way through me ... to the marrow of my bones. And then I knew: *This is not just "the flu." This pain in my bones is not a coincidence. Something divine is going on here.*

This awareness helped me surrender to the pain. Letting go of my resistance to it, I became curious about it, and entered into deep observation of my internal body experience. It was fascinating. Over the following days, the bone pain slowly dissipated until, finally, it was gone. The remaining symptoms—low energy, chest congestion, and an interminable cough—lingered on.

Dolphin Love

♡

One glorious morning in January 2003, I woke up symptom-free. And I woke up *brand new*.

This was not the temporary high of feeling wonderful after being sick for a long time. This was different. I couldn't put my finger on it. The thought kept echoing in my mind, over and over: *I am brand new*.

Over the next several days that feeling of *newness* stayed with me. Something huge had shifted inside. I was fundamentally different.

Ecstasy and bliss filled my days. My phone started ringing, after months of silence, with invitations to share my dolphin work in new ways. Without hesitation I responded to each offer with a resounding "Yes!" *I'm not holding back anymore!* With each new opportunity, my energy leapt forward with joy and enthusiasm. *This is new!*

A part of me was standing outside myself, observing my new self being in the world in new ways. *Who is this person?*

I delighted in what I was seeing. This new Linda was fearless. That terror I'd been feeling earlier? Gone. Just ... *gone*.

This new Linda was speaking to groups about the dolphins and joy without any thought or care as to what anyone might think or say. I printed prepublication copies of my book, took them to a book fair, and presented myself, for the first time, as an author.

One woman browsed through my book and said softly, "You're really out there. You know that, don't you?"

"Yep!" I responded with a big smile. "This is my life!"

This new Linda was outgoing and enthusiastic. I was expressing my true self in the world with complete abandon. I didn't care if people approved. I didn't care if they thought I was crazy. I felt absolutely uninhibited and free to be me. I was completely in my joy. I had so much fun being me ... in front of lots of people ... it was intoxicating!

Something else that was new was my energy level. I felt like the Energizer

Bunny! I woke up at the crack of dawn and created, created, created into the wee hours of the morning, working on whatever project presented itself, day after day. My energy was endless!

Gone were the self-doubts. Gone was my shyness. Most amazingly, gone were my fears!

David was observing all of this newness—for him, it was pretty bizarre. More than once, he looked at me and said, "Who are you—and what have you done with my wife?"

He was joking ... but not really. The change in me was profound. My gut-level responses to life, and my resulting choices and behaviors, were utterly unlike the me that David had known for seven years.

I had the feeling that I had been lifted up onto a magic carpet. Now I was being carried through life. Doors opened, and I passed through them with joy and ease. I was in awe and wonder at this new world—and this new self—I was discovering. Everything was effortless and imbued with magic. I was completely in flow. The days of effort and struggle were over.

A part of me wondered, and waited, for this high to fade—for my old world and my old patterns of behavior to return. That just didn't happen.

The shift was so dramatic it seemed to happen overnight. In reality, it was the culmination of a seven-year inner journey—choreographed, guided, and supported by my beloved dolphin family.

This is Grace. Grace is lifting me up above the tumult and fray of the mundane world. Grace is leading me through my life now.

I became increasingly curious about what, exactly, had happened to me. I was also curious about how this transformation was going to affect my life. At Summer's next open channeling session, I asked Dr. Peebles about it:

Dolphin Love

"My dear, what you call the flu was really a total and complete cleansing of your physical body, 100%, from the inside, out. You asked for that, my dear. You demanded no less! You are now completely *awake*. Do you understand? Now your life is about instant manifestation. *Now you are ready to put yourself in front of the public, my dear!*"

He sounded like a proud papa. A quiver of excitement passed through my body, as the most wonderful two words in the world resonated in me: *It's time!*

Another subtle shift occurred with my awakening. I became much more receptive to direct communication with the Dolphin Consciousness. In this new reality, it was as if the dolphins' thoughts *were* my thoughts. There seemed to be no separation in our "thinking." I could discern when thoughts or ideas came from the dolphins. No "thinking" was involved, actually. It was more of a feeling process that produced completed thoughts in my mind—they just popped in, fully formed.

This ongoing inner dialog with the dolphins felt so natural and normal to me I didn't even notice that it was new! To me, it felt like conversation with the dolphins had always been going on inside my mind. It was David who observed this change. He pointed out that this wasn't how my mind used to work. Thinking back to my pre-awakening reality—which wasn't easy to do!—I could see that he was right.

I've come to use the word "Dolphin" when I refer to this Dolphin Consciousness that communicates with me. The term "Dolphin" is both singular and plural. There is one "voice" that communicates with me, and it has a singular feeling. But this voice represents the collective dolphin consciousness. The dolphins don't seem to distinguish between "the one" and "the many" in the same way that we humans do. For them it's very natural that the one is the many, and the many are one.

So, in speaking about these communications, I refer to Dolphin (singular) as "they" (plural). It's both.

The first, and most precious, realization that came to me from Dolphin was that these beloved beings had found a way to give me my deepest heart's desire—a desire that, in my mind, was impossible to achieve. I had wanted, with all of my being, to *dissolve the illusion of separation between me and the dolphins.* I wanted to merge with them ... to become one with them. I wanted to *be* the frequency that they carry ... *all of the time.*

That's true for me now.

Dolphin confirmed my feeling that they had conducted an experiment on me. A peculiar message Dr. Peebles gave me, about five years into my journey, popped into my mind:

"My dear, you are undergoing a profound change at this time. Billions of teeny-tiny spirit dolphins have entered into your body and taken up residence in every single cell! These tiny spirit dolphins are making changes that will result in a complete metamorphosis of your human form. I do not have permission to tell you anything more at this time, but it is quite fantastic, my dear!"

Dolphin found a way to merge their dolphin consciousness with my human consciousness, creating a brand new quality of consciousness—a blended human-dolphin consciousness. The profound changes Dolphin made to my physical and energetic structures have enabled me to carry, and sustain, the dolphin frequencies. I am now able to radiate the beautiful healing frequencies of the dolphins out into

the world, anywhere, anytime, just by being myself! The morning I woke up feeling brand new was the moment this metamorphosis was complete.

♡

The implications of this left me spinning! I reflected upon all the times I had turned away from the dolphins, out of frustration and despair. I thought of how much energy I wasted as my head and my heart did battle. My head insisted that this dolphin journey made no sense. My heart knew that I had to persevere. I had to keep going.

Despite the struggles of my mind, I trusted the dolphins completely. Yes, I strayed from this path from time to time. Every time I did, my life fell apart. In my desperation and seeking, something or someone would nudge me back to the dolphins. The moment I felt their love again, I felt like I had come home. Each time I returned to their path of love and joy, I surrendered more deeply to the mystery and the unknown. I had no idea where this journey was leading, and it no longer mattered. I just needed to keep moving forward.

The dolphins were infinitely patient with me. They never gave up on me. They never abandoned me. I must also acknowledge myself for the perseverance, tenacity, and radical trust that enabled me to go the distance.

Ultimately, love and surrender trumped fear and resistance. Now my heart is leading the way. An incredible miracle has occurred. My impossible dream has come true. A new life has begun.

TWENTY-SIX

It's Time!

Full of excitement and anticipation, I sat down at my computer to create a flyer for introductory evenings to announce the formation of my first Dolphin Healing HeArts program. Now I was ready to embrace the full name Dolphin had given me: "Dolphin Healing HeArts ... *A Gateway to the New Paradigm.*"

The content of the flyer flowed effortlessly through me. In addition to guided meditations and other interdimensional experiences with the dolphins, I would teach Dolphin Energy Healing, and offer a certification program to those who wanted to pursue this form of healing as a career.

Dolphin told me that they needed many humans to help them transmit their healing energy on land—to people, animals, plants—to all of life! They wanted to expand the scope of their healing capacity on the planet, and to educate humanity that it's not necessary to be in their physical presence to receive their love and healing gifts. In my heart, I knew that humanity was ready to receive healing from the dolphins in this way. *It's time!*

Since one of my objectives was to emulate the dolphins' experience of Unity-Community on land, among humanity, I was inspired to call my groups "pods," and my students "podmates." I much prefer the inclusive feeling of pods and podmates to the words "student" and "class." To me, those words carry an energy of separation and hierarchical structure. That's not what the dolphins are about!

When I looked over what I'd written, it dawned on me. *I'm creating a school!* That was a surprise. Even though I knew I would be teaching something, and I would have podmates, I was still thinking of this endeavor as a little class or workshop. What was coming out of my fingers on the keyboard, and appearing on the screen in front of me, was more than I had imagined.

I'd never done anything like this before. I'd led group meditations. I'd managed staff back in my corporate days. In all of my imaginings about these deep dives with groups of people into the dolphin consciousness over time, I never thought about them being structured in this way. This was new information!

As I let this idea in, I got a bit nervous. I wondered if I was getting ahead of myself—if the concept of a school was premature.

Summer Bacon was having an open channeling that week. I decided to go, to ask Dr. Peebles if I was on track with this whole school idea.

When my name was called, even before I finished asking my question, Dr. Peebles began nodding his head vigorously:

"Yes, my dear! It's time! The dolphins are ready for many people on the planet to be doing this work! But, my dear, you will be doing more than teaching the healing skills. Rather, you will be attuning your students to the energy and frequency of the dolphins. Do you understand?"

"Yes," I replied, automatically.

Afterward, I thought, *No ... I don't understand. Attuning students to the energy and frequency of the dolphins is a whole other thing!*

The morning of my first introductory evening, I sat down to prepare my presentation. I received a download of information directly from Dolphin that gave me a very clear picture of what they were going to do with the people who would participate in these pods. I was blown away.

Dolphin told me that other humans could now benefit from the work we had done together. Others could now receive the gift of dolphin consciousness that the dolphins gave to me! I knew in my heart that a gift such as this is not meant for one person alone. This gift is meant to be shared.

Dolphin continued ... as a result of their experiment on me, they created a blueprint of spiritual initiations. I called these initiations "Dolphin Attunements," because of Dr. Peebles' descriptive words: **"You will be attuning students to the energy and frequency of the dolphins."**

Dr. Peebles had already told me that my pods needed to gather six times, and that these gatherings needed to be spread out over time. It followed that if they were to gather six times, there must be six Dolphin Attunements. With that thought, a shiver of confirmation passed through my body. Through these six Dolphin Attunements, my podmates would receive the gift of this brand new quality of consciousness. They would become human-dolphins too!

I was speechless. This little school that I was in the very beginning stages of creating was much more ... much bigger ... than what I thought I was going to be doing.

In light of this information, I saw my role more as a guide and mentor than a teacher. I'd be teaching Dolphin Energy Healing, and certifying those who wanted to become Dolphin Energy Practitioners; but my primary job would be to hold sacred space for others to receive the Dolphin Attunements, and to support and mentor them in integrating this new quality of consciousness into their lives.

Witnessing the transmission of a brand new quality of consciousness to my fellow humans felt like a tremendous responsibility.

"We are changing the course of humanity," I heard from within.

In my bones, I felt: *This is what I'm here to do.* I also knew that I would not be alone. Dolphin would be by my side every step of the way.

Dolphin Love

That evening I waited with curiosity to see who would show up to learn about my new school. The doorbell rang. My dear friend Jeanne had arrived. We waited to see if anyone else would come, and no one did. It was just us. Jeanne had received several dolphin energy healing sessions from me over the years, and had attended many of my dolphin meditations. A gifted healer in her own right, Jeanne was curious about my new adventure.

 They wanted to show me the difference between a Dolphin Attunement and a Dolphin Energy Healing session.

After my presentation, Jeanne looked at me, wide-eyed, and said, "I want this!"

My first podmate!

I felt dolphin energy buzzing strongly all around me. I tuned in and received the message that I was to give Jeanne her first Dolphin Attunement ... *now!*

This surprised me, because Dolphin had told me, rather emphatically, that the Attunements were not to be given to individuals; rather, they are to be transmitted to groups—to pods. This is part of the Unity-Community aspect of the process. Dolphin assured me that was still true. They were making an exception here, because they wanted me to experience what it was like to facilitate the transmission of a Dolphin Attunement before the first gathering of my first pod. They wanted to show me the difference between a Dolphin Attunement and a Dolphin Energy Healing session.

I gave Jeanne this news, and we practically leapt out of our seats with excitement! This felt like a profoundly sacred moment.

I led Jeanne into my healing room and had her lie down, face-up, on my massage table. When she was ready, I stood at her head and placed my hands on her shoulders. I closed my eyes and tuned into Dolphin. I told them I was turning this over to them, as I had no idea what was going to happen. I relaxed, let go, and allowed the experience to unfold.

The first thing I noticed was that the Attunement was transmitted in a matter of minutes, if not seconds. My healing sessions normally last up to an hour. I was also distinctly aware that the Attunement wasn't coming *through* me, as healing energy does. I had absolute knowing that Jeanne was receiving this transmission directly from Dolphin. My job was to hold sacred space for the transmission to occur.

There was an *otherworldliness* feeling in the room. This transmission did not source from planet Earth. It was cosmic. It came from somewhere far, far away. And the content of the transmission was far beyond my human understanding.

It felt huge.

I stayed with Jeanne for a while longer, not believing that my part was really over so soon. When I was sure there was nothing more for me to do, I told Jeanne I was going to leave her alone in the energy. When she felt complete, she could join me in the living room.

As I closed the door of my healing room behind me, I paused, overcome by the significance of what had just happened. My first thought was: *We're making more people like me now! I'm not going to be alone anymore!* Tears of gratitude and relief poured out of me.

I could barely comprehend the magnitude of what was taking place here—of the gift the dolphins were bringing to humanity through this newly created little school. I was humbled by the trust Dolphin had in me to be the bearer of this gift.

I went into the kitchen and put a tray of chocolate chip cookies into the oven to bake, for a celebration treat to share when Jeanne emerged from her first Dolphin Attunement. I closed the oven door, and the telephone rang. I laughed and cried when I heard David's voice.

He was in New Jersey on business. "I'm driving down the Garden State Parkway, and I felt a sudden urge to call."

We're so connected! I told him that I had just transmitted my first Dolphin Attunement to Jeanne.

He fell silent and felt the energy of it. Then he said, "Whoa ... I want that too!"

In that moment, David got what Dolphin Healing HeArts was really all about. Throughout my journey, David had the idea that I was special. He saw the profound connection I had with the dolphins as something that was unique to me. He could perceive it, appreciate it, and benefit from it—but it wasn't something he thought he could ever share. When David felt into the energy of the Attunement, he realized that the gift I'd received from the dolphins was now available to anyone who wanted to receive it. He wanted to receive it!

After we hung up and I took the cookies out of the oven to cool, I sat in the living room and waited for Jeanne to emerge. Soon, I heard her soft footsteps padding down the hall.

Joining me on the couch, Jeanne looked at me intensely with her big brown eyes. "Wow. That was the most powerful energy experience I have ever felt in my life. And it was powerful from the moment you laid your hands on my shoulders. It was as if a river of energy just poured into me, and ran through me, and kept on going."

TWENTY-SEVEN

Whale

The inaugural Dolphin Healing HeArts pod was scheduled to begin April 11, 2003. It was early March now, and I had a window of a couple of weeks free. I felt my Hawaiian spinner dolphin family calling me, big time. Hesitantly, I approached David with this news. I told him I really wanted to swim with the dolphins one more time before the first pod gathered. It felt like they had something important to give me, to prepare me for this next big leap in our work together.

David wanted to go too, but he couldn't take the time off work. He was so great. He didn't let that stand in the way of my going. He knew how important it was. "Next time we'll go together," we promised one another.

Next time, you'll be a dolphin too! I smiled to myself.

It was nearing the end of humpback whale season in Hawaii. I was only vaguely aware of that. As with all the trips that came before, this trip was all about the dolphins for me. I was curious about how this trip might be different, in light of my recent awakening.

Arriving at the Kona airport, taking those first steps into the luxuriously warm, moist tropical air was a feast for my senses. Bliss enveloped me as I made my way through the open-air airport to pick up my luggage.

It's always a joy to arrive in Hawaii. The welcoming ritual is a lovely custom. Friends or family members (or tour guides!) await the arrival of their traveler, floral leis in hand. When they meet, the greeter says "Aloha" and places the lei around the traveler's neck. The finishing touch is kisses on both cheeks.

There wasn't anyone there to greet me personally; as usual, I hadn't told anyone I was coming! So I partook, vicariously and shamelessly, in the joyous welcoming that was occurring all around me. The gorgeous tropical flowers, growing abundantly everywhere I turned, formed the energetic lei around my neck. The warm, salty sea breeze, wafting up from the ocean just a few miles below, kissed my cheeks.

With suitcase in hand, I giggled at the thought of wanting to strip down naked, right then and there, to discard my cumbersome mainland clothes and don my light, breezy island wear—bathing suit, sarong, and flip-flops. *Soon! Soon!*

Getting into the rental car, I made it my first order of business to turn off the air conditioning that was blasting icy cold air at me, and wind down the windows to let in the sun-drenched fresh air.

I made the requisite first stop at Walmart to buy necessities for the trip. Yes, there's a Walmart on the Big Island ... some things you can't escape! I bought sunscreen, a straw beach mat, a sun hat, a supply of underwater disposable cameras, dark(!) chocolate-covered macadamia nuts, and, of course, a box of tissues. I always cry so much on these trips!

The hour-long drive to my destination was therapeutic. As the familiar landscape passed by, and the brilliantly sparkling Pacific Ocean beckoned seductively all along the roadway, I felt all the tension and stress of the trip let go.

Upon arrival at the place where I was staying, I quickly unloaded my suitcases, changed into my island clothes *(ahhhhhh!)*, and got back into the car for my first visit to that most special place on this island. It was around 5 p.m. by the time I arrived. No other cars or people were in sight. I had the bay to myself. This pleased me.

I picked a spot to sit on the black volcanic rock wall that overlooks the bay. While settling in, my gaze swept across the wide expanse of water. There were no dolphins there now; but I didn't expect them to be here this time of day. That wasn't why I was here. This first visit was just to connect—to merge my body and soul with this place that feels like one of my sacred homes on this huge, beautiful planet.

With open eyes and heart, I fully took in the scene. Breathing deeply, I welcomed the essence of this place into me. The dolphin energy was strong here, as it always is, whether the dolphins are physically present or not.

"I'm here!" I projected telepathically to my dolphin family. I knew they already knew it, but my human self wanted to say it anyway. *"I hope to see you soon, and to swim and play with you ... maybe tomorrow?"*

I closed my eyes for a while and went deeply into myself, just being and enjoying. When I opened my eyes, my gaze fell upon a particular spot on the distant horizon, just as a flash of something disappeared into the water. Barely breathing, my eyes remained glued to that spot ... out there. Waiting ... waiting ...

A blow! A humpback whale blow! My heart pounded wildly in my chest.

"Hello!!!! ... I'm here! ... Thank you for showing yourself to me! ... You're so beautiful!"

I waited and watched some more, but there was no more whale activity I could see. That one blow was my "Aloha" welcome to the island—by the whales! What an unexpected surprise!

♡

The following morning I awoke at dawn and prepared for my first swim with the dolphins. The usual question passed through my mind and pestered me all the way down to the bay. *Will they be there?*

They were. But something was different inside of me. When I first saw the large pod of dolphins splashing in the bay, leaping exuberant invitations to come play, nothing happened inside. I felt no excitement, no rush of emotions, no pounding of the heart. I felt no sensation of urgency to rush out to them in fear that they might leave before I reach them.

I stood there, looking out at the dolphins leaping and spinning, and I felt oddly neutral inside. I didn't know what was going on, but I suited up and entered the water to begin the half-mile swim to meet them anyway. I expected my emotions to kick in as I came closer to the dolphins. But they didn't. Even when I caught that first underwater glimpse of my dolphin family, my body energy and emotional state remained steadfastly calm and neutral.

This is weird. Why am I not feeling anything?

I swam with the dolphins for two hours, all the while in that neutral state. I wanted to have feelings, but I didn't. It was strange. I missed the adrenaline rush of the emotional high.

When I called and talked to David about it when I got back to my room, I described my experience as being in the state of "Is-ness." Everything just *was*.

Over the next several days, whether I was alone in my room, or in the water with the dolphins, I remained in that state. Deep stillness enveloped me. I was in an altered state of consciousness that transcended human emotion. The thought went through my mind, *This feels strange*. But even that was just an idea. There was no *feeling* of strangeness. Everything just was. No good or bad. No right or wrong. Only the silence and tranquility of pure being.

As I was coming out of the water from my first swim, I bumped into Zoë, my Dutch dolphin sister I'd met a year earlier. We had a wonderful reunion, quickly catching up on each other's lives.

Zoë confided that she had to leave the island in a couple of weeks—her six-month visa was due to expire. She was entertaining ideas about places to go to pass the time until she was allowed back into the States. She didn't want to return home to Holland, even for six months, but she was feeling intuitively that she might have to. Zoë felt that all the time she'd spent in Hawaii swimming with the dolphins had changed her. Holland no longer felt like home. She didn't think she could be her true self there. She didn't think she could find people there she could really connect with.

I told her my news—that I was in the process of gathering my first Dolphin Healing HeArts pod! I shared about the Dolphin Attunements, Dolphin Energy Healing training, and the certification program for Dolphin Energy Practitioners.

Zoë was fascinated. She particularly resonated with the idea of Dolphin Energy Healing. "I think I'd like to learn that!" she remarked. Her enthusiastic response excited me! This beautiful woman, who swims with wild dolphins six months out of every year, was interested in learning Dolphin Energy Healing! I took that as a very good sign.

The possibility of Zoë receiving this training was a recurring topic of conversation throughout our time together. We agreed to stay in touch with one another when we both returned home, to explore how and when we could make that happen.

Meanwhile, another kind of buzz was happening on the Big Island. Peace Troubadour James Twyman's first Psychic Children's Conference was beginning in a few days. This was a big event, drawing participants and attendees from around the world.

I heard about this when I was scheduling my trip, and I asked the dolphins if I was to attend. Their response was immediate and clear: *"No."* But the timing of my trip, so close to the start of that event, seemed significant. I had a sense I would meet someone connected with the conference.

Sure enough, Merlyn and Zoë invited me to a private gathering with one of the psychic "children" who would be presenting at the conference. She was known as Grandmother Chandra.

Chandra was born with multiple physical handicaps, and as an infant began displaying extraordinary spiritual gifts. At the time we met, she was 19 years old. She was just beginning to make sounds with her voice, and to walk short distances with a walker. When she was 16, Chandra was given the title "Grandmother" by Native American Chief Golden Eagle, who recognized her as an original pipe carrier, or wisdom bearer. Over the course of her life, Chandra and her mother, Cat, mastered the ability of communicating telepathically. Cat now serves as Chandra's interpreter.

Zoë and I drove together to the private home where the gathering was being held. We were directed to a large yurt, situated a short distance away from the main house. There we joined the group that had gathered to spend private time with Grandma Chandra and Cat—about sixteen of us altogether.

When I first saw Chandra, my heart melted. She was having some difficulty negotiating the uneven terrain outside with her walker. Her physical body was quite petite. She looked much younger than her 19 years. She had dark, wavy hair and large, wide-open, penetrating brown eyes. She had on a very cute outfit. Her top was pink and sparkly. Through Cat, she told us that pink was one of her favorite colors, and that she *loved* sparkles!

While her physical handicaps were clearly evident, Chandra oozed wit and charm. Her natural, matter-of-fact way of being captured our hearts. Her sheer joy at being there with us put us all at ease.

Our host suggested that we start our time together by playing. He offered up a wide array of musical instruments to choose from. What delighted me most was a complete collection of Boomwhackers, a most ingenious percussion instrument that was invented by Craig Ramsell, a friend of ours in Sedona! We all selected our instruments of choice. I grabbed a couple of the colorful plastic Boomwhacker tubes and started whacking away—against the floor, against my body, against my neighbor's Boomwhackers. Soon we were giggling and playing like children—it was great fun! It wasn't possible to feel anything but joy by the time we were done.

In a certain moment, we all felt the energy shift. We put our instruments away and turned our full attention to Grandma Chandra. The room became quiet and still. We could feel Chandra's energy fill up the space. Cat began to interpret as Chandra gave us a group message. Then she invited any of us who wanted to, to ask personal questions.

I wasn't planning to ask Chandra a question. I was grateful to be in her energy—to listen and receive the wisdom and insights she shared with various members of the group.

Then, during a pause, an energy surged up within me. I heard myself introducing myself to Chandra, and then asking this question:

"Chandra, can you tell me a little bit about the shift I recently experienced, and what impact it will have, if any, on my work and my life?"

Chandra replied:

"Your soul's journey upon the planet is now complete. You will go home and heal the hearts of many ... both those whom you serve, and those who are in service to you."

Those two sentences were packed with meaning for me. A myriad of thoughts and impressions tumbled simultaneously through my awareness.

"*Your soul's journey is now complete.*" What does that mean? My first thought was, *Am I going to die?* But then I heard inside: *The hard part is over. Now life is about creating!*

I sensed that my focus would no longer be on healing myself, although surely there would be more of that. Rather, my energy would now be spent expanding this new way of living and being in the world, and sharing it with others.

"*You will go home and heal the hearts of many*" ... Dolphin Healing HeArts! She's confirming my new work!

The gathering with Chandra was so very special. I felt deeply grateful to have arrived in Hawaii in time to meet this precious being. Our meeting felt divinely guided.

I swam with the dolphins almost every day on this trip. But what ended up being particularly precious and new for me, was that it was my time on land, with girl-friends, that brought me so much joy!

As I was preparing for my trip, Dr. Peebles, at an open session, suggested: "*Don't plan every little travel detail in advance this time. Just go! Be sponta-*

neous! Let the magic of the dolphins, and the island, create this trip for you!"

So, with some trepidation, I booked only two nights' lodging at a local hotel. I decided to trust the synchronicity of the island to orchestrate the rest of my trip.

Meanwhile, Zoë had told me about another Dutch woman she wanted me to meet—Carla, a horse whisperer! Sure enough, the next day we bumped into Carla at the beach. She and I immediately hit it off. She excitedly shared her manifestation story of being offered an amazing house to housesit for the rest of her stay on the island. It was a really large house, and she thought it would be fun for Zoë and me to also stay there.

The next day, Carla shared the exciting news that the owners were completely okay with the idea. When it was time to check out of my dingy hotel room, I had an exquisite open-air Hawaiian-style home to move into! *Thank you, Dr. Peebles! You're always right!*

Another woman joined us a few days later, and the four of us became a yummy human girl-pod. We had so much fun! Every morning, with our underwater disposable cameras in hand, we swam with the dolphins. Each afternoon, one of us drove into town to drop off the cameras at Walmart to get the pictures developed, and to pick up the pictures from the day before. When the pictures arrived home, we all gathered around the large dining table to "ooh" and "ahhh" over all of the photos. This became a cherished daily ritual.

One day, a number of my photos were unlike any of the others—there was a series of pictures that showed the dolphins swimming into a large green energy field ... and going invisible! We thought that maybe the film, or the processing of the film, was defective. But these pictures came from two separate disposable cameras. And the rest of the pictures from those cameras were perfectly normal.

We all swam with the same dolphins the day those pictures were taken. None of us saw this green energy field with our physical eyes. But the pictures showed that something other-dimensional was going on that day. Zoë shared that some of the locals had been commenting on seeing a green energy field in the water sometimes. It was pretty trippy!

♡

We made the big decision to tear ourselves away from the dolphins for a day, so we could take a road trip to Volcano National Park, which was several hours away. Our dolphin sister Celeste joined us for the adventure. We spotted many whale blows along the way, and kept feeling compelled to pull over to watch every whale we saw. It took us a really long time to drive to the park!

At one stop, we got out of the car and stood atop a grassy open field that sloped down to the ocean's edge. The blow that caught our attention had come from what felt like a female whale, floating a fair distance from shore. Soon, we were all drawn deeply into connection with this whale. As we watched, she never left that spot at the surface of the water; her behavior was highly unusual. A ways away, we spotted her male escort. He was also staying motionless in one spot.

A tangible web of connection was created between these two whales and we four women. Each of us was lulled into a deep state of trance. Intuitively, without speaking, we spread out across the field, creating distance between us. Each in our own way, we held presence for these whales. We held sacred space.

I don't know how long we stayed in that silence. It was timeless. Then, suddenly, there was activity at the surface. We saw a series of small blows erupt. We gathered together, feeling tremendous excitement in the air all around us. "Is that a baby? Did we just witness that whale giving birth to a baby?" we asked in wonder.

Yes. There was no other explanation for our intense shared experience, and the little blows beside the mother whale. We felt incredibly honored and blessed to have been brought to this place, at this time, to lend our human love and support. It felt preordained. This was a profoundly sacred moment. I have no words.

♡

When we did arrive at Volcano National Park, we meandered slowly down the winding road through the park to the coast, where the road ends. We arrived at dusk, along with hundreds of others who were attracted to the dramatic sight of glowing lava flowing down the volcano in the darkness. We took our time eating our picnic dinner, and then started the three-quarters-of-a-mile walk to the active lava flow.

I'd been to the park once before. But at that time the hike to the flow was much farther. I didn't feel comfortable making that long walk over lava rock at night, so I only saw the lava from a distance. I felt very fortunate that the flow was much closer now.

We intended to do a "letting go" ceremony at the live lava flow. Earlier in the day, we'd each written down on paper things in our lives that we wanted to let go. With flashlights, bottles of water, and our ceremonial lists in hand, we headed out across the bed of black lava rock in utter darkness. It was magical. The vastness, silence, and stillness, with blackness above and below, felt sacred. Even though hundreds of people of all ages were making this trek, an aura of silent respect permeated the night.

We arrived at the flow. It was breathtakingly beautiful. The lava was flowing in smooth, slow, undulating waves. The color of the lava fluctuated between a glowing royal purple and the more usual deep orange-red. I remember having the feeling that the lava felt feminine. I felt deep peace here. I did not expect that.

In one moment, I felt someone standing next to me. It was Zoë. She suggested that we approach the lava together and throw in our "letting go" papers. I pulled mine out of my pocket and folded it into a small square. Step by step, we went deeper and deeper into the wall of heat that emanated from the lava. I started sweating profusely, but the heat felt good. It felt amazing. When we were a foot away from the active flow, we knelt down, said a silent prayer of release, and threw our papers into the lava. We watched them alight into flame, blacken into ash, dissolve, and disappear.

I was completely captivated by the energy and movement of this molten flow of inner earth. Even though the heat was extreme, my body didn't want to leave. This place felt immensely peaceful. After a few minutes, I willed myself to stand up and move away, so that others could approach and have closer contact. The four of us reunited and walked back to the car in silence. We'd received many gifts this day. It was a lot to let in.

I was blessed to have one more adventure with Grandma Chandra and Cat before returning home. On my last day, a group of us went out to see the humpback whales by boat. Grandma Chandra was the very special guest of honor.

This was Chandra's first boat trip in her entire life, and her first physical encounter with dolphins and whales. It was a thrill for every one of us to be present for all these "firsts" in her life. **"The dolphins are my family,"** she told us, as she was settling into the boat, being outfitted with her life vest.

We were barely out of the harbor when hundreds of Hawaiian spinner dolphins appeared, swimming toward us from all directions. Soon our little boat was surrounded. My eyes couldn't take them all in at once!

No matter where I looked, there was a mass of dolphins. They were jumping, leaping, and spinning. They swam in rapid crisscross patterns, passing under the boat and emerging on one side and then the other. They swam beside the boat, matching our speed, turning their bodies slightly to make eye contact from just beneath the surface of the water. The dolphins' high energy was contagious. We were all squealing and laughing with delight. There were more than a few tears!

The dolphins told Chandra that they were shifting our frequencies into another dimension—to prepare us for contact with the whales.

As suddenly as the dolphins appeared, they disappeared.

We continued traveling down the coast and soon came upon a pair of humpback whales—a mama and baby. The captain stopped the boat one hundred feet away, the legal distance, and we floated, marveling at the magnificent sight before us. Our presence didn't seem to disturb these whales. They appeared to be as curious about us as we were about them.

Mama floated observantly, while her baby swam more playfully, entertaining us with frequent jumps and leaps out of the water. We cheered and clapped, as this baby humpback accomplished each feat. His energy was so very sweet. We all felt deeply touched and blessed by the presence and trust of these benevolent, majestic beings.

Pretty soon our captain spotted two more humpbacks arriving ... and two more ... and then three. Looking out into the horizon, like the dolphins earlier, humpback whales were approaching our boat from all directions. This remarkable scene took my breath away.

The captain fired up the engine and we traveled along the coastline, escorted by this huge pod of humpback whales. Our boat was surrounded on all sides. My attention was glued to a pair of whales on the right side of the boat, about forty feet from where I was sitting. They swam at the surface, keeping pace with the boat. The sound of their breathing as they sped across the surface was amazing! The captain described that whale sound as chug-boating. He said it was very unusual for whales to swim at the surface like that for so long.

The whale energy washed through me in giant waves. I began to sob uncontrollably. At one point the captain tapped me lightly on the shoulder and asked, "Are you all right?" I just nodded that I was, and kept doing what I needed to do ... cry.

The captain announced we'd traveled four miles, and the whales were still with us. The experience was incredible, intense, and immense.

Chandra was also crying. The whales told her that she was receiving a healing

from the biggest and oldest Kahuna of these islands ... a whale! We were all deeply moved.

When we returned to the harbor, we were all so buzzed, it was all we could do to gather our gear, get off the boat, walk to our cars, and drive through the dense stop-and-go traffic of the tourist district. Talk about two different worlds!

I didn't have the luxury of time to integrate this massive download of whale energy I'd received. I had a homeward-bound plane to catch in just a few hours! I had to pull myself together to pack and get to the airport. Sheer will got me through those practicalities. Once on the plane, I gratefully surrendered and allowed the whale energies to have their way with me.

People sometimes ask me about the relationship between dolphin energy and whale energy. I tell them what I've learned through my direct internal experience.

During the early years of my dolphin journey, there was a period of about two weeks when I experienced a profound reconnection with Jesus, the Christ. Jesus felt like my brother. I felt him palpably present. Our connection was profoundly intimate, close, and accessible. I felt warm, safe, comforted, nurtured, and reassured by his presence. This was a spiritual homecoming for me.

Then, a week or two later, I experienced a deep connection to Buddha. I experienced Buddha as vast open space ... an endless sea of emptiness ... impersonality ... eternity ... the Void.

To me, the dolphins are very much like Jesus, the Christ energy. They're intimate, accessible, friendly, playful, warm, nurturing ... and at the deepest level, they're home to me. Whale is vast, empty space, eternity, silence, and stillness ... the Void. Like Buddha ...

Back home a couple of weeks later, Susan Palmer and I had arranged to facilitate an event together at a spiritual center in Phoenix: "An Evening of Healing and Transformation With the Dolphins and Quan Yin." Our plan for the event was that I would lead a dolphin energy meditation and group healing, and Susan would channel the healing sounds and energies of Quan Yin, the Goddess of Compassion, Mercy, and Healing.

I woke up that morning with an impulse to connect with Whale during my meditation. My mind was not on the evening's event; rather, I sensed that Whale was joining forces with Dolphin to guide my fledgling new school. I was curious if Whale had some information or guidance for me.

Into meditation I went. It took a while, but soon I began to feel my energies shift, and I drifted into a deep, deep trance. The extraordinary energy of Whale felt like a huge, huge ... pregnant pause. It was as if I was between breaths ... and I felt the immense potentiality of that in-between place. I was so deep, I was barely breathing.

At one point, I had a vague awareness of David coming in and sitting beside me on the bed. I had just enough awareness to realize that he was meditating too. I stayed in this deep, pregnant stillness for a very long time.

David started moving about. He was done with his meditation. I was still deeply immersed in mine. It felt like I could stay there forever. I couldn't have moved my body if I'd tried.

Just as David was stirring, the telephone rang. He answered the bedside phone. I knew it was for me, and that I needed to take the call. I nodded my head and turned my hand enough to let him know that I could talk. He put the receiver in my hand, and it was all I could do to hold it up to my ear. I heard Susan's voice.

Breathlessly, I spoke into the receiver, "Whale." Susan talked some more, and all I could say was, "Whale." I was barely coherent.

"Linda, our event tonight is billed as a Quan Yin and *Dolphin* event. You have to do *dolphins* tonight. People are expecting *dolphins*!"

"Whale," was all I could say.

I hung up and looked at David. I spoke softly and slowly. "What I am most aware of is Earth ... deep, deep Earth." I closed my eyes and went back in.

That was the extraordinary gift Whale gave me in this meditation. My prior energy experiences of Mother Earth had never, ever come close to the experience of her that I received through Whale. It was huge, deep, and absolutely beyond description.

The whole day, I was immersed in Whale consciousness. It was if I was in a waking dream. I kept having this inner dialog with my guides: *I have a dolphin event tonight. I have to be able to do* **dolphins** *by the time I arrive in Phoenix!*

Whale stayed with me ... all day.

Thankfully, a few hours before I was due to leave for Phoenix, a two-and-a-half-hour drive, my friend Daniel Stief phoned. He told me that he woke up that morning knowing that he wanted to attend Susan's and my event, to support us, and asked if I wanted to go with him so that I didn't have to drive.

"You're an angel," I whispered gratefully into the phone. "I accept." Inside myself, I thanked the dolphins profusely for this gift. There was no way I could have driven in this condition.

Whale was with me during the whole drive. I had no control over this intense energy experience. Once in Phoenix, Daniel made a stop at Costco to do some shopping. I stayed in the car, put the seat into a reclining position, collapsed into the relentless whale energy, and prayed. *"You guys, I have a dolphin event in one hour! Please do whatever you have to do to bring me back!"*

Whale took me into the depths again. Massive amounts of energy moved through and around me.

I had a good half-hour to lie there, immobile, in the Costco parking lot. People and cars came and went around me. I heard it all, but I was also far removed from it. I was incredibly grateful for that time alone.

When Daniel returned to the van, and we started the fifteen-minute drive to the event location, I worked and worked at getting my consciousness back into present time and space. Ever so slowly, I felt my body energy begin to normalize.

The moment I stepped into the event space, I was fully back, present, and in the dolphin energy. *Whew! That was close!*

The evening was a success. I led the group through a dolphin energy meditation and group healing. And then Susan shared the powerful healing tones and mudras of Quan Yin. Mission accomplished!

A few days later, at one of Summer's open channeling sessions, Dr. Peebles told me: "You are Whale now."

I replied, with awe and humility, "I know."

TWENTY-EIGHT

Dolphin School

Dolphin Healing HeArts ... *A Gateway to the New Paradigm* was a reality now! I asked Dolphin to bring me five more students for this first pod. I felt I could handle a group of six. Ten students appeared; David was one of them. Several of my regulars signed up for this grand adventure. And people I didn't know literally showed up on our doorstep after hearing about this unique school. Including me, we had a circle of eleven for our inaugural pod. That felt auspicious and divinely orchestrated. Eleven is a "gateway" number, a master number. This pod was the first to receive this new "gateway to the new paradigm" on planet Earth. It was perfect!

As Dr. Peebles instructed, this first Sedona pod met six times, with two to three weeks in between sessions. Four hours per session was all I could get out of everyone's schedules. This was all so new to me; I had no idea what I would possibly do with these people for four hours anyway!

When the pod arrived for our first session together, the eleven of us sat in a circle in my healing room. Excitement and anticipation filled the air. Every one of us was intensely aware that something brand new was about to happen in this little room, in David's and my home, in Sedona.

The energy in the room was electrified. The air was thick with a multitude of spiritual presences. Like me, these ten podmates were spiritual pioneers. Their hearts guided them to be here, and they answered the call. They showed up with no clue what was going to happen for them, but with a knowing that whatever it was, their lives would be forever changed for the better.

I opened the session with a meditation in which each person met their personal dolphin spirit guide, who would swim by their side throughout their Dolphin School experience. It was great fun to go around the room and hear the names of the dolphin guides, many of which were quite normal human names—not what one would expect a dolphin spirit guide to be called! The dolphins want to be accessible to us. They want us to perceive them as friends and helpers. They have no interest in being placed on a pedestal.

David's guide was named Archie. I've asked David to tell this story himself:

David:
On Meeting Archie

About six months before the inauguration of Dolphin Healing HeArts, Linda and I were invited to attend an event in Phoenix. The gathering had been organized by our friend Ann Albers, in honor of World Angel Day. During one of the guided meditations at this event, I had a very deep and profound experience of Archangel Michael.

After that day, Michael became a frequent visitor in my meditations. He became my primary spiritual guide.

This was a pivotal time in my life. I had been making my living as a software designer and programmer for almost thirteen years. For the first ten of those years, I worked for a small firm that wrote software for hospices and home health care agencies. The firm was in New Jersey, but I worked from my home in Sedona, set my own hours, and I had a great amount of creative freedom. In 1999, that little firm was purchased by a much larger corporation, and my life changed.

I was now the lead Software Architect for a large division of a nationwide firm, responsible for a product with many millions of dollars in annual sales. Suddenly I had to deal with multiple layers of management and bureaucracy. I was still able to live in Sedona (I had that written into my contract!), but I had to travel frequently, spending at least a week of every month on the east coast. Even though I liked the project, and I liked the people I was working with, I gradually became dissatisfied with the corporate environment. It just didn't fit me. I started imagining alternatives. I couldn't see myself taking another job; if I left this one, it would be to go out on my own.

But my job was very secure, and Linda and I had gotten used to having this reliable source of income. The idea of moving on to something new was pretty scary.

Michael was my guide during this critical period, as I gradually worked up my courage to make this major life change. I received a pretty cool confirmation of this one day. Linda and I attended an open channeling session with Dr. Peebles. When it was my turn to ask a question, I started out by telling Dr. Peebles that I had decided to give notice at my job.

Dr. Peebles interrupted me to say: *"We know! Michael told us!"*

Six months later, in our first dolphin pod gathering, Linda led us through the meditation to meet our dolphin spirit guide. A most remarkable dolphin swam up in front of me. He seemed huge! And he was surrounded by a bright golden aura. When I asked him for his name, he told me, *"I am Archie."*

The name made me giggle. All I could think of was Archie from the old *Archie and Jughead* comics. In my youth, people used to kid me about being Archie, because of my bright red hair.

The next morning I meditated in our bedroom. Soon, I felt Archangel Michael's presence. And then Archie was there too. I felt disoriented, almost dizzy. Archie … Archangel Michael … Archie … Archangel … I saw Archangel Michael in flowing robes, with wings. And Archie was a great big dolphin! But somehow their energy was the same. And then I received a communication from Archie, like a bubble of light: *"You can think of me as the Dolphin aspect of Archangel Michael."*

After the meditation, I gave my first Dolphin Energy Healing training. It was an intriguing challenge for me to teach others to do something that I do naturally and intuitively, without thought. I got better at that over time.

Then the big moment arrived. It was time for my beautiful podmates to receive their first Dolphin Attunement.

Throughout our time together, the dolphin energy in the room kept building. Now, the energy was so strong, it felt like we were all inside a huge bubble that was about to burst. The atmosphere was thick, and our bodies were buzzing from the high frequency of the dolphins. We were already in an altered state of consciousness, and the Attunement hadn't been delivered yet!

I invited everyone to lie down so that they could fully relax and receive the Attunement deeply. I remained standing and followed the instructions Dolphin gave me to lead the pod into their first Dolphin Attunement.

In the silence and stillness of the desert, far from the nearest ocean and physical dolphins, a new human-dolphin adventure began.

When our Dolphin School gathering was complete, and everyone had hugged their goodbyes, there was no time for me to rest. That night, I was giving a very special birthday party!

When I met Grandma Chandra in Hawaii, her mom Cat told me their home is in Scottsdale, Arizona—just two hours away from Sedona. I also learned that Chandra's birthday was coming up. In fact, it was the same day as my first Dolphin School gathering! As Chandra, Cat, and I were talking (remember, Chandra communicates telepathically through her mother), Chandra said, *"I want to go to Sedona for my birthday!"* Chandra had never been to Sedona, and we all giggled about how much fun that would be. But when I got back home, and dove into preparations for Dolphin School, the Chandra birthday idea faded away.

Then one day I received an e-mail from Cat saying that Chandra still wanted to come to Sedona for her birthday, and did I have suggestions of a place for them to spend the night? I checked around and sent her back some names and contact information. Once again, I let it go.

And then thoughts began passing through my mind. *If Chandra is coming to Sedona, I'll bet the local community would love to meet her!*

I was a little bit nervous to suggest this idea, as I didn't know Cat or Chandra all that well. But I shrugged off my resistance, wrote up a quick e-mail suggesting the possibility, and sent it off. Cat's answer came quickly:

"YES! Chandra would love to have a gathering while we're there. We're planning to be there on the night of her birthday, but that's okay."

I had one week to put something together, in addition to my own preparation for the initiation of Dolphin School! But we dol-

Cat and Grandma Chandra

phins love being spontaneous. I felt tremendous joy and excitement around creating this little gathering for Chandra. She's such a special being. I want lots of people to know about her and to meet her!

It was meant to be. Everything fell quickly and easily into place. I found a reasonably priced space that happened to be available that night, which was pretty amazing. I wrote up an e-mail announcement and sent it out to my small e-mail list. In the email I included a couple of photos of Chandra from our whale-watching trip, so that people could see her and make a visual connection. I even whipped up a quick

flyer, also with pictures of Chandra, and posted them around town. I knew that simply seeing pictures of Chandra would immediately open people's hearts.

And then ideas began coming in for Chandra's birthday celebration. *She needs a cake!*

I had no idea how many people would attend the event, so I decided to buy a small cake for Chandra to enjoy after the event with her family. I would present it to her at the event, in front of everyone, so we could all celebrate and sing "Happy Birthday" to her.

So what kind of cake should I get? I thought about e-mailing Cat to ask what kind of cake Chandra liked. Then I wondered if it was even possible to e-mail Cat a question like that without Chandra already knowing about it. She's so psychic! She's completely awake.

And then, inside myself, I heard, "Chocolate!"

Huh?!

"I like chocolate!"

Oh my gosh. "Chandra, is that you?"

I felt her huge giggle ...

Oh my gosh! And then I wondered to myself, *How does one give a surprise birthday party for someone who's completely awake?!*

"One doesn't!"

By now I was giggling myself. What a predicament!

I went to the bakery to order Chandra's cake. "I want a chocolate cake with chocolate frosting," I told the saleslady.

"What kind of filling?" she asked. "Fruit or buttercream?"

"Strawberry!" I heard.

"Make that strawberry!" I smiled, chuckling to myself. *If this woman only knew!*

I e-mailed Cat to fill her in on this hilarious string of events. She wrote back, "I'm just curious, what answer did you get to your question about what kind of cake Chandra likes? I'll tell you if the answer really came from Chandra."

"Chocolate, with strawberry filling," I replied.

"Yep! That's Chandra!" her mom assured me. I had no doubt!

After spending my afternoon initiating my new podmates into their Dolphin School journey, I was riding an enormous high as I arrived at the birthday event. I smuggled Chandra's cake into the back room of the space, and went to the door to greet the guests.

More than a hundred people came that night to meet Chandra! I knew some of them, but most of the faces were brand new to me. It was a stunning turnout, considering that my little e-mail list had about twenty locals on it, and the invitation only went out five days before the event!

Chandra was a hit. Communicating through her mom Cat, she was adorable, charming, utterly sweet ... and also deep, intriguing, and wise. We all hung on her every word, spellbound by her presence. Toward the end of the evening, Chandra opened the space for questions, and many received deep and meaningful answers to their personal inquiries. Finally, someone asked, "Chandra, what is it that has brought you to Sedona now?" All of us waited to hear the deeper, metaphysical meaning behind Chandra's appearance in Sedona at this moment in time. But Chandra's answer was much simpler:

"Linda Shay promised me cake!"

The whole room burst into laughter. My face turned a few shades of pink as I turned to face everyone and shared my own adventure story about Chandra's birthday cake. Then I went to the back room and lit the candles on the cake. As I brought out the cake and presented it to Chandra, everyone sang "Happy Birthday" to this precious soul. It was a glorious, joy-filled moment.

Our Dolphin Healing HeArts pod met every other week, for five more four-hour afternoon sessions. Our time together flew by. We began each session seated in a circle, gazing at one another in amazement. We were all fascinated and curious to discover how the Dolphin Attunements affected everyone. I was curious about what the lasting effects of the Attunements would be. How would these podmates' lives be different now? I wasn't interested in transitory highs. I wanted these Attunements to result in the kind of permanent growth and transformation that happened for me.

The changes in each podmate's energy and physical appearance, from session to session, were remarkable. We witnessed each podmate opening up and becoming more vibrant and alive, right before our eyes. Many looked and felt years younger.

Each podmate was given time to share what was new for them since receiving the most recent Attunement. Many expressed that they were feeling more openness and spaciousness in their lives. There was less fear, which created room for more love, joy, and freedom. They were becoming more powerful. Some delighted in reporting that for the first time in a very long time, they were giving themselves permission to play! One podmate shared that the dreams she'd had her entire life didn't feel like just dreams anymore—they felt real. They felt achievable now.

One woman, who had been a very private person, reported that she suddenly found herself being very social and outgoing. Friends of hers noticed this sudden, marked change and asked her why she was acting so differently. She told them, "I've been dolphinized!"

There were some challenges too. Long-held, deeply hidden emotions, such as anger, pain, and fear percolated up to the surface to be acknowledged, felt, embraced, and released. Flulike symptoms developed as podmates' cells released toxins that were stored in the body.

Intimate relationships were affected. The two married women in the pod reported that their husbands were going through Attunement-like integration processes right along with them. To the degree the spouses were willing, Dolphin made adjustments to their frequencies as well, to ensure that their energies remained in alignment with their mates.

Podmates shared that their bodies were communicating with them as never before, serving as barometers to inform them when they veered from this dolphin path of higher love, truth, and joy. It became physically painful to pursue old patterns and beliefs that were not in alignment with their soul's highest expression. Because of this, they felt inspired to take risks and speak their truth—to stand up for themselves—as never before.

Each podmate experienced tremendous healing, growth, and transformation in such a short time. We watched as a pod as, one by one, each of us stepped into authenticity and empowerment. It was an incredible gift to bear witness to these profound shifts.

Dolphin Love

In addition to everyone sharing their Attunement experiences, I managed to squeeze in a little bit of healing training during each session. For sure, the highlight of each gathering was the transmission of the next Dolphin Attunement!

David:
My experience of receiving the Dolphin Attunements

By the time I participated in Linda's first Dolphin School pod, I had been on a conscious spiritual path for almost thirty years. During this time I attended many workshops and trainings, followed various teachers, practiced many different disciplines, meditated in many different ways, and learned to channel. In the course of all this, I had a number of profound and life-changing mystical experiences. And of course I had been around Linda for seven years. I had gone with her to swim with the dolphins, I had attended many dolphin meditations, and I had received many dolphin energy healing sessions—which were always amazing.

But the Dolphin Attunements were completely new.

One difference I noticed was that, when Linda would give me a dolphin healing, it was clear that the dolphin energy was coming *through* her. She was the vehicle. But that wasn't true for the Attunements. Linda played a part, but the Attunements didn't come through her. They just ... *came.*

I was happy that we always lay down to receive the Attunements. I had the sense that if I had been standing up when the Attunement came in, or even sitting, my body would have just fallen over.

One of the women, sharing after our First Attunement, called it the "Ka-pow!" Attunement. The energy that came in was that sudden and that strong. And it's not even right to call it an "energy." It was more like a group of profoundly advanced beings were performing some kind of surgery on very high parts of me, parts of me that were far beyond my experience of myself as a human being in a human body, parts of me that I hadn't known existed.

Dolphin Love

And it happened outside of time. In linear time, we would lie down, and it would be forty-five minutes to an hour-and-a-half before any of us would be ready to get back up. Still, it was very clear to me that the Attunement was happening outside of linear time. I could say it happened "in an instant" or "in a moment," but that's not quite right. The experience was that the Attunement hadn't happened yet … and then it had. And then I could do nothing but lie there for a long time, while my body and energy system slowly began to absorb and integrate what had happened. Eventually I would become aware that I was ready to slowly get up.

There was never any fear; instead I felt absolute trust, complete safety. And I felt profoundly honored and grateful to be receiving this gift.

After each Attunement, when we were finally ready to get up, we would all walk outside. Each in our own timing, in silence, we would slowly walk the streets of the neighborhood where Linda and I lived. Each time, I felt like a brand new being, in a brand new world. I found myself stopping at every bush, tree, and cactus, communing deeply with the spirit of each plant I encountered. The plants seemed to understand.

It was probably a lucky thing that we were in Sedona. In another town, a neighbor might have looked outside, seen this bunch of crazy, stoned-looking people, and called the police! I do remember running into one neighbor on one of these walks, who looked at me and asked, "Are you all doing some kind of workshop?" All I could do was nod and smile.

Sometimes, during the Attunements, there were visions. During my Fourth Attunement, I had the sense that I was in a basement, below ground level. Suddenly, all of the matter above me broke into pieces and dissolved. It was like all the lights were turned on. I looked up, and there was no longer a ceiling above me, and not even a sky. Just massive amounts of gold-and-white light, streaming in, enveloping me, brighter than anything I'd ever experienced. I stayed in that light for a long time.

All of this led up to the Sixth Attunement, which was the most remarkable by far. During my Sixth Attunement, I found myself gliding through the water, surrounded by four dolphins. There was one above me, one below me, one to my left, and one to my right. We were all moving together, at the same speed. Gradually the dolphins came closer and closer. Their bodies became all shimmery, and so did mine. We weren't matter anymore; we were light. As the light dolphins kept coming closer, our bodies began to overlap. We overlapped more and more, until we merged completely. And then there was only one body, glimmering with light, gliding through the water. It was dolphin, and it was human. And it was me.

Later that night, alone after everyone had gone home, I became aware of a new, strange feeling around the middle of my back. I reached my hand around and felt my back. Physically, there was nothing there. But energetically, I could trace the outline of something very distinct and real. My dorsal fin.

TWENTY-NINE

Surprise, Surprise!

After David received his Fourth Dolphin Attunement, his passion for teaching rose to the surface. He realized he had a contribution to make to Dolphin School.

David's spiritual journey began much earlier than mine. He was in his freshman year at Princeton, on track to achieving his childhood dream of becoming a nuclear physicist, when he had his first psychic experience. Here's how David tells this story:

> I was sitting in math class taking a midterm exam, and I noticed that Valerie wasn't there. Valerie was dating my roommate, and she and I were friends. It was very strange for her to miss such an important exam. As I was wondering about this, an image came into my mind. I saw Valerie being hit by a bus on Washington Road, the road that runs alongside the Princeton campus. This image was so vivid, and so disturbing, I couldn't stop thinking about it. I wondered what was wrong with me, that I could have such a violent thought about my friend.
>
> Three hours later, I asked my roommate if he knew anything

about Valerie, and he told me that she had been hit by a bus on Washington Road. She had a broken arm, but she was OK. The accident had happened exactly as I had seen it.

The next day, sitting in my physics class, I pondered the uncomfortable realization that the science I was learning did not allow for the reality of what had just happened to me, and had no explanation for it. The experience felt more important to me than what I was learning in my classes. This set my life off in a completely different direction.

Six months later, David made the difficult decision to leave school and embark upon a journey to seek understanding of the new awarenesses he was discovering. He moved into New York City and got deeply involved in the vibrant spiritual scene that was bubbling there in the 1970s. To support himself, he took a nine-to-five job writing computer software. Most of his evenings and weekends were devoted to workshops, seminars, trainings, conferences, and retreats. This went on for five years, until David found his way to a small community of students who were devoting their time and energy to one man's teachings. David became a member of this community, and devoted himself fully and completely to these teachings that had utterly and profoundly changed his life.

After years of volunteer work, David became a teacher of these courses in personal and spiritual development. He was convinced he would spend the rest of his life teaching, and living, in this community. Then, ten years into this extraordinary life experience, his relationship with the community came to an abrupt and painful end, when he came to the conclusion that the leader was no longer in integrity with the teachings. Hurt and betrayed, David left his living companions of ten years, and re-entered the world at large. Once again, he took a job writing computer software to earn a living, and eventually he found his way to Sedona. This is what he was doing when we met.

It was a huge step for David to open to the idea of teaching again. A tremendous amount of healing must have occurred, for his spirit and soul to feel safe and strong enough now to come out of hiding. It was time for David to let his spiritual light shine again. He declared his wish to join me and Dolphin in our service to humanity.

At first, the idea of teaching Dolphin School with David was a big shift for me. David had been such a wonderful source of support for me throughout my journey; but our paths, and our ways of living and being in the world, were so different! He was a computer guy, and I was a dolphin girl! The mere possibility that our seemingly opposite energies could blend together in such a way that we could create and teach together was beyond my imagining!

But I also knew that David had a lot to contribute to my new school. He had years of experience conducting seminars and workshops in front of large groups of people—I'd never done anything like that before! And I knew I was taking on a lot with this new creation—it would be good to have a partner. David has a huge heart, and he is a highly intelligent, wise, kind man. I saw that David could bring essential traits, skills, and knowledge that I was still learning and mastering. I would hold the vision, the energetic connection to Dolphin, and the qualities of consciousness that David was still manifesting and integrating.

I also loved the idea that we, as a couple, would be teaching Dolphin School together. Having a balance of male and female energies to guide our podmates through their journey felt important, and beneficial, for the students. So much of what Dolphin School is about is creating, and sustaining, harmonious relationships. The dolphins are the masters of this, and we humans have so much to learn! It would be perfect for a couple, in loving relationship, to be doing the teaching.

Immediately upon graduating from the first Sedona pod, David joined me as co-creator and co-teacher of Dolphin Healing HeArts. This was a miracle to me!

♡

The same week David first expressed his desire to teach, he also came to me with an e-mail announcement for a workshop that was being given at an intentional community in Eugene, Oregon, by some friends of his. The workshop was called "Naka-Ima: The Practice of Honesty." Naka-Ima is a Japanese word that means "Inside of Now." The workshop was founded by people who had been involved with the community that David had spent so many years with, and one of the leaders was his old teaching partner.

David had stayed in touch with some of these people over the years, and he had been hearing great things about this particular workshop. It seemed to be a kinder, gentler evolution of the work he had devoted his life to years before. David had a hunch that attending this workshop would be a valuable experience for both of us, before we began collaborating and teaching together.

Throughout my whole seven-year journey with the dolphins, never once had I been guided to attend any kind of healing training or spiritual workshop. Except for Dr. Peebles, the dolphins seemed to not want me to muddy the waters by exposing myself to a lot of different energies or teachings. So I was quite surprised to notice that I, too, felt attracted to this workshop!

I think it was because of the community-building aspect. All my life I had been a one-on-one person. There were times I felt inexplicably uncomfortable in groups. Even in my own meditation circles, while everyone else was joyously talking, hugging, and connecting after their experience with the dolphin energy, I sometimes experienced feelings of separation and loneliness. In those moments, I didn't know how to reach out and make a connection.

Dolphin had told me that one of the big-picture outcomes of our school was to create Unity-Community among humanity. As the founder, creator, and teacher of this program, I knew that inner quality had to start with me. And I suspected that, even after my awakening, I still had a lot to learn—and perhaps some healing to do—in this area.

As I read about Naka-Ima, shivers went up and down my spine. Dolphin was, indeed, encouraging me to do this! We signed up and quickly rearranged our life so we could attend this workshop, a thousand miles away, in just a few weeks.

♡

And then, out of the blue, I received a phone call from Zoë, my Dutch dolphin sister. She had returned to Holland from her annual six-month stay in Hawaii, and she was feeling restless. One reason she called me was to further explore the Dolphin Energy Healing training I'd told her about during my recent Hawaii trip. She told me that ever since we'd talked about it, it kept coming into her mind.

Zoë had to stay in Holland for six months. She was sensing that there was something for her to do there—that there was, indeed, a purpose for her being there—but she didn't know what it was. Her passion was the dolphins. Her greatest wish was to live in Hawaii all year round, so she could swim with the dolphins all of the time. But the visa rules limited her time in Hawaii to no more than six months each year. She was back in her native country now, feeling displaced and confused.

After Zoë shared, I brought her up-to-date with the amazing things that were happening with my first Dolphin School pod. When I paused to take a breath, Zoë said, with great enthusiasm, "I want to receive this training!"

My mind whirled. "You'll need to come to Sedona for several months to do our school," I told her. We both knew, with Zoë's visa issues, that that couldn't happen for at least six months. But throughout the rest of the call, Zoë kept affirming her desire to receive this training.

"Well, where there's a will, there's a way!" I told her, before we hung up. "I'll meditate on it, and I suggest that you have a talk with the universe. Say out loud what it is that you want, clearly and firmly!" We agreed to stay in touch, and then we hung up.

As soon as I hung up the phone, the top of my head started buzzing intensely, and dolphin energy was streaming through my body. Dolphin's not waiting for me to meditate! I couldn't have moved if I'd wanted to.

Still standing by the phone, my eyes closed, and my hand reached out to my desk for balance. Questions formed in my mind faster than I could "think" them, and then the answers came as "yes" or "no." With each correct answer, energy poured through me in confirmation.

Is Zoë to receive this training?
Yes.

Will she come here for it?
No.

She's to receive it in Holland?
Yes.

Am I to give her the Attunements over the phone? Will she do this alone?
No.

Am I supposed to go there? My heart was racing ...
Yes.

She'll organize a pod for me to teach there? Breathe, Linda ...
Yes!

Powerful streams of energy flowed through my body, confirming that my interpretation of this communication was correct.

My head was spinning. *Already? You want me to take this school to Europe already? My first pod hasn't even graduated yet!*

I told David what I'd just received. He was as shocked as I was; but neither of us could deny the confirmation shivers that were pouring through us.

"You have to call Zoë back and tell her this news."

"I don't know how! I've never placed an international call before." I fumbled through the telephone book, trying to figure out how to place an international phone call. Then I called Information and asked them. The woman who answered gave me the country code for The Netherlands and hung up. I attempted a number of dialing combinations, without success. We kept getting funny ring tones! Finally, I gave up. "I'm going to send her an e-mail, and pray that she reads it right away!"

I wrote everything down in an e-mail and closed the message by asking Zoë to call me immediately. When I hit "send," I put out a really strong telepathic communication: *"Read your e-mail, Zoë!"*

Ten minutes later, the phone rang. It was Zoë. I was so relieved to hear her voice! David picked up a second phone so we could all talk.

Zoë was in a bit of a panic herself. "After we hung up, I started to wash my dinner dishes, and I did what you said. I told the universe what I wanted. *I want to do something with people. I want to do something with dolphin energy. I want to create something that's really joyful, fun, and playful!* It felt good to do that. And then when I finished, I was going to go to bed, but the thought popped into my mind to check my e-mail one more time. I really hadn't intended to do that, because I had already done my e-mails not long ago. But I felt strongly that I needed to check my messages one more time. And there was your message! I was so surprised. But I have to tell you, I don't know if I can do this. I've never organized anything before. I've never done anything like this before!"

My nervousness came up again. *I've never been to Europe.* But, as the three of us talked it over, it felt right.

"Neither have I!" I responded. "We just have to trust that everything we need will come. The dolphins will help us!"

We all relaxed a little, and began to talk about possibilities. Zoë said that September felt like the right time to start a pod in Holland. It was now May. September was only four short months away!

"I think you need to come here for a promotional trip. If people are going to do this, they need to meet you and feel the energy of the dolphins."

My nervousness came up again. *I've never been to Europe.* But, as the three of us talked it over, it felt right. We came up with a plan. I would make this first trip alone, in June, just after the Sedona pod received their Sixth Attunement. In September, David and I would travel together to teach the Holland pod. David had frequent flyer miles left over from his job—I could use those to pay for the first flight. Zoë told me I could stay with her this first trip. She'd talk to friends and see about lining up some introductory events, and call us back in a few days.

My nervousness had turned into excitement. We hung up the phone and I looked at David. I felt like I was spinning. "I'm going to Holland!"

THIRTY

Archie Speaks

I awoke the next morning in a panic. The idea of traveling to Holland six times to move one pod through the six Dolphin Attunements was overwhelming to me. It just felt like too much. As luck would have it, Summer Bacon's monthly open channeling session with Dr. Peebles was today. I asked David to go with me, in the hopes that one of our names would be called to receive a personal message.

Summer's open sessions with Dr. Peebles had become quite popular and well-known. I remembered the old days, when five or ten of us sat in a circle in Summer's living room, and there was time for each of us to talk with Dr. Peebles at length. Now, Summer was using a local auditorium for these sessions, and over a hundred people came each month. Dr. Peebles would start the session with a message for the whole group, and then ten or twelve people would get the opportunity to ask one question apiece. If you wanted to ask a personal question, you put your name into the basket, and hoped to be called—one of Summer's helpers would pull names from the basket at random. It was always wonderful just to hear Dr. Peebles and be in his energy, but I realized how fortunate I had been to have so much of his time and personal attention during the early years of my dolphin journey.

Midway through the hour-and-a-half session, a huge bubble of energy arose inside of me—and at that moment my name was called! I waited while the microphone was passed to me. Then, with my arms held out in front of me, holding that bubble of energy, I said, "I'm feeling the expansion of my school right here ..."

"*Yes my dear! And are you ready to stand at the helm of the boat and* **oversee** *it? Are you ready to* **oversee** *it, my dear?*" Dr. Peebles asked with great enthusiasm.

"Yes," I replied. I didn't really know, yet, what I was saying yes to. Our exchange happened so fast, it didn't occur to me to mention the phone call with Zoë and the invitation to go to Holland. I did notice that Dr. P. repeated the word "oversee" three times, with great emphasis, which seemed odd.

A friend of ours was sitting in the row in front of us—she used to come to the dolphin meditations in our home, years earlier. As soon as the session ended, she turned to me and said, "Linda, did you get what he was saying to you? Are you willing to oversee it? Oversea it? You're supposed to take your program overseas!"

"That's exactly right!!" I leapt into the air with this realization. "I was just invited to take this program to Holland!" The puzzle piece fell into place. This was the confirmation I had been seeking.

And then I thought ... *How will we possibly do that?*

I looked at David with big eyes. Both of us had nothing but questions. Big questions. Lots of them.

After socializing with a few friends, David and I drove home in silence, each lost in our own tumble of thoughts. We were both feeling the magnitude of what was happening. Urgency was in the air.

We walked through our door, went silently together to the living room couch, and sat down. All of the sudden, I saw David's posture shift so that he was sitting quite erect. A huge energy came into the room.

"Should I get a tape recorder?" I asked.

"Yes," a deep, unfamiliar voice responded. This had never happened before.

I quickly grabbed our tape recorder. David came out of trance for a moment, to help me get the tape recorder set up. "I think this is Archie," he said. David spoke an introduction into the tape recorder, then immediately he was back in trance, and Archie began speaking.

Archie spoke for an hour and a half. I am honored to include extensive excerpts of Archie's channeled message in this book. Up until now, much of what follows has only been shared with podmates of the Dolphin Healing HeArts school—and only after they received their Sixth Dolphin Attunement. And some of this material has never been published before anywhere, in any form.

David (speaking into the tape recorder, before going back into trance): Today is Saturday, May 17, 2003. We are talking about the pods and the Attunements and Holland, and the process by which these will expand out into the world. Specifically, what to expect for people who have completed the Sixth Attunement, which so far no one but Linda has. And so of course, we don't know what that is going to look like.

The Sixth Attunement

Archie: The Sixth Attunement should be looked upon as a birth, a birth of a new being upon the planet. The word "rebirth" can also be used, but simply a new birth is actually more accurate. The being, having received the Sixth Attunement, will begin to approach life in a radically new and different way than any that they have experienced before. They will be coming from a place of freedom and security which did not previously exist.

However, they will at that point be at the beginning of a process of expressing that freedom out into the world, and expressing that nature. It is unrealistic to expect the being at that point to be entirely clear of attachments, to be entirely clear of their previous ways of thinking, doing, and interacting with the world. And in fact, each being will express this new beingness of the completed Attunements process in their own new and unique way.

And so a primary function of the school going forward, will be to provide the support system for these new beings walking the planet Earth. And that will be one of the prime values of the skills you will begin learning in your Naka-Ima workshop—learning to efficiently and quickly release any attachments to the old ways of being, and to old natures.

Those who have attained the Sixth Attunement, who have received the Sixth Attunement, have become your children. That is how you should look upon them. And that is also the level of understanding which will be required as you see the broad and various ways in which they choose to express these energies into the world, while continuing with their own evolution. They will in fact be entirely free and self-sufficient. And, at the same time, you will see that they will need you more than ever—as a friend, as a guide, and as an example, by continuing with your own evolution and your own explorations; and continuing to bring your own explorations out for the benefit of all. That is one of the reasons that your work with the whales has now begun.

So, in approaching the being who has completed the Sixth Attunement, there must be a dual view; at one level perceiving and understanding and expecting the level of perfection that has been attained, while at the same time, knowing that essentially this is a brand-new being. There is a youngness, there is an inexperience, there may very well in some cases be a clumsiness.

And for some there may be great temptations to deny, to go back to old comfortable ways of being. These will dissolve over time. There is an inevitability, after the Sixth Attunement, of expressing a new way of being into the world. However, do not be surprised by anything that anyone experiences in this brand-new reality. *After the Sixth Attunement come the biggest lessons, and the biggest jumps.* This is a process that will require deeper integration than anything your students have experienced so far.

Archie and Archangel Michael

You are very curious about the relationship between the Dolphin energy you experience as Archie and the Angelic energy you experience as Archangel Michael. We are giving you an image now. Understand that the universe is in fact organized in such a way that if you were to set off in one direction and continue on until Infinity, you would ultimately return to the place where you started. It is not a circularity, but a question of higher dimensions. Perhaps one way of thinking of it is that these two entities are simply coming to you from opposite directions, from opposite ends of the universe. There is a complementarity to the dolphin energy and the angelic energy. The thing in common is our love for you.

The Dolphin Consciousness

Linda: *Let's follow that up with the difference between the Earth dolphins and the spirit of the dolphins that's coming through in my work, that seems beyond anything that I've experienced with the physical dolphins in the water.*

Archie: Physical Earth dolphins are imbibing* of, and being sourced from, the same galactic dolphin consciousness as is being expressed through you in your work. They are much farther along the path of imbibing and realizing and expressing this energy in physicality. Yet they also are, in many cases, limited by the limitations of physicality. They do have the capability of taking you to other dimensions and parallel worlds, and actually that is a better description of where you were taken to. It was a parallel world.**

In particular, the spinner dolphins, as you know, are perhaps the farthest along on the planet in realizing or actually incarnating this energy. Each dolphin species has its own particular role, its own particular gifts and talents, its own particular mission. In this specific regard, most other physical dolphins are not quite as far along as the spinner dolphins, while still in most cases being far, far beyond any level that humanity has experienced to this point.

Linda: *I think my question is what is it that I'm accessing in the healing work? It seems to be unlimited.*

Archie: Precisely. It is not being sourced from another physical being. It is being sourced from the cosmos. It is being sourced from the galactic, universal,

---

* I looked "imbibing" up in the dictionary: (1) To drink. (2) To absorb or take in as if by drinking: "The whole body... imbibes delight through every pore" (Henry David Thoreau). (3) To receive and absorb into the mind and retain; as, to imbibe principles; to imbibe errors.
** Here Archie is referring to what happened during my second Hawaii swim trip (Chapter 13), when the dolphins and I "disappeared."

pan-universal consciousness that expresses itself into this universe as well as others. This is not the only universe. And this consciousness extends across the multi-verse, across multiple universes. Even "intergalactic" is not an adequate description, because galaxies are physical. This phrase "intergalactic energy" is useful for the human mind, in order to describe the vastness of what you're accessing. However, it is not technically correct.

"Pan-universal" implies that this energy stretches across the multi-verse, across multiple universes. This is a new term, and it may not be useful for your talks in public at this time. The truth is, a single experience of the dolphin energy will be far more useful to the vast majority than any of these conceptual frameworks that we're discussing. We are offering this conceptual framework to you because you are curious about it, and because your mind still finds ways to attempt to limit the source of that which you have befriended, that which you have chosen to be an ambassador for.

The Nature of the Attunements

Linda: *Is each Attunement ... is everybody receiving the same quality of frequency with each Attunement, or is it an individualized process for each person, that ultimately by the Sixth Attunement, they end up in the same place?*

Archie: Each Attunement has its own nature. This nature is the same for each person who receives the Attunement. The essential nature of the First Attunement is the essential nature of the First Attunement. The essential nature of the Fourth Attunement is the essential nature of the Fourth Attunement.

Linda: *Is there a value in us knowing what the essential quality of each Attunement is, and sharing that with the students?*

Archie: No. No. This is simply not currently possible. The Attunements are taking place at a level beyond your current understanding, and beyond what can be conceptualized or put into words. The greatest benefit is to be had by each individual entering into each Attunement in a state of unknowing. It is best for them simply to receive in a state of trust.

Linda: *Is this school the only means for people to receive these Attunements, or is this something that people can get in other ways?*

Archie: The most useful answer to that question, is that it is no concern of yours. This is not a criticism. For the vast majority of those who are attracted to you, the opportunity that the school is offering them will not be available to them by any other means. This is simply the reality at this time. It is also true that there will come a time when a critical mass is attained, and when this opportunity is simply in the air, and all that one has to do is breathe. However that time is still many years in the future.

Linda: *I think my fear is setting up an energy around this Attunement process. What I've experienced with some people who swim with dolphins in Hawaii, is "Well, I had this experience, was that an Attunement?" So I don't want this energy around it that's elitism; that has the thing that you can only get it through me. I don't want to create that kind of a scenario.*

Archie: Your caution is well-founded. However, what you're discussing has to do with your communication, rather than with the essence or the reality or the nature of what is really happening here. At this point, and by "this point" we are talking about the next several years, it is extremely unlikely that you will meet anyone who has independently received more than one or perhaps two of the six Attunements.

The Difference between Dolphin Energy and
the Dolphin Attunements

Understand that the difficulty that you are having in conceptualizing and understanding the nature of the Attunements has to do with understanding and comparing and contrasting them with simply the reception of the Dolphin Energy. Which, in itself, can be and often is life-transforming. And so, the best way to think about it is to understand the difference between *receiving of the source* and *becoming the source.*

It is the difference between the man who drinks of the Fountain of Youth, and the man who actually *becomes* the Fountain of Youth, so that everyone around him begins to drink of *him*, as of the water. And so, it is not necessary in any way to compare or to invalidate these experiences. In particular, your friends in Hawaii have had many deep and profound experiences of the Dolphin Energy. And they have drunk of this energy, as have you! And that is an extraordinarily deep and profound and significant experience. And so you must clear your mind of any concept that it is necessary to hold the Attunements even in relationship to this experience. It is not one or the other.

Linda's Role

Archie: Your perception that your existence was an experiment, in the early years of this experiment, was essentially correct. There are others. There are three others, this on a planet of six billion people. You have struggled with that awareness. Your ego has struggled mightily with that awareness. The ego desperately wants to be special, and yet it cannot deal with the reality of your uniqueness. That is because it will attempt to use the uniqueness in a way that the uniqueness is not meant for. This is simply your path, and your gift.

Your business, if you will, and your mission, requires others to perceive your gift, so that they can perceive first of all that such a gift exists upon the planet, and that imbibing of this gift is worthy of their time and effort. Your humility serves you well. However, any minimization of your mission here upon the planet is a false humility. That is why your friend Dr. Peebles is continually challenging you with the grandiosity of your nature. This stretches you in a way that you need to stretch.

And what will serve those who you come into contact with is a simple matter-of-factness, neither grandiose nor self-effacing. Simply: "This is what is happening in my reality, this is what I have been given to share. To my knowledge, I'm not aware of anyone else who has been given this to share at this point."

And in particular, the difference between imbibing of the Dolphin Energy, and choosing to *become* this energy. That is a good way of expressing the essential difference. Choosing to become the source. Choosing to allow your very nature to be transformed, so that you are the source. This will become very clear after the Sixth Attunement.

After the Sixth Attunement

One of the things that you have not prepared yourself for, is that some, initially, will have a great experience of loss after the Sixth Attunement. It is the loss of, in a sense, their humanity, their small humanity. And their personality. Their personality will still exist; however, it will be increasingly irrelevant, and may struggle mightily against this irrelevance. Like all of the processes that your students go through, this must simply be met with love, and with compassion, with understanding, with patience. Some of your students will have the Sixth Attunement and immediately begin expressing this new level of freedom and creativity in the world. And some of them will embark upon a process that may take months or years. Some will do both at the same time. *Life begins with the Sixth Attunement.*

Linda: *So, in my personal experience, what is coming up for me as an example of what you're referring to, is the impersonality. Things becoming impersonal - they just are. And that awareness overriding anything else.*

Archie: Yes. You can understand, to one who has identified with the small self, with the ego, how profoundly disturbing these experiences may be. And so, some will have an alternation of experience, where they will enter into that space, and then will spend weeks struggling with it.

Linda: *Because it's so foreign...*

Archie: Well, because it places that which they have devoted the bulk of their time and attention and love to into its proper perspective, which is a perspective of nothingness. And so, this is why your process took the seven years that it did. And of course, that is really miscounting. Fifteen or twenty or thirty years would be more appropriate, if one were to mark the beginning of the process. We love you so much. We are enormously grateful for your willingness to experience what you have experienced.

Linda: (crying) *I couldn't have done it without my sweetie ...*

Archie: Yes, he studied his entire life to prepare for this, for this role that he is playing. And that is part of his problem, that he has completed his mission and so has nothing but choice. However, when we said to you what we said to you before, about how we look upon you, understand that this is the proper way for you to look upon your students. In understanding our appreciation for your journey, you can choose to appreciate their journey. And not in any way to minimize it, but to hold it in the most profound respect and gratitude.

Do the Attunements Require Linda's Physical Presence?

Archie: You are aware that you do not provide the Attunements. And it is not entirely accurate to even describe you as the vehicle for the Attunements. You are aware of that also.

Linda: *It's more of an invitation. I create the space and invite the students to receive it.*

Archie: What you don't understand is that you invite the Attunements themselves. It is as though you are the flower, and the Attunements are the bees. What is most accurate to say is that your consciousness has now evolved to a level which attracts the Attunements. Bringing in is another phrase, holding the space is another phrase, opening the window, opening the dimension.

Linda: *So it's dependent upon my level of consciousness. So giving the Attunements would be limited to people who have attained a certain level of consciousness.*

Archie: Yes, this is correct, and even "level of consciousness" is not an appropriate term, as it implies the greater than/less than dichotomy that you are so desperately trying to avoid. "Quality of consciousness" may be closer to the truth. It may be simpler, simply to understand that this is your mission.

At this time, unlike the Dolphin Energy, which can be delivered remotely, it is not yet time to attempt to deliver the Attunements remotely. The danger is that the student will simply receive the Dolphin Energy.

[*Happily, as of this writing, this limitation has been lifted. I began facilitating remote Dolphin Attunements to podmates in November 2010. It is an extraordinary experience to sit comfortably in my home in Arizona, and facilitate Dolphin Attunement transmissions for podmates in multiple countries, all over the globe, all at the same time, all receiving this gift in the comfort of their own homes. The land beneath each receiver also receives the Attunement frequencies.*

It came as a complete surprise to me when this first became possible. I had been delivering Attunements, always in person, for more than seven years. As I was reviewing this channeling, in preparation for the book, it was lovely to rediscover that Archie had told us, back in 2003, that remote Attunements would eventually become possible—just "not yet." I had forgotten that!]

Linda: *And after the First Attunement, people can begin doing the healings…*

Archie: The most beneficial at this point would be for them to begin doing healings on each other. Ideally, doing the healings with others outside the pod would be best begun after the Third Attunement. Now, in the case of your initial pod, some were experienced healers, and this supported them in going out into the community. However, this has also led to some degree of difficulty and confusion, in that they have not created for themselves a clear delineation between the Dolphin Energy and the energies that they were previously transmitting.

[*Archie went on to give us a great deal of information. Some of this was personal, and some of it was specific instructions for how to structure our school, how to organize the weekends, where and how to give Introductory Evenings about the school, and so on.*

In reviewing this information, years later, I'm struck once again by Archie's clarity] *and wisdom. In addition to being a wonderful spiritual guide, he's a great business coach!*

The channeling ended with the following sections, which Archie has given permission to share …]

Archie on Publicity

You are in the phase of your creation in which it is necessary to devote a significant amount of your time and attention toward publicity. We prefer the word publicity to marketing, in that it is not necessary to attempt to influence, in the sense that the word marketing usually means. It is, however, necessary to get the information out.

The vast majority of those who will most benefit from the school do not yet know of its existence. Understand that everyone who hears about the school will be uplifted, simply through the information. Simply through being given the opportunity to be aware of the new energy and the new existence and the new reality which is becoming real upon the planet.

There are those who will hear, who will not act for many years. That is not your concern. And there are those who will be drawn to you to support this process. There are those who will simply call you, who will not be able to tell you how they found out about it. But that does not change your responsibility to announce, and to reach out; to make aware, and to show.

There is a deeper issue here. You have a desire for those around you to be comfortable. What is it that one is most comfortable with? That which is familiar, yes? …You are *doomed* to make people uncomfortable. Do you understand?

Archie on Channeling

Archie: We would like to speak about the nature of these communications. The more frequently the two of you put aside specific time to receive these communications, the more useful they will be, and the more easily the information will come through. This should begin with simply the two of you, and ultimately others can be invited and included as well.

Your creation, your mission or school is a collaboration between yourselves, as physical Earthly representatives, and spiritual sources. This type of communication is not a key part of your teaching, simply because the experience of interdimensional communication is becoming widespread. It is not part of what is unique about your contribution. However, it is useful to you, and to others.

(As the session ends)
Linda: *Thank you, Archie.*
Archie: It is our privilege.

THIRTY-ONE

Oversea-ing It!

A few days later, Zoë phoned to report that she had me scheduled to give five introductory events in locations all throughout the country—thankfully Holland is a small country! She excitedly shared that everything flowed effortlessly. All the help she needed did magically appear. We were so excited!

I got off the phone and booked my first flight to Europe—to Amsterdam! Three weeks later, I was on my way.

Zoë met me at Schiphol Airport. She was radiant! And she had even more exciting news. While I was in flight crossing the Atlantic, a journalist phoned her from Holland's popular spiritual magazine, *Paravisie*, asking for an interview with me. The woman had seen our tiny ad in a spiritual newspaper, and wanted to be the first to write an article about this new spiritual program that was coming to Holland. Of course I said yes, and the next day, Zoë called the woman and made the appointment.

Two days later, the journalist and her photographer came to Zoë's apartment in Utrecht for our interview. She was an attractive, dark-haired woman, about my age. The photographer was also about my age, casual and friendly in dress and appearance. Kindness radiated from his eyes. Both of them were warm, curious, and open.

We all sat down together in Zoë's living room and talked for about an hour and a half. The journalist started out asking questions from the perspective of someone completely new to the whole idea of dolphin spirituality. She asked about who the dolphins are, and about my own journey with them. Many of her questions were ones I wasn't used to answering, which helped me learn how to deliver my message to a broader audience.

When we were done talking, the photographer took me outside to the large grassy courtyard in front of Zoë's apartment for the photo shoot. At first I was nervous, and feeling conspicuous with all the people passing by, but the photographer did a great job of making me feel comfortable and at ease. I had a lot of fun!

The resulting story was an in-depth, five-page color article. It told the story of my journey with the dolphins, and what the dolphins were now bringing to humanity as a result. They even put my picture on the cover! When Zoë and I envisioned this trip, we didn't imagine that. My spirit dolphin publicity agents did a great job!

I presented six introductory events that trip. Five were planned and publicized. The sixth was an unplanned, impromptu gathering hosted by one of Zoë's beautiful friends in her home. This friend suggested the gathering as a "trial run" for me. I was happy for any opportunity to share!

When Zoë and I arrived at her friend's home, the living room was filled to capacity with men and women of all ages. Everyone was so excited to hear about the dolphins from this American woman. It was so sweet to be so warmly welcomed by these friendly Dutch people! My heart was overflowing with joy and appreciation.

The next event was the first official introductory, held in historic Zutphen, in the center of Holland. Traveling to Zutphen was reminiscent of driving to my very first public sharing of my dolphin story back in Sedona, so many years ago. I could feel the dolphins in my field, swimming about with so much excitement. The energy kept building and building.

When we arrived at the event location, many excited guests were already there. As I walked into the space and took in the scene, streams of energy started pouring through my body, and it didn't stop! People kept arriving, and more energy moved through me. *Goodness! The dolphins are soooo excited about this evening!* The excitement and energy level was almost overwhelming.

I don't remember much about what I said and did that night. It was all so much newness for me to let in! I mainly remember the incredible energy and excitement I felt.

One very special woman was there that night. Johanna van Wijk was soon to play a big role for Dolphin Healing HeArts in Holland. She wrote of her experience at this evening:

Dolphin Love

Johanna van Wijk:

In 1991 I traveled on holiday to Glastonbury, England—a very spiritual place. There was a visionary artist there, he had many dolphin paintings. All of the paintings were about dolphins giving energy to the world, making a circle around the earth.

While I was looking at these paintings, I received an inner message, a knowing, that the dolphins would be bringing a great gift to the earth and to humanity. I never forgot this. For many years I was watching and waiting for this gift to appear, really searching everywhere for this gift of the dolphins to begin. Where is it? And what is it?

I was in Crete in April 2003 for a healing class. Each time I visited the local markets, local people would look at me and tell me "you have something with dolphins." "You will be doing something with dolphins." The people in Crete have such a strong relationship with the dolphins, they once had a king who had dolphins as his advisors ...

Then, two months later, finally after twelve years, this gift of the dolphins came right to my home town of Zutphen, brought by Linda herself, accompanied by Zoë at that time.

For Linda it was all so fresh and new to be in the Netherlands, having had the dolphins' message to go to this far away country to remind people about unconditional love and unity, community ... To teach, about what?

At that time a lot of spiritual knowledge was opening up already in Dutch people. We were blessed with a roller coaster of spiritual teachings and workshops and so forth. Yet Linda was convincing enough that she would bring a completely new awareness for us over here.

Throughout that evening, tears kept flowing from my eyes, and nothing could stop that. To my surprise, the dolphins really touched my heart so intensely.

My mind tried to stay in control by bringing up all kinds of judgments and non-believing ideas of what Linda spoke about, but dolphin energy opened up my heart that night.

A beloved friend, Haniël van der Meer, insisted that she would pay for me to participate in the first Dolphin Healing Hearts class in Zutphen. I will be forever grateful to Haniël, for sure. She knew that it would be of tremendous importance to me and Dolphin Heart World.

Haniël was 80 years old at that time, and she also signed up as a student herself! Within days, I started to help with recruitment, e-mailing and phoning to so many people from the large network I was involved in ...

And so the first Dolphin School class in Zutphen started with twenty-seven students, only three months later!

Zutphen was the largest attended introductory of the trip. Sixteen people were present that night. At the remaining four evenings, the groups were much smaller–four, three and even two! I knew that the number of people who came didn't matter. Even though I'd traveled all the way from America to be there, it honestly didn't matter to me that so few people attended the remaining events. I knew that what mattered was that I was there, the dolphin energy was flowing, and the people who did come were being touched. Each event was pure joy for me to share.

One more woman, an accomplished animal communicator, wrote about her experience at her introductory evening. It made me laugh!!

> **Marjan Vrins:** Linda, when I first met you in Amsterdam, I thought, "My god, that lady is hyper. I do not know if I can stand that for a whole evening."
>
> But when I looked into your eyes, something shifted inside me, a kind of recognition. For one split second I had the feeling that I knew who I was, and that it was all right. With that moment of eye contact, you had me.

I was in Holland for ten days, and presented our Dolphin Healing HeArts program to perhaps forty people. Zoë did so much to make that trip happen, and gave me incredible support the whole time I was there. I could feel the dolphins' excitement the whole time.

At some point during that trip, Zoë and I, with David on the phone, set a goal for twelve students to register for the first Holland pod by the time I left. We knew we would certainly attract more before September. On my last morning, while I was packing to return home, the phone rang, and our twelfth person signed up. Zoë and I squealed with excitement and jumped for joy in her living room. I phoned David immediately. "We have a pod! We're coming to Holland together!"

We were all rather stunned and overjoyed by all that was happening. Magic and joy was in the air! Dolphin was leading the way …

THIRTY-TWO

Opening to Human Love

I got home from Holland, and just a few days later David and I flew to Oregon to attend the Naka-Ima workshop there.

My goal for this workshop was to heal my issue of feeling separate and alone in groups. And I did! It happened on the second day of the workshop, during an interactive exercise with two other participants.

The three of us were a triad, and now it was my turn to be the receiver. As the receiver, my role was to just *be* ... in connection. My two partners served me as sacred witnesses. Their role was to give me their undivided energy and attention for forty-five minutes. Most of that time, they were in silence. The idea behind the exercise was to discover, and heal, whatever resistance might come up in response to the experience of simply being seen by others. What, inside of me, prevents me from being my authentic self, in relationship with others?

The workshop leader told us, as receivers, to do our best to remain in eye contact with one partner at all times. I alternated between having my eyes open and closed. It was intense for me to sustain eye contact, in silence, for so long.

At one point in the exercise, at a time when my eyes were closed, I became aware of a protective shield in my energy field. It was a paper-thin metallic shield, rectangular in shape, and curved to match the contour of my energy field. It hovered about eight inches in front of my body, and covered my torso. I was only aware of the shield in the front of my body, but I suspect it surrounded me completely, front and back.

This is what it's like to be fully grounded, fully present, in my human body.

Realizations surged through me. *It's easy for me to receive love from nature, animals, and spirit. Somewhere along the way, I became afraid of humans. The human world feels dangerous to me.*

Inside of me, Dolphin declared firmly: **That's an illusion.**

A strong desire to choose differently welled up in me. *I no longer want to go through my life protecting myself from humans. I want to love humans —all humans— and I want to let humans love me.*

I opened my eyes and briefly told my partners what was occurring inside of me. I closed my eyes again, focused all of my attention on this shield, and commanded out loud, "Shield, dissolve!"

Instantaneously, the shield dissolved. An incredible amount of energy... *love... human love...* flowed into me. I collapsed on the floor in a heap, crying in gratitude and relief. *It's so much ... who knows how long this shield has been holding this love energy at bay, out of my fear of letting it in!*

When I was able to pull myself together, and share my new reality with my partners, I told them how amazing it was to feel—*really feel*—connected to my human family again. I felt free. I felt fully alive. It was an indescribable relief, really.

At the break after my session, I had an extraordinary experience walking through the virgin forest to the cabin where David and I were staying. With every footfall onto the soft, yielding earth below, I felt every cell in my body jiggle. I was acutely aware of every single cell inside of me!

This is what it's like to be fully grounded, fully present, in my human body. I'm not only connected to my human family again. I am now connected to myself, as never before!

This was a brand new experience. Never before had I felt the exquisite sensation of truly inhabiting every cell and space of this body. It was incredible. Incredibly joyful!

Thoughts flowed. *Sure, humans will still do the hurtful things that they do, but I can handle it now. I'm no longer willing to block the flow of love, out of fear of being hurt.* A Tom Petty song played in my head, "It's only a broken heart." I giggled. *That's right! And broken hearts heal!*

In this workshop, Dolphin supported me in healing this core wound. It makes complete sense that I needed to be in a group in order to heal this issue. This wasn't something I could heal at home, alone—or in the water with the dolphins! Being in a group with attentive, loving humans created a safe space for this wound to be triggered, and then healed. My strong intention to heal empowered me to see the shield that I had erected subconsciously, no doubt in an attempt to keep myself safe. But what the energetic shield was really doing was limiting my ability to give and receive love.

I am extraordinarily grateful to Dolphin, and to the folks at Naka-Ima, especially my two exercise partners, for holding sacred space for, and witnessing, this profound healing.

The remainder of the workshop was spent learning simple, yet powerful, connecting skills. Now, I was really ready and able to do that! We learned how to connect to ourselves first, and then how to reach out in authentic connection to others, without losing ourselves. I had never been taught these basic skills!

I came away from that weekend with a deepened compassion for the human condition. A fire got lit in me. Even more than before, I wanted to do something tangible to make a positive, sustainable change in the human condition on this planet. I wanted to help people learn how to live in connection. David and I returned home to Sedona, passionate about incorporating what we'd learned and experienced at this workshop into our school.

This was the beginning of the element of Dolphin School that we call the Dolphin Living Skills.

♡

Imagine you are a spinner dolphin. You spend your entire life in deep connection with all of the members of your pod—seventy or eighty of your closest friends. With your powerful hearing, far beyond human hearing, you continuously hear the heartbeat of each of your podmates, as well as all of their expressive sounds. With your sonar, you "see" inside your podmates' physical bodies. You feel each other's emotions, know each other's thoughts. If a member of your pod is out of harmony in some way, everyone in the pod knows it instantly.

You are transparent to one another. There are no secrets in the pod. You live in a state of constant connection, but you never lose yourself. You're grounded in your own identity, and fully connected to the pod, and there is no conflict between the two. You live in a state we humans can't even imagine.

The Dolphin Living Skills are the *how* of Unity-Community. With the Dolphin Attunements, and the Dolphin Energy Healing training, the Dolphin Living Skills became the third element of *Dolphin Healing HeArts ... A Gateway to the New Paradigm.* They began with what I had learned in Naka-Ima, along with elements of David's learnings from years before. Soon, Archie and Dolphin brought us many more practices, teachings, and experiences to share with our podmates.

With the first Sedona pod, in April 2003, I had wondered what I would do with my podmates for four whole hours together. Less than a year later, Dolphin School consisted of six full weekends, with one Dolphin Attunement each weekend, and three months of integration time between each weekend. And the major challenge David and I faced when we planned the pod's activities for each weekend was figuring out how to fit everything in!

THIRTY-THREE

A New Beginning

When the time came for David and me to travel together to The Netherlands to initiate our first Dutch pod, I was truly ready.

As we sat in the opening circle of our new pod that first Friday night, in September 2003, twenty-seven beautiful, warm, loving, open, and very excited Dutch faces looked back at us. There was so much love and acceptance in that room, David and I felt immediately at home. We spoke all together about how we would flow with the language issue, the cultural differences, etc. We were all in this grand experiment and adventure together. The bond we created that night was beautiful, strong, and deep. Our love affair with Holland, and our Dutch podmates, had only just begun ...

Archie's description of life after the Sixth Attunement perfectly matches my own experience of waking up that morning in January 2003, feeling brand new. When I try to remember who I was before my awakening, it's as though I was living my life in black and white. The morning of my awakening, I opened my eyes to a world shimmering in bright, brilliant Technicolor.

Dolphin Love

As I move through my new life, every aspect of it feels new. When I try to access who I was before my awakening, it feels as though *that* Linda, and *that* life, aren't real. The past seems dreamlike–vague, illusory. I have memories from that life, but they don't define me. They don't inform my current decisions and actions. They're just stories. *That* Linda, and *that* life, no longer exist.

Now, there's a vibrancy and vitality to my life that didn't exist before. Not only am I brand new ... the world that I'm living in is also brand new. I, and others around me, absolutely feel the frequency of the dolphins flowing through me. The most frequent adjective people use to describe my energy is "sparkly." This flow is natural, spontaneous, and effortless. I don't "do" anything to activate the flow. It just is.

Now, I am blessed to extend this sacred gift out into the world. It is a joy, an honor, and a privilege to hold space for, and to witness, my podmates as they receive this extraordinary gift from the dolphins. I get to witness the journey *through the gateway* ... from the old paradigm of duality consciousness and separation, to the new paradigm of love, joy, and unity consciousness–oneness with All That Is.

Witnessing that moment when the spark of love and joy alights in a podmate's eyes, and then watching that spark deepen and grow, completely transforming her quality of life, is an extraordinary thing. Seeing our podmates evolve, over the course of our journey together, into gorgeous, open, sexy, free, empowered, juicy, and fully alive human-dolphins, makes all that we do to bring this revolutionary gift to humanity worthwhile.

The new paradigm is uncharted territory for humanity. There are no road maps, no blueprints for how to live in this new world, in this new way. As our new adventure unfolds before us, our hearts lead the way.

In a 2007 channeling with Archie, the Dolphin Council elevated my awareness to the bigger picture of what we are doing together:

It is our desire to heal the hearts of humanity —all of humanity.

You have used these words, but you are only beginning to let yourself feel them, let alone think about what that will mean, and can mean.

If we were to speak in terms of time, this school that you are creating for us—and for yourself, of course, and for humanity—but this school that you are creating for us, is part of a progression in time which, of course, goes back thousands of years, but most directly began, let us say, sixty years ago and continues 200 to 250 years into the future. And your personal role in this plan extends for ... it would be helpful to think of it as extending for the next forty to fifty years.

This message stirred me to my core, and even further deepened my commitment to this path of sacred service.

Dolphin weaves an exquisite tapestry of Love and Joy in and around our planet, for the purpose of human and planetary healing and evolution. There are many gifted and dedicated dolphin ambassadors in the world today; more are answering the call all the time.

I feel honored, awed, and blessed to be a part of this interspecies, interdimensional pod of humans and cetaceans. It is with sheer joy and delight that I weave my rainbow thread into the tapestry, making my contribution to the Dolphin vision of a healed and whole humanity, and a healed and whole planet Earth.

People can learn a lot from dolphins ...
to live in harmony, to create love between people,
to live the life they were meant to live.
When people come into contact with dolphin energy,
they realize their source ...
and their future.

Thank you, Thank you,
Thank you, Thank you,

The writing of this book was a journey that, in many ways, paralleled my seven-year inner journey with the dolphins. I'm embarrassed to admit that it took even longer than that to complete this book. I was two months away from finishing it—for about four years!

My first words of gratitude and acknowledgment must go to my dear friend in spirit, Dr. James Martin Peebles, and to Summer Bacon, my dear friend who channels him. It's not an exaggeration to say that Dr. Peebles played quite a large role in my journey. I don't know where I would be without the wise and loving counsel I've received from him over the years.

My first draft of this book was a mere shadow of what you hold in your hands. I owe a debt of thanks to my first readers, for persevering through that clumsy first draft—Sandra Bond, Tracy Bychowski, Lorraine Custodio, Michael Eason, Carolyn Fumia, Paula Green, David Green, and Patricia Kerschner. A later version was read and critiqued by Joe Nicely, Michael Eason, Jeanne Michaels, and Joyha Baker. Thank you, thank you, thank you my friends!

When I was finally ready to bring this book to completion and publish it professionally, a magnificent team appeared to support me in doing so. What a joy it has been to work with: Sharon K. Garner, copyeditor extraordinaire; Jamie Saloff, supremely gifted book designer and guide through every step of the self-publishing process; and our friend Manjari Henderson, the brilliant graphic artist who designed the book cover. I feel enormously blessed to have manifested a creative team of such high caliber. My heartfelt thanks to each of you for the exquisite contributions you have made to this finished product. It was a joy working with you. Let's do it again!

I offer a warm thank-you to all who found their way to me over the years to receive the beautiful healing frequencies of the dolphins. Every one of you has touched and enriched my life.

There are no adequate words to express my feelings of love, joy, and gratitude for my beautiful podmates, who journeyed deeply with me through the Dolphin Healing HeArts experience. Never would I have imagined feeling such depth of love and connection for my fellow humans as I feel for all of you.

What an adventure we're on! Together, we've taken baby steps and giant leaps toward creating Unity-Community on land, among humanity. I'm so proud of us! I know the dolphins are too. We will surely continue to ascend the spiral together, to greater love, harmony, joy, peace, and play in this Earthly lifetime.

Thank you, beloveds, for trusting me to hold sacred space for your journey. I'm privileged to know you and to have you in my life. I love you with all my heart.

My heart swells with gratitude and love for my family and friends—both physical and those in spirit—who have loved me and journeyed with me through all my human wanderings. You know who you are. I love you and thank you, with my whole heart.

To the Shay family—ILYSM xoxoxoxoxommmmm!! For sure, I have walked (or swum!) a path less traveled, and while you may not have understood my journey, you've always accepted it, and me, without judgment. Not many are blessed with families such as you. Mom, you went the extra mile when I most needed help. Enormous thanks for your gift that made this book a reality. My dad is not with us, in the physical, to celebrate this accomplishment. But he's joyously celebrating this momentous event "on the other side." *"Hey dad, meet me at our treehouse for a toast?"*

This next thank-you is a bit unusual ... but if you've made it through my book this far, nothing should surprise you! The poem: *"People can learn a lot from dolphins..."* that precedes this section was given to us by a cat named Mikey! Mikey's person, Gerda van Gemert, is a gifted animal communicator who participated in our second Holland pod. Shortly after her first Dolphin School weekend—The Frequency of Joy weekend—Gerda sent this e-mail:

> When I returned home from the weekend, one of my cats, Mikey, was running around my house and garden. When I asked him why he was running so hard, he gave me a big smile and said: "**You saw them! The dolphins! I am very glad that you went. You did it!**" I was amazed by this, and I sensed that Mikey had a lot more to say! So I quickly got a notebook and a pen and started writing down all that Mikey was telling me. His message took three pages!

Gerda thoughtfully translated Mikey's message into English for us—naturally, he speaks to her in Dutch! Mikey's words were incredibly wise, deep, and accurate.

With his beautiful poem, Mikey gave us the perfect way to describe who the dolphins are, and what this work is about. The next time we updated our Dolphin Healing HeArts brochure, we asked Gerda for Mikey's permission to use his words in our materials. Mikey graciously said "Yes!" Mikey, Gerda, thank you both for the gift of these beautiful words. I love you both so much!

By the way, Mikey ended his message to Gerda with this pithy statement:

> *Dolphins are very good teachers. Do not underestimate their skills. Their teaching methods are really sophisticated. They are almost as good as cats!*

Dolphin Love

Finally, I thank my beloved husband, David Rosenthal, for not only supporting me and then joining me on this journey, but also for taking on the enormous task of editing this book. Thank you, sweetie, for caring for and nurturing this book as if it were your own. You skillfully massaged my ramblings into a clear and polished narrative that I'm immensely proud of. Your contributions have improved the readability of this book tenfold. I loved that as the end was in sight, you were almost more excited about the book than I was!

David, thank you for being my best friend. Thank you for your unconditional love and support every step along this magnificent journey we're sharing. I love you. I adore you. I am blessed to have you as my mate. *Thank you, dolphins, for choosing David for me. He's perfect!*

Etiquette and Protocols for Swimming with Wild Dolphins

It is natural for books like this one to cause some readers to strongly desire the experience of swimming with wild dolphins themselves. It is a magnificent experience to have!

And there are conflicting views as to whether such encounters benefit, or harm, these beautiful beings of the sea. In some places, swimming with wild dolphins is illegal. In other places, boats and swimmers are closely monitored to ensure that interactions are respectful toward the dolphins and within established guidelines.

Should you feel the heartfelt desire to seek out such an encounter, I offer these protocols and tips to ensure a mutually nourishing and respectful experience for all involved:

- It's very exciting to be with the dolphins and to see them in their natural habitat. To the best of your ability, stay connected to your heart. Be mindful and respectful in your attitude. Don't try to force anything.

- The ocean is the dolphins' domain. You're entering *their* world. Be observant for cues that you are there at their invitation. The more you observe the dolphins' behavior from moment-to-moment and respond to their cues, the greater the chance of a wondrous close encounter that will change you forever.

- Select boat captains whose primary concern is for the well-being and safety of the dolphins. Ask them, in advance, what their protocols are for dolphin encounters. If they do not follow the protocols that are given below (for example, if they feed the dolphins to attract them to their boat), voice your concerns and take your business elsewhere.

- If you are not participating in a group swim trip, or going on a boat with an experienced captain and crew, consider hiring a personal dolphin swim guide to support you in creating your perfect experience.

Etiquette for human behaviors when swimming with wild dolphins:

- Don't feed them.

- Don't touch them.

- Don't dive on top of them when they are resting.

- Don't cut them off by swimming directly at them; rather, approach them much like entering into traffic from a freeway on-ramp. While swimming parallel to the pod, make your approach, closing the gap between you, little by little—merging with them.

- The proper swim technique is with your arms at your sides. Swimming free-style can be frightening to dolphins, and may cause them to create more distance between you. (Refer to Chapter 4, which describes the "dolphin kick" swimming technique.)

Visit **www.dolphinheartworld.com** for resources and references to create the dolphin encounter that's perfect for you. Many of our Dolphin School pod-mates organize and lead dolphin swim trips for groups—to Hawaii, Bimini, Panama, the Red Sea, and the Azores!

When you meet the dolphins in the wild, blow them a kiss from me!

Unity—Community

This book has told the story of Linda's seven-year journey with the dolphins that led to her awakening, and to the founding of Dolphin Healing HeArts ... *A Gateway to the New Paradigm*. Now, this is no longer just Linda's story ... it's humanity's story. Here, podmates reflect on their Dolphin School experiences:

The power, joy, and love that the dolphins allowed me to experience in my own energy field was beyond overwhelming. It allowed me to feel the dolphins' flow, dance, shine, and sparkle throughout each and every cell, fiber, and part of my being in an electronic sea of light and love, bringing great joy to my soul. Thanks for making this possible. ~ Fred F., Florida

I remember feeling completely safe during the school and able to share anything that I felt inside with Linda, David, and my podmates. It truly was a pod experience of complete transparency. It is hard to describe how my life has changed. One very huge way is this: No matter what is happening in my life,

I never feel alone. I feel the dolphins with me always, and anytime I need support, I just have to mentally call them and I feel them with me, supporting me. Recently a short film producer commented to me, "We want your calm, wise energy as part of our crew. You bring a peaceful joy wherever you go." ~ Anne G., Panama

Since I am attending Dolphin School, there is this true, sparkling, joyful hope that fills my heart over and over again. It is beyond hope—it is a true, deep conviction that together with the dolphins, we really can take part in the co-creation of a New Earth for humanity and all other creatures living on this planet. *And it is simply starting within our own deepest self! Connecting with our own deepest joy!* For me, as a laughter coach, who invites people to reach out to their inner joy through laughter, joy, and playfulness, the Dolphin Healing HeArts school was the perfect next step in my life! ~ Leen G., Belgium

What an incredible weekend! I didn't get an opportunity to express my gratitude and profound wonder for what you have given us. It still seems like a miracle that I was ever able to find you in the first place, and now, a year-and-a-half later, our pod has just received its sixth and final Attunement! Thank you for your love, your light, your devotion, your ability to see each and every one of us for our unique individuality, your unwavering focus and intention, your beauty and joy, and your integrity. ~ Deni B., California

It still is a complete mystery, but I feel it is also a total gift. When I first began Dolphin School, one of my biggest intentions was to come closer to myself so that I could better give to the world and in my massage practice. I've come to the insight that this school is bringing me closer to myself—and that *that is enough.* The world and serving others comes after that. I think I've waited lifetimes for that insight! ~ Maegan G., Berlin, Germany

To me, swimming through the Dolphin School was a very special, valuable experience—a great gift, and still is, and always will be. The Dolphin School felt to me as a warm welcome, a homecoming. Truly being together with kindred persons felt like a warm loving shower, and now after three years, my contacts with podmates are still important to me. Now, when I look at the past few years, I really can say that the things I learned within the Dolphin School I use and apply in my daily life. It empowered me. ~ Ellen O., Netherlands

The dolphins are masters at teaching us how to energetically hold space so we can fully embody the highest spiritual energy we are ready for. I have the deepest gratitude for them. They have helped me to remain in my body as I am one with the energy of Whale, Christ, and Buddha. Within the last month, I have recognized deeper, and can hold the presence of God's Love as it pours through my heart. I am honored to know that I am "worthy" and can stand in that. It's been such a blessing! ~ Eric E., California

I resisted the call of the dolphins for quite some time, but I certainly remember the feeling of joy and happiness when I answered the call. The first weekend of the Dolphin School was like coming home for me, and I was on the verge of tears almost the whole weekend. I felt homesick, and I wanted to be a dolphin. Now I can't imagine a life without the dolphins and the whales. They are guiding and accompanying me. ~ Emmy V., Netherlands

To connect with Linda and learn more, visit:

www.dolphinheartworld.com

Are the Dolphins calling You?

About the Author

Linda Shay is a Dolphin Ambassador who travels internationally in her mission to bring the gifts of the dolphins ... from sea to land. Linda does this through her teaching, healing, speaking, and writing. Linda is the founder and teacher of *Dolphin Healing HeArts ... A Gateway to the New Paradigm*, a revolutionary spiritual school, affectionately known as "Dolphin School."

After leaving her corporate job behind, Linda found herself on a spiritual journey that led to a momentous event in her life. While in Hawaii, swimming with a pod of wild spinner dolphins, Linda had a magical encounter with one wild dolphin that set her life on a radically different course. Her true-life spiritual adventure story, that takes place both in the high desert of Arizona and in the Hawaiian waters swimming among wild dolphins, is contained in these pages.

Linda lives with her husband, David Rosenthal, and their two cats, Tyler and Cinnamon-Girl, in the Sedona, Arizona area. A true human-dolphin, Linda is always exploring new ways of living and being in body on this planet. Her current passion is walking, and running ... barefoot! ... on the land. Being in skin-to-skin contact with Mother Earth in this way brings Linda great JOY!

CPSIA information can be obtained
at www.ICGtesting.com
Printed in the USA
FFOW03n0134070317
33162FF